14.95

THE EMPTY PLACE

From left to right: the author, Abeabo Waibo, Kora Midibaru.

THE

POETRY, SPACE, AND BEING

EMPTY

AMONG THE FOI OF PAPUA NEW GUINEA

PLACE

JAMES F. WEINER

INDIANA UNIVERSITY PRESS
BLOOMINGTON AND INDIANAPOLIS

The paper used in this publication meets the minimum requirements of American
National Standard for Information Sciences—Permanence of Paper for Printed
Library Materials, ANSI Z39.48-1984.

∞™

Manufactured in the United States of America

Library of Congress Cataloging-in-Publication Data
Weiner, James F.
  The empty place : poetry, space, and being among the Foi
of Papua New Guinea / James F. Weiner.
      p.   cm.
  Includes bibliographical references and index.
  ISBN 0-253-36382-9 (alk. paper)
  1. Foi (Papua New Guinea people)—Philosophy. 2. Foi (Papua
New Guinea people)—Social life and customs. 3. Folk-songs, Papuan.
4. Papuan poetry. 5. Spatial behavior—Papua New Guinea.
I. Title.
DU740.42.W4   1991
306.4'0899912—dc20   90-49766
                                                            CIP

1 2 3 4 5   95 94 93 92 91

To Fiona Gai McMaster and
Fabiana Estelle Weiner

Even though the world keeps changing
quickly as cloud-shapes,
all things perfected fall
home to the age-old.

Over the changing and passing,
wider and freer,
still lasts your leading-song,
god with the lyre.

Not understood are the sufferings.
Neither has love been learned,
and what removes us in death

is not unveiled.
Only song over the land
hallows and celebrates.

—Rainer Maria Rilke,
Sonnets to Orpheus, no. 19
(translated by M. D. Herter Norton)

CONTENTS

LIST OF FIGURES

LIST OF MAPS

FOI ORTHOGRAPHY

The Foi language was first analyzed by the missionary Murray Rule. Aided by his wife, Joan Rule, and his fellow missionary David Donaldson, he produced an unpublished grammar and lexicon of Foi during his stay at the Asia Pacific Christian Mission station at Inu, Lake Kutubu. Rule's orthography has been adopted by the Foi people, and I have followed his conventions in this book (see Rule 1977: 8–10):

Consonants

/b/	[p]	WI[1]
	[b]	WM[2]
/t/	[tʰ]	WI and WM
/d/	[t]	WI
	[d]	WM
/k/	[kx]	WI and WM
/g/	[k]	WI
	[g]	WM
/r/	[ř]	WM only
/ʔ/	[ʔ]	WM only
/f/	[f]	WI and WM
/v/	[v]	WI and WM
/s/	[s̪]	before /a/ and /e/
	[s̪][3]	before /i/, /o/, /u/, WI and WM
/h/	[h]	WI and WM
/m/	[m]	WI and WM
/n/	[n]	WI and WM
/w/	[w]	WI and WM

Vowels

/a/	[a]	before /a/, /e/, /o/ in following syllable

---

[1]WI = word initial
[2]WM = word medial
[3]Tongue slightly retroflex

	[∧∧]	before /i/ and /u/, AP[4]
/ã/[5]	[ã]	or [∧∧] as for /a/ above
/e/	[e]	AP
/ẽ/	[ẽ]	AP
/i/	[i]	AP
/ĩ/	[ĩ]	AP
/o/	[o]	AP
/õ/	[õ]	AP
/u/	[u]	AP
/ũ/	[ũ]	AP

In addition, there are two tonemes, high and low, that affect only a small number of word pairs, for example: *haẽ*, "egg, fruit, seed," and *haẽ* [high tone], "dog."

---

[4] AP = All Positions
[5] The tilde (˜) indicates nasalization

ACKNOWLEDGMENTS

The research for this book was carried out between 1979 and 1989. It was made possible by an Australian National University Research scholarship and an Australian Research Grants Scheme award.

I would like to gratefully acknowledge the following people who read various parts of this manuscript and who offered comments and critical suggestions that I found essential to the book's completion: Keith Basso, Aletta Biersack, Steven Feld, Alfred Gell, Dell Hymes, Michael Jackson, Charles Langlas, Alan Rumsey, Marilyn Strathern, Roy Wagner, Wayne Warry, David White, and Michael Young. In particular, I am grateful to Michael Jackson for pointing me to the core of Heidegger's relevance to Foi poetry, and to David White for his explication of some of Heidegger's more difficult terms. In addition, Don Gardner argued with me about art and speech-act theory to my ultimate enrichment.

Every man and woman and many of the children of Hegeso village helped me with my inquiries at one time or another and tried to make my stay as comfortable and memorable as possible. But I would like to acknowledge my great debt to my two closest friends and field assistants, Kora Midibaru and Abeabo Waibo. Over the years that I visited Hegeso, these two men worked toward establishing a rapport and friendship with me. Through them I enjoyed the satisfaction of watching my project among the Foi emerge over time. Through our dialogue, they came to understand why I was there, and to share some of the delight I experienced in coming to understand the Foi language and way of life. Many times I savored the moment when, unbidden and unelicited, one of these two men would offer an insight that capped a long period of interrogation. When I think of Hegeso, I invariably picture the three of us sitting on the verandah of my house, against the background twittering and screech of the birds in the nearby trees, translating a difficult Foi text, looking at the pictures in old *Time* magazines, sharing a meal, a smoke, a story, fashioning in an awkward, self-conscious, humorous, irritating, trusting way a mutual world. Viya Iritoro shared many of those moments with us, and for his friendship I would like to express my deepest appreciation.

As well as being skilled singers themselves, Kora and Abeabo provided most of the help I required to translate the songs, and through the years they patiently elucidated some of the more complex nuances of Foi poetic and metaphoric usages.

In neighboring Barutage village, Fahaisabo Ya'uware and Maniname Ya'uware contributed integrally to the translation of Barutage songs. But it was the incomparable Kunuhuaka Deya whose compositions first spurred me to take an interest in Foi poetry, and I would like to acknowledge her creative genius as a poet.

Finally, Cathy O'Sullivan, a professional musician and anthropologist, transcribed the musical texts which appear in the appendixes to chapters 6 and 7 and provided the description of the beat, timing, and measure employed by Foi singers. I would like to thank her for all her observations on the musicological properties of Foi song poetry.

THE EMPTY PLACE

INTRODUCTION

In January 1983, Dabura Guni,[1] an elderly man of Hegeso village, related to me the various spells that are used during the construction of the communal men's longhouse. One by one he recited into my tape recorder the spells uttered when fastening the door lintels, upon completion of the fireplaces, upon the erection of the four main structural posts, and so forth. Afterward, he told me how he had learned these spells. Dabura had sought to achieve contact with a ghost in a dream. He prepared himself by fasting and abstaining from sexual intercourse. He then traveled to a spot along the Mubi River where it made a tight bend, what the Foi call an *ibu geno*, next to which he slept one night. That night in a dream, an old man appeared. He taught Dabura the longhouse construction spells and assured him that he would have a long life. Dabura continued to contact the ghost through dreams over the ensuing years.

In that same first dream, Dabura, though unmarried at the time, saw that his wife was going to give birth to a female child near Isa, a ridge immediately south of Hegeso village, and that the child would therefore be named *Isaka*, "Woman of Isa." When some years later he did marry, the first child his wife bore was female. At this time, Dabura wanted to name the child Maruti, which he had earlier learned was the name of the ghost man's eldest daughter. But he heeded his original dream, which he felt was prophetic, and named the child Isaka.

Abuyu Ka'anobo and his wife, Kagua Karage, have two female children. The second daughter is called Hikuka. *Hiku* in Foi means a point of land, a spit, a headland. They had originally wanted to name the child Siyuka, after Abuyu's deceased sister's child. But Abuyu's father's sister, an elderly woman named Kubinu, had a dream in which a ghost appeared to her at a point of land along the Mubi River named Igiri, and this ghost told her that the child should be named after that place.

Kora Midibaru told me the following: Suppose you dream that you are paddling a canoe upstream from Hegeso longhouse. If you reach all the way to the Sumani Creek, the farthest point upstream at which Hegeso people live, it means you will live a long life. If you get only as far as Gofofo, or Namanihimu, both places close to the longhouse, it means you will not live long.

The Foi consider dreaming a talent, or an art, if you will. The man or woman who is skilled in divining the significance of dreams becomes privy to their hidden prescient messages. These messages are sent by ghosts, the disembodied souls of the departed. Dreams are the only way in which the deceased can communicate directly with the living.

The dreams that Dabura, Kubinu, and Kora had were fairly typical of Foi oneiric experiences (though as I have discussed in a previous article [Weiner 1986], the Foi recognize a wide range of dream images). Names are crucial to the Foi, since things with the same name are considered to have an affinity with each other and thereby to affect each other. A person named after a place becomes identified with all of the events associated in the past with that place, all of the people whose lives have been linked to it. Foi parents are quick to detect whether a name they have bestowed upon a newborn is inauspicious, usually indicated by the child's unrelieved ill health or bad temper. Perceiving a named locale in a dream is often taken as an indication that a ghost has taken an interest in the child and has lent the force of its special abode to the child's well-being.

Ghosts therefore are essentially part of the landscape. The swirling whirl-pools found in sharp bends in a river, the bases of certain trees that attract brightly colored birds, places where powerful magic spells were once performed—these are the spots that attract ghosts. Men—the seeking of dreams is charac-terized as a male activity in Foi—go to these places to seek contact with ghosts through dreams.

These are the places which, to Foi perception, are associated with *stillness*, with the *halting of motion*, with the capturing and *rendering motionless of some movement of flow*—the whirlpool that stops the flow of water; the nectar-filled tree flowers that gather the passing birds; the spells that bind the wandering spirits to a particular spot. Anything that holds that flow or movement in place has a potential, a pent-up energy, a possible source of power or revelation.

There is another way in which names are "revealed" to the Foi, however. In the men's longhouse, men perform the *sorohabora* memorial song poems. Typically, these poems link the life course of a deceased man to the places he inhabited during his lifetime. In the closing lines of every Foi memorial song poem, the name of the deceased man who is the subject of the song, his father's and mother's names and clan names, and the deceased's "private" or "hidden" name are recited. In stark contrast to men's lonely ghost-haunted outposts in the bush, the setting is the interior of the longhouse, crowded with living people.

These songs, as I have said, are performed by men and constitute the most elaborate aesthetic form the Foi possess. But the songs themselves are composed by women. Here it seems Foi women are arrogating to themselves the revelatory talent of ghosts. Perhaps that is not exactly the right way to put it: men hear their wives and female relatives singing their memorial song poems while the women make sago, and it is men who, in their ceremonial performance of those songs, reveal men's names publicly.

The association between women and death is an abiding one for Foi men. Women as widows are closely identified in a literal way with their dead husbands: in pre-Mission times they applied a mixture of mud and urine called *kaemari* to their skins for the thirty-seven days of their formal mourning period. Wearing this foul-smelling mixture, the widow evoked the decomposing corpse itself, which was kept in state for that period. In addition, the dead man's ghost, not yet reconciled to leaving the living community, was thought to remain near the widow, anxious to discover whether his wife had conspired with a lover to bring about his death.

Like ghosts, then, women also reveal hidden names to men in the bush. And men take these names and make of them the songs that are the medium of their flamboyant ceremonial performances. They take the names they perceive in dreams and give them to their children to ensure their healthy and speedy growth, and they take similarly revealed words and turn them into the magic spells that are the adjuncts of their assertive male productivity.

As I noted, ghosts are drawn to places where a flow or movement has been encapsulated, redirected, stopped. But women embody within themselves a continuous, periodic flow, that of menstrual blood, as well as its encapsulation —in the form of children. Their flow is associated with life, but as with ghosts it is a life that includes death, finality, surcease: for women's menstrual and childbirth fluids are lethal to men.

Not all the dreams that people have are as easy to interpret as the first two dreams I described. The ambiguity of ghosts' life condition perhaps explains why their communication itself is devious, elliptical, and ambiguous. Most dreams, like the one Kora related to me, need to have their elusive meaning revealed through metaphor. Ghosts live in a sort of parody world, according to the Foi, where words do not mean what they normally mean, where inedible things are staple foods, where mice and lizards are domesticated animals. Ghosts are usually ill disposed to humans because they are frustrated with their inability to participate in living society. At the same time, they maintain a wistful interest in the living, particularly their surviving relatives. While ghosts most often are the sources of sickness, delirium, or death, they do attempt on infrequent occasions to communicate benevolently.

Like their communication, the parody world in which ghosts live is a result of their fundamentally different existential relation to human being. Dead, they can neither live nor die—they cannot experience life as temporal or spatial process. Ghosts are said to exist in a place called *Haisureri*, which traditionally the Foi located far downstream (that is, southeast) where they presumed all water eventually wound up. At *Haisureri* the movement of water presumably ceased, and deprived of such a life-orienting flow, ghosts existed in a motionless dimension. That perhaps is why they are drawn to places where motion has been brought to a halt. If my characterizations of ghostly existence seem tentative and dubious, it only reflects the Foi's own difficulty in understanding the motives, intention, and mode of life of ghosts.

In the often opaque images of dreams, men seek the revelation of some metaphoric link that will allow them to exert the ghost's power in their own world. If ghosts reveal pearl shells as birds of paradise, or pigs as cockatoos, men assume that these equations in themselves constitute a key to exerting a leverage on the world. The Foi man then knows that by invoking the bird of paradise or the cockatoo in a spell, he will gain access to shells and pigs. He does not have to understand the link between the two domains, though it may be readily apparent to him and anthropologist alike (in these cases, it is the red color of birds of paradise and pearl shells and their common use as male decorations, or the white color of cockatoos and pigs and the similarity of their raucous squealing and shouts).

It can be said that what women's songs reveal is also a metaphoric link: most commonly they depict the life of the deceased in terms of the series of places he inhabited, so that a temporal and a spatial interval are equated. But the link in this case is not an arcane or arbitrary or adventitious one imputed by a nonhuman agent. In the case of the poem it is the revelation of the fundamental lived experience of life and death as spatially and temporally constituted states of being. Time and space acquire their significance for the Foi, as they do for all of us, as a result of human action in a world, and it is this fundamental existential synopsis of being that lies at the heart of every Foi poetic "metaphor." Here, then, is the contrast with which I wish to begin.

Foi men and women attribute distinct modes of life to their bush houses, scattered throughout the riverine territory of the Mubi Valley, and the longhouse village, where they assemble primarily for formal occasions. From their bush houses, women process the sago planted there by their husbands; men relocate and build a new bush house every three to seven years to take advantage of the different maturation rates of the sago in the various groves they own, and also to make maximum use of available garden land. A man and his wife (or wives) and children are separated from other families while engrossed in these activities. Men are usually separated from their wives as well, who spend their day in the sago groves while their husbands are working in gardens, setting and inspecting animal traps, building and repairing houses and implements. Subsistence activity—and by this I mean *all* the daily intentional movements and actions through which the Foi inscribe their agency and identity upon the earth—is not, by and large, communal activity, at least not nowadays.

But the isolation of each Foi household in the bush must be seen against the stylized and complex sociality centered on the longhouse village. Not more than a forty-minute trip from even the remotest bush house is situated the longhouse, an impressive structure over fifty meters long, flanked by over a dozen smaller houses which face it on either side. Inside, the Hegeso men sleep when in the village, while their wives and other women sleep in the women's houses along the sides.

In the village men and women practice their vigorous, pedantic, didactic, sometimes egregious, always experimental collectivity—and always with one eye on the crowd, as if it were an activity that they have to practice regularly lest their skills of politesse and urbanity wane and become dull. Gathered around the fireplaces, men orate to each other, discussing current events, disputing ownership of various property, asserting their individual points of view with all the verbal skill at their disposal. Women do likewise in their nearby houses and also raise their voices to participate, sometimes unwantedly, in men's discussions.

Men also sing the *sorohabora* memorial litanies on ceremonial occasions in the longhouse, very much a piece of this public, communal discursive "theater." The performance of these songs is a quintessential male activity and is based on their most profound notions of display, self-assertion, discursive and performative skill, sexual attractiveness, and malehood. The men celebrate these values, give shape to them, give homage and honor to those men most remembered for having lived these values during their lives. The men in fact discursively create and celebrate *the longhouse of men*.

But in another sense this activity is *not* creative. For the men freely admit that they are not the authors of their song poetry. The women compose the songs; men merely perform them. Men hear their women singing these songs while the latter are making sago. Perhaps a man has gone to tap *kara'o* tree oil[2] while nearby his wife is making sago. As he works, he hears the rhythmic chant of her sago song, the *obedobora*. Later on, he and his regular ceremonial singing partner, his *soro ira*, may put the words to the men's *sorohabora* melody and practice it in anticipation of a future performance.

In *The Heart of the Pearl Shell* (1988), I suggested that in mundane subsistence activities, men are the *initiators*: they clear gardens, cut down trees and sago palms, fashion fish traps and animal traps, build houses. Women, by contrast, *maintain* the initial efforts of men: they tend gardens, process sago, fish with nets in dammed water, check rat and small animal traps on a regular basis, care for pigs and children in houses. But poetically, we are confronted by an opposite situation: it is women who are privileged with poetic creativity, while men are merely copiers and performers: they maintain women's poetic originality. Furthermore, this differential access to discursive modalities is not "arbitrary": it is consonant with a more general Foi perception of male and female qualities, as I will discuss shortly.

Just as ghosts reveal the link between names and places, so do women reveal the same link in their songs. The invocation of place names is a central feature of Papuan poetry, as Schieffelin (1976) has effectively described in his study of the ceremonial performances of the Kaluli, geographically and culturally close to the Foi. People's lives are recalled in terms of the places they inhabited and transformed through their life activity: the gardens they made, the traps and weirs they built and set, the paths they habitually used. The temporal span of life is more compellingly and authentically envisioned in spatial terms by people such as the Kaluli and Foi. By serially listing place names, a temporal span is automatically invoked, a sense of life *movement* is appealed to.

This contrasts quite radically with the static, timeless, conceptual equations of men's metaphoric usages. The intent of magic spells, as we shall see, is to turn a movement into stillness; the poem, on the other hand, turns the final stillness of death into what was its original constituting life movement. Women are the true source of the central *moving* images in Foi society: their menstrual flow, which is so akin to the flowing water which orients the Foi in their cosmos; and the "flow" of place names and personal names they initiate in the memorial songs.

In both cases men assert themselves as *interrupters* or *controllers* of these flows: their semen blocks the flow of blood and allows it to coagulate and form a fetus. They also take names and render static their moving characteristics. Magic for the Foi involves the ability to *fix* ghostly power, and to that extent —to the degree, that is, that they bring continuity to a halt—men become more "ghostlike" in their social impact than women, who, though possessing a ghostlike "lethal influence," nevertheless are the true sources of life-sustaining motion.

The Foi number about forty-two hundred and inhabit the alluvial valley of the Mubi River on the fringe of the southern highlands of Papua New Guinea. They subsist chiefly on the products of sago manufacture, gardening, tree-crop cultivation (chiefly marita pandanus, breadfruit, and *Gnetum gnemon*), foraging, fishing, and hunting. Both men and women cooperate in caring for domesticated pigs, which are killed and exchanged for shell wealth and PNG currency, both informally by individuals and on ceremonial occasions in large numbers.

The Foi are organized into a number of dispersed groupings called *amenadoba*, literally "man-line," and which I have translated as "clan." Men and women belong to the clans of their fathers, providing the proper bridewealth was transferred from their fathers' clans to those of the mothers' relatives. Any-where between three and fifteen dispersed local clans constitute a community, which centers its collective life around the men's ceremonial longhouse village.

In *The Heart of the Pearl Shell* I suggested that the central Foi conception of human action was the dynamic between the repetitive, rhythmic motions of water, pearl shells, procreative energy, and life itself, and the moral necessity to cut, channel, and redirect such flows for socially and cosmologically impor-tant purposes. While in that book I was concerned with the *sociological* implica-tions of that contrast, it should not be forgotten that if such an image truly lies at the "heart" of the Foi's most encompassing perception, then it will be composed and sustained by their most central life activities. Robert Armstrong, in his book *The Affecting Presence*, has suggested that there is a core trope that is at the heart of any society's aesthetic.

> The creator does not build into his work cues to some real or imagined affective state external to the work itself, but rather strives to achieve in that work the embod-iment of those physical conditions which generate or are causative or constitutive of that emotion, feeling, or value with which he is concerned. (1971: 30)

Because the work of art grows out of and alongside all the actions of our life, the embodiment that the artist strives for is essentially a *spatiotemporal* one. Art does indeed "grow out of its society as an expression of the deepest qualities and motives in it" (Yasuda 1957: 37), providing we realize that these values are not presented in abstract form but are those experienced in the daily confrontation with life itself. If it is *in this embodied, sensual meaning* that art is the "total social fact" we want to make of it, then we should expect Foi poetry to make use of such imagery of movement and flow; such imagery invests the social world of discourse with the compelling immediacy of lived experience.

The focus on repetitive, rhythmic, periodic movements finds its most encom-passing cultural elaboration among the Foi in the form of *seasonality*. They recognize a yearly dimorphism between the rainy monsoon season of midyear and the relatively drier half of the year which begins around October and lasts until about April.[3] These months were traditionally spent in the swamps and riverine gardens of the Mubi Valley, and Foi men and women spend this time gardening, making sago, and caring for pigs. But around April, the southeast-erly winds start to bring more constant rain and drizzle. It is also around this time of year that the fruits of various *Ficus*-species trees begin to ripen and fall to the forest floor. These fruits are avidly sought by the marsupials, casso-waries, and megapodes of the more remote bush areas. With the onset of the mists and fogs of winter, these animals descend from their home in the sky, so the Foi say, in search of the *baí, bángo, waria,* and other *Ficus* fruits. It is at this time that, one by one, Foi nuclear families used to move out of the Mubi Valley to their hunting lodges in the Yo'oro River Valley to the north, the area they call Ayamo.

In *The Heart of the Pearl Shell*, my attention was captured by the idea of seasonal variation in *social morphology*. I wanted to demonstrate that for the Foi, their two seasons corresponded to two distinct modes of sociality, which they did. I mentioned only in general terms the spatial and temporal dimensions of these contrasting modes of life: that hunting was associated with the fragmentation of Foi communal life, with the isolation of nuclear families in the hunting preserves, and that the gardening season, on the other hand, was associated with communal life in and around the longhouse and the values of gregariousness, competitiveness, and confrontation. I was content to leave the contrast in those terms because I took the whole question of Foi sociality for granted. But here I want to consider the manner in which the Foi's central images of their life condition, the raw material for their aesthetic, are condensed within the phenomena of movement, seasonality and spatiotemporality.

Seasonal variation is but the expression of a translated landscape, a topographical image in its temporal dimension. And time, when considered as the life span of people, is a record of their movement through space. It is on this interchangeability between landscape and temporality, summed up in the image of *season*, that much of Foi poetry (as well as Oriental and Papuan poetry in general) focuses.

In this book I describe a nexus of Foi discourse that includes their geography and spatial relationships, their existential confrontation with death, their architecture and dwellings, the iconism of the Foi language (phonological, morphological, and syntactic), their poetry, song, magic, and performance. I want to preserve the essential unity of this nexus, *not* to portray the above phenomena as a bundle of separate things with semantically homologous structures. I want instead to convey the ideas that language and movement across the earth both involve bodily activity; that the deictic iconism of Foi articulation and the spatial relationships that are found in Foi dwellings and territory are products of the same discursive creation of subjectivity within a communally lived world; that poetry is not confined to a game of supercharging ordinary metaphors but is a fundamental property of the discursive life of a community.

These considerations lead us away from structuralism, still the orthodox analytic framework of anthropology, and toward phenomenology and existentialism, and to the attempts made in this century to get around the a priori distinctions between language and other activity, between building and dwelling, mind and body, between the being of life and the being of death, all of which are smuggled in by the Cartesian foundations of structuralism. In the following chapters I want to dissolve the factitious boundaries between these phenomena and by doing so reveal the aesthetic constitution of Foi society. Foi poetry exposes the basis of this aesthetic not as a mystery that has to be decoded but as the revelation of the most fundamental spatial and temporal life conditions, death and language.

NOTES

1. The Foi today append the names of their fathers or grandfathers as "surnames" when they are called upon to give official names (such as during census taking). They call these names "tree names," a "tree" being a line of men of two or three generations in depth (see Weiner 1988).

2. A viscous, reddish-colored sap used to decorate the body during ceremonial occasions, and exported by the Foi to highlands populations to the north (see Weiner 1988: chap. 3).

3. For a more technical discussion of seasonal variation in interior Papuan economies, see Weiner, ed. 1988.

1   IMAGE AND METAPHOR IN FOI POETRY

IN AN ARTICLE ENTITLED "Sound Structure as Social Structure," Steven Feld spoke of inequalities in the "distribution
of expressive resources" (1984: 383) for men and women
among the Kaluli people of New Guinea. One of the ideas
he discussed, which he had elaborated in his book *Sound and Sentiment* (1982),
was that the Kaluli drew a distinction between two kinds of structured sound
forms, weeping and song, and that these are "separate but complementary struc-
turings of sound for social evocation" (1984: 397). He summarized this distinction in the following way:

> Women's funerary weeping, which turns into wept song . . . expresses immediate
> sorrows over loss and abandonment. Men's ceremonial *gisalo* song ultimately moves
> listeners to weeping. . . . Women are highly valued and evaluated as funerary weep-
> ers, and men are highly valued and evaluated for composing and performing persua-
> sive *gisalo* songs. (Ibid.: 397)

He goes on to conclude:

> For men, the composition and performance of ceremonial songs creates a grand
> social focus around them and their powers of evocation. . . . What weeping achieves
> for women is far less sweeping. . . . No persuasive social ends and no long-term
> changes in social life are effected by weeping; largely, it is an intensely aesthetic
> display of personal grief. (Ibid.: 399)

These differential expressive resources seem to parallel a more general distribution of social agency in Kaluli society, Feld goes on. Men value the qualities
of assertiveness, of being able to move others in emotional ways—through
fear, sexual enticement, grief. Less clear is what women evoke through their
weeping, as Feld himself admits (ibid.: 400). Women's influence over men is

negative rather than socially impressive. Men feel that they are continuously drained of vitality through prolonged sexual contact with women; as Raymond Kelly has succinctly put it for the neighboring Etoro, heterosexual contact is antisocial activity (1976: 45). In suggesting that contrasts in Kaluli sound structure are coterminous with other social contrasts, Feld thus speaks from "a perspective that considers structured sound as 'un fait social total' " (ibid.: 383).

I would like to comment upon these ideas of Feld by considering the Foi, close neighbors of the Kaluli geographically, culturally, and linguistically. Looking at contrastive emotional states may not be the proper way to begin a consideration of the availability of differential expressive resources, for these may in fact be subsumed under definitions of male and female identity and fundamental ideas of agency, power, and personhood. Indeed, in a more recent publication (1988), Feld cites approvingly those philosophers of aesthetics such as Nelson Goodman who have questioned the "expression" theory of art,[1] by pointing out the false dichotomization between cognition and emotion that is at its foundation. If aesthetic form is only the "expression" of certain internal states, then it is these contrasting states that are sexually dimorphic, not merely the expressive resources per se. This, it seems, is a characterization harder to justify yet implicit in Feld's dichotomy.

If aesthetic discourse is not viewed in terms of expression, however, we can examine its constitutive role in social imagery in wider terms. I would thus like to discuss Foi men's and women's differential use of and access to image making itself. Granted that the affective and cognitive dimensions of image and trope are inseparable, I would still like to suggest that the pragmatics of Foi discourse polarizes this unity in the interests of *stipulating distinct male and female existential conditions*.

I suggest that we begin by making a distinction between *image* and *metaphor*. Although they are both rooted in the analogic capacity of human perception, they are, at least among the Foi, models for *the ontological status of contrastive modes of socially valued discourse*. To put it simply, Foi men manipulate metaphor in its *conventional* and *semantic* capacities. Because they employ metaphor as an extension of conventional *referencing*, Foi men *objectify* the definitional aspects of Foi words. Women, by contrast, are the *image makers* in Foi society; to paraphrase Mallarmé, they repair the deficiencies of the Foi language by restoring the *experiential* and *apperceptive* qualities to communication. Men make magic, the most crudely instrumental use to which metaphor can be put; women make poetry, which restores trope to its existential foundation.

I draw on a variety of disparate sources to provide a methodological and theoretical underpinning for this exercise, notably Ezra Pound, who drew a sharp distinction between image and metaphor; the existential philosophers Heidegger and Merleau-Ponty, who situated discourse as we in fact encounter it, as part of our manipulatory engagement with the lifeworld; and finally, certain anthropologists such as Alfred Gell, Paul Friedrich, and Feld himself

who locate the beginnings of poetics and discursive style in the appreciation
of the embodied, material nature of speech and communication, or in other
words, who comprehend language to be iconic at all levels—phonological, morphological, semantic, and, in the present case, even metapragmatic.

The sparse, terse form of Foi poetry that we will examine shortly brings
to mind Ezra Pound's formula for imagist poetry: "Use no superfluous word,
no adjective which does not reveal something" (1913: 200), and "no metaphors
that won't permit examination" (Paige, ed. 1950: 11). The imagists sought
to hold fast to immediate perception, to eschew conception. They correspondingly distrusted metaphors that unnecessarily clothed or ornamented the object
of poetry—the American poet Jack Spicer, for example, wrote, "I want to make
poems out of real objects" (1957: 413). Indeed, in his book *Ideogram*, a history
of the imagist influence in modern poetry, Laszlo Gèfin suggests that Pound's
theory "with some simplification . . . may even be summarized as a critique
of and an alternative to metaphor" (1982: xiii).

All this is echoed by Japanese poets and literary critics who have described
haiku (which heavily influenced Pound). Kenneth Yasuda says that "haiku has
something in common with painting, in the representation of the object alone,
without comment. . . . [The haiku poet] does not give us meaning; he gives
us the concrete objects which have meaning" (1957: 7). And elsewhere: "Metaphor is always an interference for the haiku poet. His aim is to render the
object so that it appears in its own unique self, without reference to something
other than itself" (ibid.: 51).

These sentiments are intuitively satisfying when considering a great deal
of non-Western poetry. The following two fragments from Dobuan poems,
so beautifully rendered by Reo Fortune, as well as being models of imagist
austerity, are very close to haiku in form:

> A canoe at midnight
> the widow Leionai
> mourns softly at midnight
> a canoe at midnight

> He is singing, singing inland
> from the straits of Natuwa
> black satin bird singing inland

>   (Fortune 1932: 301, 255)

But intellectually, we may find it hard to dismiss so easily some theory of
metaphor as a constituent of poetic usages and meaning. The definition, nature,
and effect of metaphor have been debated since Aristotle's time, but let us
begin with the idea that metaphor exerts an *ecstatic* or "displacing" effect—
"trope-ic," in Ricoeur's phrasing (1977)—on conventional usages. In other

words, metaphor cannot be defined or invoked apart from an imputed set of *conventional* or "definitional" (lexical) significances which metaphor obviates or realigns in some way, as, for example, Silverstein and Jakobson suggest.[2] But unlike conventional, referential usages, metaphor provides its own context; it is, in Wagner's felicitous terms, a "symbol that stands for itself" (1986). Metaphor "refers" only self-consciously, as it were, and poetry goes beyond metaphor, to the image which, it seems, involves a complete by-passing of reference. A poem, especially an imagist poem, or a haiku, or a Foi or Dobuan song poem, is so self-contained and self-referencing that it obstinately resists reduction in semantic terms. Poetry coheres the evocative power of imagery, rather than the referential power of words; by holding fast to the object, it shatters the conventions that insulate us from experience. Metaphor is a play on words; poetic image is additionally a play on the world.

The distinction between metaphor and image I am suggesting itself "stands for" a fundamental dichotomy in linguistic function. At the end of his book *Consciousness and the Acquisition of Language*, Merleau-Ponty stated:

> Language is characterized by two contradictory needs: *a need for uniformity and a need for expressivity*. It is necessary that a form be used to be understood, and yet a form that is used too frequently loses its meaning—for example, "terrific," "unbelievable." . . . The need for expressivity fights against the wearing out of words and forms; it even arouses linguistic creations at certain moments. (1973: 89)

It was Martin Heidegger, however, who associated this functional dichotomy with contrasting existential states of being. Heidegger founded his approach to being (*Sein*) through an analysis of what could be called "human nature," *Dasein*. This approach was grounded in Husserl's notion of intentional consciousness: the idea that consciousness is always consciousness *of* something, or *toward* something (Husserl 1960). It is by the things in our environment toward which it is directed that consciousness arises. Heidegger characterized the attitude which directs consciousness toward things as that of *care* and *concern*. In other words, our perception is directed by our own concerns and projects, and the world so constituted is thus a humanly resolved world.

In the absence of a relation to human projects, things in the world exist in a sort of "brute facticity." They may exist side by side, but have no real relation with each other. The consideration of entities in this *ontic* state means that they exist apart from constituting human concerns (Heidegger 1962: 32–34; Sefler 1974: 31–32; Harries 1978: 72). Human beings are aware of things in their ontic state, but only in their sheer *facthood*, that is, uninvolved and *detached* from them.

In this state, neither humans nor the things they encounter are intelligible. Only when humans turn their attention to the world, only when the world acquires a *structure* (Vycinas 1961: 27), does being become *existential*, that is, defined by the scope of a human being's engagement in and with it. The world then becomes *ontological*—that is, setting the conditions for human knowledge of and relationship with it.

The attitude of *care* (Heidegger 1962: 84) that is necessary to this state is "the kind of concern which manipulates things and puts them to use" (ibid.: 95). Without this constituting attitude, the world is essentially the Cartesian universe in which entities need no other entities in order to exist. But as Heidegger pointed out, "Descartes' conception of the world is ontologically defective" (ibid.: 128). It views the ontic properties of entities "as something . . . [which] must have priority and take the lead in the sequence of those dealings with the 'world' in which something is discovered and made one's own" (ibid.: 101).

Now, for Heidegger it is language with which being-in-the-world is "built": "Language is the House of Being," he wrote (1971a: 132). It is the way in which the structure of being is fabricated. Just as the act of building brings forth the spaces within which human time and history unfold, so language builds the doors, passageways, and rooms within which we locate ourselves as speaking beings. Yet language is not "a mere tool," Heidegger maintains; "rather it is that event which disposes of the supreme possibility of human existence" (1949: 276–77).

As the "house of being"—a metaphor I will return to toward the end of this book—language has its ontic and ontological dimensions. What Heidegger calls "representational" language is language in its purely descriptive or referential function. "Language [in this sense] is an assertion and the 'primary significance of assertion is pointing out.' [It is] letting an entity be seen from itself" (Sefler 1974: 135, quoting *Being and Time*, p. 196). The thing which is pointed out is extracted from the contexts of meaningful use which constitute its existential "environmentality," as Heidegger describes it (1962: 200).

The value of this procedure is manifest: words as representations can then be readily equated with other words, and meaning can be artificially restricted to a context of labels rather than things themselves in lived use. It is what make structuralism possible, of course, and it is no less than the original Saussurean dichotomy between signifying vehicle and thing represented.

But language also has its ontological properties, and it is in these properties that Heidegger is most interested. The ontological properties of language arise from the fact that speaking is an activity like other bodily activities, and mirrors the world as a reflection of our concernful engagement in it. Language in this sense places things in their existential relations of relative nearness to and distance from the speaker. It "names" a thing not by attaching a factitious, arbitrary label to it but rather by revealing it in all its various contextual relations within our world. Language reveals the "world," which as Heidegger defines it is the most encompassing term for activities that pertain to "involvement in one's surroundings" (Halliburton 1981: 28).

Language in this mode does not *represent* things. To represent something is essentially a distancing act which substitutes for the thing in its primordial reality a manipulable word whose only context is speech itself. Heidegger is describing a language which preserves the true thing in its human dimensions, rather than a code which assigns a token label to a thing abstractly conceived. This language, this existential language, is what Heidegger calls poetry.

Heidegger does not mean by this that such language must take the form of verse and meter; that all language is originally couple, rhythmic and rhyming form. These are the laborious forms with which poets have had to reinvent the poetic out of a language that has succumbed to formalism, a language that has become dominated by its signifiers instead of its signifieds.

Heidegger instead is referring to what Ezra Pound and the imagists surmised language to be in its pristine state. Pound's notions of image and ideogram were inspired to a great extent by Ernest Fenollosa's essay "The Chinese Written Character as a Medium for Poetry." Fenollosa's far-sighted consideration of the iconic nature of the Chinese ideogram led Pound to conclude that "a language written in this way simply HAD TO STAY POETIC" (1951: 22). Fenollosa concluded:

> The Chinese written language has not only absorbed the poetic substance of nature and built with it a second world of metaphor, but has, through its very pictorial visibility, been able to retain its original creative poetry with far more vigor and vividness than any phonetic tongue. (1967: 378)

Fenollosa's most valuable contribution is this assertion of a phenomenological theory of metaphor itself. It is not that imagist poetry or haiku does away with metaphor—hardly, since metaphor lies at the heart of what poetry reveals. But poetry does more than offer novel metaphoric juxtapositions. It embodies the fundamental relations between people and their lifeworld; it is the first language of experience itself. "Metaphor, the revealer of nature, is the very substance of poetry," Fenollosa wrote, and the first metaphors were "at once the substance of nature and of language" (ibid.: 377, 378). Andrew Welsh, in his valuable assessment of Fenollosa, put it simply: "Language can structure the world as well as it does because the world once structured language" (1978: 126). E. F. Kaelin in his lucid summary of Heidegger's aesthetics said much the same thing when he characterized Heidegger's approach to poetic language as "so constituted as to produce this contact with the world and [engage] the entire structure of perceiving being" (1967: 73).

The question of *ontology*—that is, a consideration of the preconditions of our knowledge of and action in the world—is of course critical for anthropology. The existentialist position I am borrowing from Heidegger and Merleau-Ponty seems to me preferable to the orthodox, unreflective assumption of a superorganicism as our taken-for-granted subject matter. I want to avoid considering the question of the constitution of social life from a consideration of the constitution of the world at large. What we are interested to call "meaning" cannot exist prior to perception; rather, it is part and parcel of the perceptual act itself. Perception, of course, does include the perception of "recognizable, relatively enduring patterns in the interactions of many individuals" (Kultgen 1975: 382)—it is not that I want to deny the effects of communal intersubjectivity; it is only that it seems improper to assign a transcendental and determining force to this perception over others. By so doing, we destroy the individuative, creative half of perceptual symbolization in favor of its collectivizing half; we preempt a consideration of all that Michael Jackson reminds us is "spare, original, strange" in life. As Wagner suggests, there is nothing "more" cultural in art or artistic creation than there is in "ordinary" apprehension:

> The difference between ordinary perception and artistic creativity is not that between a naturalistic "sensing" of the world and an artificial, meaningful "interpretation" of that sensing, but rather it is a difference between one kind of meaningful act and another one, of greater concentration, organization, and force, within the same semiotic focus. The power of a great music, of a compelling tradition in poetry or painting, is the power of concentrating and preempting, organizing, orchestrating and distilling, the significance that serves us in our ordinary apprehension of reality. (Wagner 1986: 27)

One destroys the work of art "by deploying between oneself and the work"

> all manner of representations, such as the concept of a dichotomy between form and content or the concept that the work stands over against some other reality, as a signifier stands over and against a signified. The effect would be to diminish the transformational power of the work. (Halliburton 1981: 39–40)

At the same time, neither am I advocating some crass materialism or some vulgar mimetic theory (any more than was Lévi-Strauss when he noted the role of natural speciation in totemic thought). I am merely trying to situate a study of language as we confront it, as a mode of engagement in a lifeworld. I am suggesting that we take seriously the observations made by many modern poets and critics, both Western and Japanese, that poetry begins with the "inevitable desire to express the objective," the effect of which is "a progressive expression of the eternally objective within the temporarily subjective" (Wadsworth 1914: 120). In representing the world, men and women also reconstitute their characteristic modes of engaging with it.[3]

Let us first look at several examples of the kinds of discourse to which I have been referring. One of the most important forms of Foi men's use of metaphor is what they call *kusadobora*, "spell talk" or magic. As I noted briefly in *The Heart of the Pearl Shell*, spells in Foi have a standardized format which focuses on the invocation of a semantic parallelism. This format is as follows:

I am not doing x
I am doing y

or:

> This is not an *x*
> This is a *y*

For example, a man who is about to plant *wasia* pitpit (*Setaria palmifolia*) recites a spell, the central equation of which is:

> I am not planting this pitpit
> I am planting the feathers of a hawk as it flaps its wings

As I and others have noted (for example, Wagner 1972; Schieffelin 1980), the intent of this format is to effect a transfer of properties from one domain to another. In this case, the sudden enlargement of the hawk as it spreads its wings is used to represent the desired sudden and rapid growth of this cultivar.

A more important category of spell contains references to mythical characters. For example, in a spell for transplanting sago shoots of the *honamo* variety, a man says:

> I am not planting this sago sucker
> I am planting the skull of Tononawi

Tononawi is the name of a character in a Foi myth that deals with the reciprocity of revenge killing (see Weiner 1988: chap. 11). There are no references to the spell in the myth, which is freely recounted publicly. Only men who know the spell, which, by contrast, is private property, realize the link between it and the actions of Tononawi in the myth. The point is that the magic spell deliberately proposes two separate domains which it then compares, equates, or draws together. It is a *semiotic* relationship pure and simple, and a use of metaphor in its most basic Aristotelian definition. In its dependence on the *contrast* between things being compared, this kind of metaphor opens the door for structural analysis, itself originating in the original Saussurean dichotomy between form and meaning.

Now let us compare this format with Foi song:

(Song 8):[4]

1. *duma   yefua sabe ya   erege*
   mountain Yefua ridge bird cockatoo

   auwa fore   iba'ae
   wing broken is

   ibu sumani habo   ya   namuyu
   creek Sumani water end bird cockatoo

   vira hua   uboba'a
   shot struck gone

2. *duma   faī hesabo   ya   erege*
   mountain side following bird cockatoo

   auwa forabo'owa'ae
   wing broken

   duma   ka'afa hesabo   ya   namuyu
   mountain edge   following bird cockatoo

   vira huiba'ae
   shot killed

3. *ira farabo haū   bobo ya   namuyu*
   tree farabo break off leaves bird cockatoo

   auwa gefodiyo'owa'ae
   wing spear pierced

   ira sonane haū   bobo ya   namuyu
   tree sonane break off leaves bird cockatoo

   auwa fore   iba'ae
   wing broken is

4. *yiya amena ira so'one*
   we   men   tree so'one

   hedawabo
   dawabo

   yiya amena ira namani
   we   men   tree namani

   dawabo
   dawabo

5. *yo hūa   ka   mege bamo*
   his mother woman only that

   kabe Suibu
   man Sui

   yo hūa   ka   mege bamo
   his mother woman only that

   kabe Sui
   man Sui

1. The ridge of Mt. Yefua, the sulphur-crested cockatoo
   Its wing is broken

At Sumani Creek as it flows underground, the cockatoo
Its wing is broken

2. Following the side of the mountain, the cockatoo
Its wing broken

Along the edge of the mountain's base, the cockatoo
Arrow shot and killed

3. The cockatoo breaks off the leaves of the *farabo* tree as it flies
Its wing broken

The leaves of the *so'one* tree, broken off by the
   cockatoo's flapping wings
Its wing broken

4. We are the men of the *so'one* tree clan
Ibu Duwabo

We are the men of the *namani* tree clan
Dawabo

5. His mother, the only woman
Her son, Sui

His mother, the only woman
Her son, Sui

This song, as in principle do all Foi songs, commemorates a deceased man, in this case, Yabokigi of Hegeso village. The dead man is spoken of as a bird who falls to the earth with a broken wing. The subject of the song is not overtly named until the last refrain (termed the *dawa* in Foi song terminology). Yet he is identified as a member of the So'onedobo clan because the sulphur-crested cockatoo is one of the principal totems of So'onedobo, and the places named in the song—Mt. Yefua, the end of the Sumani Creek—are So'onedobo clan territories which Yabokigi inhabited during his lifetime. Further, the falling leaves of the *so'one* tree, the eponymous totem tree of that clan, suggest the loss of a clan's male members, as do the falling leaves of the *namani* tree, another totem species of So'onedobo (so that this clan is often referred to as "Namanidobo" in songs). Finally, the *furabu* tree is a large *Ficus* variety that is identified with head-man status, and a fallen *furabu* tree is a conventional metaphor in dream and song for the death of a head-man, again identifying the former head-man Yabokigi.

This song thus relies on the most conventional of metaphoric designations for its imagery; how does it differ, then, from the magic spell? The efficacy of the magic spell lies in its rote memorization and recital; the substance of the analogy is backgrounded to the purely magical or instrumental effects of the words. The effect is perceived by Foi men in large part as a function of the esoteric nature of the magical words themselves, many of which are often in foreign languages.

But a Foi song, unlike a spell, is always an individual composition. It is an attempt to render an emotion or interior state in terms of a concrete object or sensual experience. The song *evokes*; the magic spell does not. The song produces a direct emotional response; the spell seeks a pragmatic transformation. The song does not, as does the spell, focus on the equation between two putatively *separate* domains; it reaffirms the more fundamental affective and evocative properties of such cognitive manipulation.

It is important to note at this point that unlike the Kaluli, the Foi do not focus on the *instrumental* properties of this imagery. The success of a song is, it is true, measured by its ability to evoke emotion in people, but this property is not made into a ceremonial contest, as is the case with the *gisaro*. Emotion itself is not commoditized or objectified, as it seems to be among the Bosavi peoples, and perhaps it is this externalized quality of emotion in Bosavi that fosters the idea that song and emotion can be linked as expressions of each other. Nor, like their nearest neighbors to the east, the Kewa, do the Foi use such songs as an adjunct to rhetorical encounters between competing political units (LeRoy 1978), although the ability to employ creative metaphor is essential to the Foi's own rhetorical contests.

Like the love songs of the Avatip of the Sepik River region of Papua New Guinea (Harrison 1982), Foi memorial songs arise in the perception of the tragic dimensions of the life condition. For the Avatip, this is the perception of the frustration and longing that stem from thwarted or unrequited love; for the Foi it is the alienation that results from the death or loss of loved ones. Kunuhuaka of Barutage village, living in Hegeso, was not only one of the most accomplished poets of my acquaintance but also the most articulate when it came to explaining the sources of her poetic inspiration. One of her loveliest songs, however, was actually taught to her by her mother, who explained that one day in the bush, her little boy, Ta'anobo, became lost. She wandered around the bush in the region named Ayamo calling Ta'anobo's name, but all she heard in reply was the sound of birds crying out *"i! i!, wo! wo!"*

(*Sago song 4*):

1. In this uninhabited place I hear the *sisiyu* bird
   But I hear no men

2. The mountainside, the *u* bird
   But I hear no men's speech

3. At the place of the *yamo* sago, the *sisiyu* bird
   But you only I hear not

4. Where the *gabe* sago is, the *muri* bird
   But to me you do not speak

5. At the bend in Ama'afu Creek, the *sisiyu* bird
   But you alone do not speak

6. At the mouth of the Fifigiri Creek, the *u* bird
   But you alone speak not

7. At Segenabi Creek, the *u* bird
   But you do not call out

8. At Saburuba Creek, the *muri* bird
   But you do not speak

9. At Dāri Creek, the *sisiyu* bird
   But you do not speak

10. At the base of Mt. Sobore
    You only do not call out

11. At the mouth of Guratõa Creek, the *u* bird
    But you do not sing out

12. At the place of the *dāre* sago, the *sisiyu* bird
    But you do not speak

13. At the place of the *yamo* sago, the *sisiyu* bird
    But you I hear not

14. At Yegena, the *muri* bird
    But you do not call out

15. At the place of the *geroa* cane, the *muri* bird
    But you do not call out

16. At the empty place Yegena, the *sisiyu* bird
    But I hear no other sound

17. At Mt. Weyeru, the *muri* bird
    But you do not call out

18. At Īsa Creek, the *yiyo* bird
    But you alone do not call out

19. At Dāri Creek, the *muri* bird
    But you only do not speak

20. At Aboragemo Creek, the *u* bird
    But you alone do not speak

21. This sago mallet
    Strike quickly

22. Ta'anobo is calling out
    He keeps calling out

23. Ta'anobo's namesake, the bird
    He keeps calling out

This song seems to me a splendid example of what Pound referred to as the "one-image poem": "a form of super-position, that is to say, it is one idea set on top of another. . . . in a poem of this sort one is trying to record the precise instant when a thing outward and objective transforms itself, or darts into a thing inward and subjective" (1916: 103).

The Foi of the Hegeso area, the uppermost part of the Mubi River inhabited by people, call their region *awa hao*, "the empty place," and they refer to themselves as *awamena*, as opposed to, for example, the people who live around Lake Kutubu, the *gurubumena*, and the Lower Foi people, the true *foimena* (see map 1-1). When I asked them why they call it the empty place, they replied:

> The people of the Lake, or the Lower Foi people around the end of the Soro River, they have their hunting area and their garden area in one place; they live where there is meat. But as you know, we live in the Mubi Valley here where there is only sago, and we have to travel a long way to Ayamo, where the animals are, where people do not live. So we call the Mubi Valley the empty place, or the dry place, because there is no meat here.

Kunuhuaka's song evokes the *awamena's* view of their habitat as an encompassing life condition: that where there is meat, yet there are not people; that the search for meat pulls people apart from the gregarious effects of life that centers around the communal longhouse village. As the songs will make clear, the Foi ultimately make of this a tragic image: that the male quest for meat, the exemplary activity of men, isolates them from other members of the community as effectively as death.

As Kunuhuaka and numerous Foi men explained to me, certain experiences of sound and sight have the power to evoke sentiments of abandonment, grief, and loss (as they do for the Kaluli [Feld 1982]). The memory of dead kinsmen is a constant and engaging conceptualization for the Foi; the sound and sights of the forest and the innumerable creeks and rivers where one shared one's life and experience with the departed emerge as poignant evidence of a landscape now rendered empty by the loss of those who quickened it through the significant and "concernful" acts of living.

Thus, sago melodies all begin as mourning songs; though they become thematically more varied, the "poetics of loss and abandonment" remain a substrate of imagery throughout the entire range of song themes.

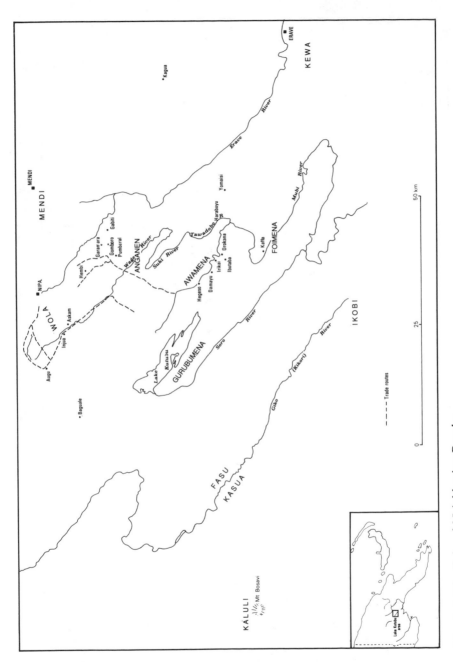

Map 1-1. The Foi and Neighboring Peoples

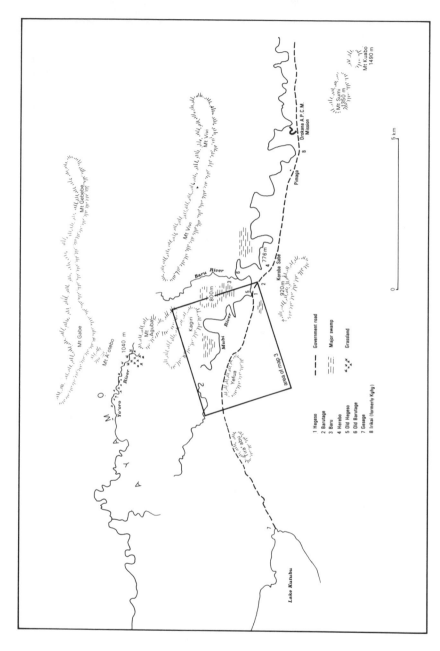

Map 1–2. The Mubi Valley (Maps 2–1, 2–2, and 3–4 below depict the area within the square)

A common way of depicting death is given in the following sago song, which was performed as a women's ceremonial *sorohabora* by two Hegeso women:

(*Women's Song 6*):

1. He who planted the *sa'ara* pitpit
   His hand is cold

2. He who planted the *kamua* pitpit
   His hand is stiff and lifeless

3. He who planted the *wayane* pitpit
   His hand is dead

4. He who planted the *diame* pitpit
   His hand is still and without life

5. He of the clan of the *namani* tree, Yaroge
   Dawa

6. She of the clan of the *wa'ari* tree, Hasobe
   Dawa

7. The man of the *namani* tree clan
   Yaroge

8. The child of the *wa'ari* tree woman only
   The boy Sega

This is a song beautiful in its simplicity, in the way it so clearly evokes contrasting images of life and death for the Foi. A garden is the very epitome of regenerative life; it grows and swells as a man's and woman's life does, and to the Foi it is the most convincing index of the vivacious appropriation of space. And dead vegetation grows sere and yellowed, suggesting the yellow hue of dead or aged flesh.

All Foi clans have numerous totemic species associated with them, and any of these species can "stand for" both the clan and its component individuals. The most important series of totemic designations are tree species, and in referring to the deceased (in this case, the man Sega) as the child of his father's and mother's clan trees, the song tacitly suggests regeneration, as of the fruit of these two *Ficus*-species trees. In this simple melody, then, is contrasted the vegetative regrowth of manmade gardens (and the tenuousness of such regeneration, because it is interrupted by the death of the gardener) with the more permanent regeneration of the trees, which need no human intervention to bear their fruit. Like the trees themselves, the clans live on despite the fact that their individual fruits ripen and fall to the ground. Thus, this song, like all Foi songs, seems to bear out Pound's general definition of poetry: "the most concentrated form of verbal expression" (1951: 36). It is by this concentration of "discursive value," if you will, that the spatiotemporal world of the Foi is affirmed and made accessible. Let us now explore the linguistic capacity which enables this.

In *The Heart of the Pearl Shell,* I analyzed the procreative ideology of the Foi, and the constellation of social relationships that derives from it, as a working out of the implications of their bipartite view of men's and women's corporeal attributes. With respect to reproductive functions, men consider that women are *self-sufficient*: that is, they have the spontaneous and continual ability to produce menstrual blood, the most important procreative substance. Men, by contrast, produce only small amounts of semen in the course of their lives, and moreover, semen has, though a necessary, yet a quite limited role in conception. Since men cannot control reproduction by virtue of any corporeal advantage, they manipulate women's menstrual capacity by giving bridewealth to a woman's male kinsmen. This gives the husband the right to claim that woman's issue as his own, rather than as the woman's brothers', to whom children are "naturally," or unproblematically, related. Men's reproduction is *contingent*, therefore, on the manipulation of exterior objects, namely, the pearl shells and other wealth items that constitute marriage payments.

This ideology embodies in a fundamental sense the *experience* of male and female vitality for the Foi: their perception of the difficulties in impregnation; the periodicity, regularity, and predictability of women's menses; the paucity of semen as opposed to the great quantities of blood women produce; the fact that human bodies are filled with blood, which is the female contribution during gestation.

But the notions of contingency and self-sufficiency, being essential subjective evaluations of experience, are not limited to this narrow definition of physical reproduction; they embody a general apperception of men's and women's total life condition and underwrite a moral appraisal of action and social purpose. For the Foi, the world is experienced as a collection of distinct though analogous rhythmic, periodic, and ceaseless movements: the movement of water from west to east; the journey of the souls of the dead to the afterworld in the same direction; the alternation of monsoon and dry seasons and the periodic ripening of annual crops; the continual flow of women's procreative substance; the journey of the sun through the sky. It is men's responsibility to cut, channel, and redirect these flows for morally appropriate ends: they set traps in the forest and rivers to catch edible animals and fish; they pay bridewealth to a woman's relatives to transform her procreative capacities into a male analogy of female continuity; they manipulate cult objects so as to "fix" the power of ghosts in particular places for their own ends.[5]

The perception of men's and women's characteristic productive activity—and I mean this in an encompassing sense of all concernful acts through which individuals become aware of, manipulate, and leave their imprint on their world —models this basic dichotomy. Men carry cutting tools, the axes and knives that are an extension of their active, manipulatory being, and use them in the most important male tasks—collecting, felling trees, making canoes and houses, and, in traditional times, fighting. Women carry string bags, fishing nets, and sago baskets, which hold, encompass, and embody the product of certain important natural flows: children, food crops, sago starch, fish, and foraged semidomesticates.

As another activity of being, speech is no more or less instrumental than the exertions of the limbs, no less implementary than clearing a garden or making sago. I would therefore like to suggest that there are distinct male and female approaches to signification and linguistic embodiment themselves among the Foi, and that these approaches are coterminous with the characteristics of male and female "equipment" in general. I mean "equipment" in Heidegger's sense: that of *pragmata* appropriated in the course of our dealings with the world (1962: 97). More important, as the carrying and using of distinct tools and implements "stands for" distinct acting male and female identities among the Foi, so do characteristic modes of signification and topics of discourse delimit the male and female speaking Foi subjects.[6]

The forms of speech with which men constitute their assertiveness as males are all examples of what has been conventionally called "metaphoric" speech in New Guinea. There are many reports of forms of discourse whose purpose is to conceal and "cut off" signification rather than reveal or explicate. Usages which "preempt" lexical signification by substituting a figurative for a literal meaning in this way are variously called "turned over words" among the Kaluli (Feld 1982), "veiled speech" among the Melpa (A. Strathern 1975), "tree leaf talk" among the Foi, and "pandanus talk" among the Kewa (Franklin 1978). In Foi, for example, one can refer to a person by any of the totemic species of that person's clan; a man can refer to his penis as "pandanus fruit" or "bamboo"; men speaking circumspectly of murder talk of "rolling a smoke"; "mushroom" often means a gift of meat; and so on. But "tree leaf talk" is also a term for concealed or hidden signification in general, as well as these standardized usages that everyone knows. A man, for example, indignant that he was being left out of the negotiations for the marriage of his clan niece, chose to express this by complaining about those of his clansmates who were in the habit of borrowing his prize hunting dog when they went to the bush. Such usages are part and parcel of men's oratorical encounters, and because the hidden meaning of the discourse will become apparent only to some men present, these forms of concealed speech allow men of status to converse at several levels at once and in effect to conduct private dialogues in the midst of public oratory.

Finally, both men and women, but primarily men, have a stock set of metaphoric equivalences which they use to interpret the allegedly portentous significance of dream imagery. And as with tree leaf talk itself, there is a distinction between those equivalences which are commonly known (for example, the equation between a dream of sexual intercourse and portended success in hunting;

between a dream of a house falling down in disrepair and the imminent death of a man; between a dream of red bird feathers and future success in pearl shell acquisition) and those dreams which require the interpretation of particularly skilled men.[7]

The crucial feature of the metaphors of dream interpretation, magic, and much of tree leaf talk is that a great deal of them are *standardized*: the appearance of certain conventional dream images means the same thing in any man's dream; magic spells rest on the rote learning of metaphoric equivalences which again are invariant in the context of the spell. Such standardization collapses the impact of these metaphoric usages into a variety of referential signification: metaphors though they still remain, the degree to which they impinge upon conventional usages has become attenuated.

In all cases, knowledge of these metaphoric equivalences is jealously guarded and can be transferred from one man to another for a payment of shell wealth. They are not thought to have individual *authors*. In effect, they constitute an alternative—and restricted—referential *code*, and they do not transform or enhance conventional usages as much as they *restate* them.

The images of poetry, as opposed to the metaphors I have just described, on the other hand, are individually authored; knowledge of who wrote them is indispensable for construing and interpreting them. They don't reposition conventional usages; they truly preempt them by laying stress on speech's more basic *evocative* function. Poetry is not merely a more complicated way of interlayering additional metaphoric equivalences. It is a resynthesis of our experience of the objective, and, as Hugh Kenner says, "it is in precisely this dimension that poetry is most resistant to exegesis" (1951: 64).

This is not to say that all women are poets, or that men are incapable of poetic imagery. The rhetoric of men's oratorical encounters relies heavily on image, just as the imagery of many women's poetry becomes almost standardized and conventional itself. Men and women display virtuosity in both modalities, since they are a feature of the linguistic condition generally. I do not want to be interpreted as reifying male-female *opposition* in Foi society, because faith in the self-evidence of sexual bipolarity is no less a feature of Cartesian thinking than a belief in the absolute division of mind and body. The use of metaphor always evokes the image, just as the image has no vehicle other than metaphor for its embodiment. The distinction I am appealing to is therefore a matter of sexual *habitus* in the use of one of these components to elicit the other.[8] In these terms, the linguistic functions I have been discussing *are* accorded distinct social valences by the Foi.

The key feature of the true image is that it cannot be rendered into other terms. Alexander Baumgarten and Karsten Harries[9] have insisted upon the self-sufficiency of the poetic image: it resists rephrasing in others' terms, and it is positively adamantine in its resistance to semantic decomposition. Women thus are the *image makers*; their use of metaphor is also self-sufficient, like their bodies, and thus assumes poetic, rather than formulaic, shape. Men, on the other hand, are the *semanticists*: they employ discourse as a means to an end, defined by them as revelatory power. They commoditize semantic equivalence so as to cut off the flow of meaning rather than enhance it. They reposition reference rather than by-pass or obviate it, as women's poetic usages do. Women's images embody a self-signifying world of evocation distinct from the conventional tropes of quotidian experience; they reveal the flow of analogy between discursive domains that experience confirms. Men's secret codes sever the discursive and conceptual links between experiential realms themselves, and attempt to render meaning stationary for the purposes of their individual self-aggrandizement.[10]

Thus, I maintain that poetic usages contrast with semantic ones in Foi as image contrasts with metaphor, and that, furthermore, this contrast itself models a dichotomy within the total Foi practico-discursive *hexis*. Men initiate metaphoric conventions by lending to dream interpretation, magic, and oratory a utilitarian and political currency. Women "extend and maintain" the metaphors that men deal in by imagistically revealing their spatiohistorical implications. Women articulate the sensual, spatiotemporal qualities of the human life course; men implement magical and oneiric equations between the various tokens that are adjuncts of their male identity: primarily pearl shells, birds, and animals. This states in more general terms the contrast between women as *producers* and men as *transactors* that Marilyn Strathern (1972) has observed to be a general feature of intersexual mediation in interior highlands New Guinea societies. One might say that Foi women *produce* images in the course of their feminine life activity as they produce vegetable food and children. Men *reify* these flows of feminine productivity into the adjuncts of their own contingent productivity: they turn male children into clansmen; women and pigs into shell wealth; vegetable food into the currency of their own relations of nurturative indebtedness. And of course they take women's songs and make of them the performative accessory to male display and assertive vainglory in public ceremonial. Men, in other words, *transact* with the product of women's self-sufficient imagination.

> Lived experiences first become meaningful . . . when they are explicated *post hoc* and become comprehensible . . . as well-circumscribed experiences. Thus only those lived experiences are subjectively meaningful which are memorially brought forth in their actuality. . . . (Schutz and Luckmann 1973: 16)

What I am calling the memorial songs of the Foi—they are sung only to the memory of deceased men and have no other subject—accomplish this precise function of providing a communal assessment and recognition of the central existential features of lived experience for the Foi. As an *aesthetic* form, they also provide the ceremonial form for the Foi's most poignant reconstruction of male and female capacities, the nature of life, death, and territoriality, and the continuity between parents and children. The next chapter details the spatial dimensions within which the images of living poetry acquire their impact.

N O T E S

1. See also Glickman 1978; Goodman 1978; Tormey 1971.

2. For example, in Silverstein's paper "Metaforces of Power in Traditional Oratory" (1981).

3. Michael Jackson in his discussion of the centrality of body metaphors has suggested that it is

> not enough to say that they arise because subjectivity can identify itself only through external objects . . . or that anthropomorphic metaphors simply reflect the fact that, ontogenetically, the first "language" of life is gestural, postural and bodily. . . . For to emphasize the psychophysical or social aspects of metaphor construction and use is unhelpful as long as it implies a dualistic conception of human behaviour. . . . My argument is that metaphor must be apprehended non-dualistically and that the idea or sensation and its bodily complements (social, mechanical, physiological, geographical, etc.) betoken, not an arbitrary or rhetorical synthesis of two terms . . . but a true interdependency of mind and body. (1983: 132)

4. The number given to each Foi song in this book refers to my own cataloguing.

5. An analysis of such cults is given in Weiner 1987.

6. Benveniste evinces a Heideggerian approach to the *Dasein* of discourse when he suggests that "every utterance assumes a speaker and a hearer, and in the speaker, the intention of influencing the other in some way" (1971: 226). In terms of language-as-equipment, "Language is . . . the possibility of subjectivity because it always contains the linguistic forms appropriate to the expression of subjectivity" (p. 227).

7. I discuss details of Foi dream imagery and interpretation in Weiner 1986.

8. I am grateful to Roy Wagner for illuminating this point.

9. From Baumgarten's *Reflections on Poetry*, quoted in Harries 1979: 71–88.

10. This distinction has parallels among the Navajo. Witherspoon (1977: 142, 160) notes that Navajo men are exclusively sand painters, a form of art that stresses the static quality of things, whereas women weave, an activity that emphasizes the fluid, mutable, and dynamic qualities of movement.

2

SPACE AND NAMING

The Inscriptive Effects of Foi
Life Activity

Bright, Bright, the flowering tree
That's taken root upon this spot.
The blossoms that it shone with in the
    morning,
It will have lost before the night has fallen.
Human life is like a sojourning
Yet for melancholy there is time to spare.
Brooding long in silence on these things
My heart is filled with bitterness and grief.
        —T'ao Ch'ien (365–427)[1]

LET US BEGIN with the assumption that it is only through language that the world and its contents become accessible to us. By language do I mean only speech, words, grammar, and so forth? By no means. Speech is only one of all of our kinesthetic, bodily activities. All of our postures, attitudes, orientations, movements, and actions, as intentionally constituted, mark out the world in the same way as does our lexical labeling. In fact, to separate the two is to invoke the orthodox Cartesian dichotomy between the mind and the body.

Our intentions and concerns structure the world; they "polarize" the world's objects and dimensions in terms of their relation to such concerns. Lived space is constituted as the graphic record of such intentional consciousness over time. Through our acts of concernful appropriation of objects which we put to use, we turn the ontic, inchoate, qualityless environment into *existential space*: the space in which human intention inscribes itself upon the earth, as Eric Dardel puts it.[2] Relph suggests that "places in existential space can therefore be understood as centres of meaning, or focusses of intention and purpose" (1976: 22). This *inscriptive* activity of the body is encompassed within a comprehensive "linguistic" capacity, of which the verbally *descriptive* function of speech is only one manifestation.

For Merleau-Ponty, lived space is structured by our patterned acts within it, by the meaning and end of our intentions within it. To structure space in this way means

> to mark out boundaries and directions in the given world, to establish lines of
> force, to keep perspectives in view, in a word, to organize the given world in

accordance with the projects of the present moment, to build into the geographical setting a behavioural one, a system of meanings outwardly expressive of the subject's internal activity. (1962: 112)

In this chapter I would like to describe the lineaments of the Foi spatial world and to explicate the role that naming plays in constituting this world as an intersubjective, social one. I maintain that Foi song poetry *is* poetic because it reveals to the Foi in their maximally intense moments of social engagement the existential foundations of that world. The poem precisely encapsulates a set of "meanings outwardly expressive of the subject's internal activity," which, as I noted in the last chapter, Ezra Pound suggested was the essence of imagist poetry and which Merleau-Ponty above described as the essence of humanly inscribed space.

Heidegger maintained that the poet *names* things: not in the sense of labeling them, for they already are represented to us by such labels. Names, on the other hand, expose things in their being, that is, in terms of their true relation to our life condition. David White has provided one of the most incisive interpretations of Heidegger's writings on this subject:

Names bestow what Heidegger calls a measured command over entities. The measure is the extent to which any given name is a locus wherein may be experienced relations between the being of the entity named and being as totality. (White 1978: 25)

In other words, a society's place names schematically image a people's intentional transformation of their habitat from a sheer physical terrain into a pattern of historically experienced and constituted space and time. "Space is a society of named places, just as people are landmarks within the group," Lévi-Strauss noted (1966: 168). The bestowing of place names constitutes Foi existential space out of a blank environment; it reveals what Merleau-Ponty described as the figure-ground reversal of nearness and remoteness. Let us first examine how this existential contrast emerges for the Foi.

FOI EXISTENTIAL SPACE

In contrast to the Euclidean space of absolute, geometric dimension, I would like to describe the way existential space is constituted for the Foi through their life activity. Relph has suggested that such space consists of a threefold division:

First there is a set of *districts* or regions of particular significance, defined by the interests and experiences of the [people] concerned. . . . They are organized and opened up by *paths* . . . which reflect the directions and intensities of intentions and experiences, and which serve as the structural axes of existential space. They radiate from and lead towards nodes or centres of special importance and meaning which are distinguished by their quality of insideness. These are *places*. (1976: 21)

Relph also makes the crucially important observation that "this pattern of places, paths and districts is repeated in some form at all levels of existential space" (ibid.). It is evident on at least two levels in the creation of the spatial world of the Foi of Hegeso.

Foi Hunting Territory. First, there is the division of the major regions of Hegeso territory: (1) the centrally located territory which is the domain of permanent human occupation, the land around the Mubi River, and (2) the region called Ayamo, the hunting preserve north of this inhabited territory. Ayamo is delimited by the valley of the Yo'oro River (a tributary of the Augu River northeast of it). This area is reserved for hunting, trapping, fishing, and collecting. No one dwells permanently at Ayamo, though traditionally, most men and their families spent several months of the year there. There is one major path from the Mubi Valley to Ayamo: it crosses a small ridge that lies between the Baru and the Yo'oro rivers (actually, the Yo'oro is the northernmost extension of the Baru, though they are separated by an expanse of porous karst through which the river flows underground). On the north side of the ridge one descends to the Yo'oro River. There, the people of Barutage and Hegeso keep canoes which give them access to their various properties by way of the Yo'oro, which is navigable.

I am not acquainted with the details of everyday life at Ayamo in the same way I know life on the banks of the Mubi. I spent one four-day period in 1981 with three men, during which time we hunted with dogs, dammed a small creek to find fish, and gathered bush-fowl eggs and tree grubs. Because of the responsibilities now incumbent upon the Foi to attend weekly church services, allow their children to attend local primary schools, provide labor for rotational maintenance projects, and seek wage employment, the men and women of Hegeso spend far less time at Ayamo than they did traditionally. Whereas in the past, so I was told, certain times of year would find nearly the entire village at their hunting retreats, nowadays at any given time no more than several members of the village are at Ayamo. Two Hegeso men habitually spent much time there over the last ten years. Many young men with no responsibilities went regularly for short trips. Older married men with families spent the least amount of time at Ayamo. These are just impressions on my part, as I kept no records.

The dwelling we stayed in during our trip was, men assured me, typical of Ayamo houses: a sleeping platform built right on the ground (in contrast to all other Foi dwellings, which are built on posts) and a lean-to roof sheltering one side of the sleeping area. There was one narrow firepit, and four men and two dogs slept rather snugly under the roof.

Hunting with dogs at Ayamo involves allowing the animals to smell out trees where marsupials are sleeping. As we followed the dogs through the bush, those trees in which they showed interest were inspected for claw marks or other signs that they were inhabited by marsupials. When a game animal is located, the nimblest member of the party is given the task of climbing the tree and scaring the marsupial into dropping down to the ground, where it can be attacked by the dogs and the men with their axes. Alternatively, men remarked to me that the tree could be felled to the same effect.

No gardens are made at Ayamo, but people do plant small amounts of sago and certain greens characteristically eaten with meat. The owner of the house in which we stayed had planted quantities of the broad, banana-shaped *kā'i* leaf, used by the Foi for lining earth ovens, and some *Hibiscus manihot* (Foi: *ga'ana*). The Foi seem to make an exaggerated contrast between the activities one pursues at Ayamo and those one engages in when living in the Mubi Valley, as the next section details.

SEASONAL VARIATION

In contrast to the present-day situation, in traditional times, so I was told, the people of the Mubi Valley used to devote a great deal of the year between March and September to hunting and life at Ayamo. It is during this time that the southeasterly monsoon brings an increase in rainfall, lower temperatures, much cloudiness, and drizzly weather to the Mubi Valley. In addition, the fruits of certain *Ficus*-species trees such as *gofe* (*Ficus pungens*), *bāngo*, and *waria* begin to ripen from March onward. These fruits are avidly sought by rodents, marsupials, and cassowaries. Around March the bush fowl also begin laying their eggs inside their large mounded nests. Many Foi men and women thus spent much time during this part of the year trapping, hunting, fishing, and gathering at Ayamo. With the cessation of the southeasterlies and the return of dry daytime weather in October, these people would return to their bush houses along the Mubi and begin preparing their gardens (see Weiner 1988: 33–40).

It is important to understand the "locus" of seasonal variation for the Foi. They do not, for example, reckon that the rain has started to increase, and so it is time to abandon the village; they do not time their movement by the ripening of the fig trees, nor do they inspect the ground for evidence of increased traffic of animals. Their seasonal residential alternation, such as it is, begins with one or more men deciding to move to Ayamo for a time. Others may wait for a while, or not go at all. How the Foi *conceptualize* their yearly cycle is only as good (or bad) a "model" of people's actual movements as the anthropologist is willing to grant.

It is sufficient to note that movement between Ayamo and the Mubi Valley was traditionally periodic, that the Foi speak of it as seasonal. Ayamo is a place in time as well as a region in space. As a time, it is also a product of people's inscriptive, bodily activity. Temporality, like spatiality, is also created by intentional consciousness-*toward-things*. Seasonal variation, then, begins and ends in the *movement* of Foi people between Ayamo and the Mubi.

The dispersion and isolation of Hegeso people are at their most visible at Ayamo. Houses there are empty most of the year. Not everyone is there at the same time. The region is much bigger than the Foi's gardening territory, and people are more spread out; hence they encounter each other less frequently. One doesn't enjoy the neighborly feeling of seeing people's houses go by one by one while paddling along the Mubi River. At Ayamo there are no gardens, no large plantings; the visible signs of people's presence are smaller and less noticeable: traps which are made of forest materials themselves and which are further camouflaged by overgrowth; the small framework of fish dams just visible along the surface of a creek mouth; a recently disturbed bush-fowl nest. During our hunting trip we walked through pathless bush: there are no paths through Ayamo.

In every sense, Ayamo is *remote*. Although it is a relatively short distance away by Foi standards (people can reach their territory in Ayamo in well under a day's travel), to cross Mt. Aguba and descend to the Yo'oro River is to enter another world. It is distanced from communal life in the village by its very exoticness. There, men seem to live a fantasy caricature of their life; they can spend all day hunting and indulge their appetite for meat (if they are lucky). In quiet evenings in the longhouse, during meal breaks in the garden, wherever they have the chance to gossip, men exchange stories about life at Ayamo, savoring the minor triumphs and frustrations of the hunt. Remote in space and time as it might be, it is never far away from men's concerns.

Mubi Valley Territory. The regional contrast between the Mubi Valley and Ayamo is the first level of existential space for the Foi. The second revolves around the contrast between longhouse and bush within the Mubi Valley itself.

It is not, by and large, a man's public, longhouse-centered life that is memorialized in song poetry (though I examine several examples of just that in chapter 7). Rather, it is in terms of his purposeful activity away from the longhouse, in the bush, that a man's life course is usually depicted poetically. Let us turn to the bush house and see what are the inscriptive effects of men's life in the bush.

The shelters that people occupy in their hunting areas such as Ayamo are called *aya a*, "hunting houses," or, as *aya* also means "up, upward, ascending," they could be called "houses up above." From such houses people carry out only those activities associated with hunting. The *sabu a*, by contrast, is where men and women live while they are engaged in their nonhunting subsistence tasks of sago making, gardening, and pig raising. These houses line the Mubi

River near the longhouse and are also scattered in and near the swamps in intrariverine territory. Some men build their houses at a spot remote from other houses; other men prefer to live in what can be called compounds with their fathers or brothers and families. The houses themselves vary greatly in size and condition. A few of them are little more than elevated sleeping platforms with a firepit and a roof; most are quite substantial and are as large and well made as the women's houses in the village. A Foi *sabu a* site is surrounded by characteristic cultivars: There is usually a cordyline and flower garden next to it (indeed, finding cordyline in the bush is evidence of previous habitation). Many houses and compounds have small fenced gardens alongside. Men usually plant banana, *Gnetum gnemon* (Foi: *hagenamo*), and marita pandanus near their houses, the latter two of which are fairly fast-growing fruit trees (pandanus bears fruit about four years after planting). They also plant *kā'i*, the plant whose leaves are used to line earth ovens; these are then always on hand when meat is cooked at the house.

Men care for their pigs from their bush houses. Pigs roam the nearby bush during the day, foraging for food, but often wander back to the house at night. One man fenced the area under his house, making an effective pig enclosure where the animals were fed and protected.

Although Ayamo is the hunting area and, as I have said, the Foi tend to draw a spatial and temporal boundary between their hunting and their gardening activity, men set deadfall traps around all of their permanent habitations, in the hopes of snaring rats, bandicoots, and the occasional possum. Deadfalls are typically set in trap lines around the bottom of a gully or near streams, positioned to take advantage of animal movements (see Kelly 1977; Schieffelin 1976). Certain fruit-bearing *Ficus*-species trees are commonly found in secondary-growth areas where people live. Men place a wall of stakes around these trees, leaving one gap. Into this gap is inserted a deadfall trap, designed to capture small animals that have come to eat the fruit that has fallen within the circle of stakes.

The ground is not the only surface exploited in the Foi habitat. The Mubi River is fed by numerous small creeks, streams, and smaller rivers, all of which, in contrast to the Mubi, are the property of specific clans. All small creeks that lead into the Mubi have dams placed across their mouths. These dams are kept in regular repair by their owners. People take advantage of the pronounced rise and fall of water levels to place weirs into gaps in the dams in order to trap fish returning to the main river when water levels recede.

While much attention and time are devoted to gardening, casual trapping, and fishing in the Mubi Valley, it is sago making which is the *raison d'être* of *sabu a* life. The major sago swamps are all located near the Mubi River. The large sago groves contain the haphazardly interspersed palms of many different men. Men like to have sago in as many different groves as possible, primarily for reasons of convenience and mobility, but also to assure a supply of usable starch for their sons in the years to come. And, despite the generally swampy nature of Hegeso territory, there are really only a few swamps large enough to provide good sago resources all year round. These swamps, such as those at Faibu, Oyane, and Gigisabu (see map 2-1), contain sago palms owned by men representing every clan of Hegeso.

One of the first things I learned during our sodden walks through the sago swamps was that every palm was owned. Moreover, there is a slight conflict between the desire of men to keep the extent of their resources hidden and the obvious social advantage of the community at large having exact knowledge of whose palm is whose. When a young man is about to get married and start out on his own, the first thing his father will do, if he hasn't already, is take him on a tour of the sago groves where his father has planted palms for him. The state of his father's sago holdings determines in large part where a man will build his bush houses in the coming years.

A man acquires knowledge of territory in a piecemeal fashion, as his father or guardian shows him one by one the places available to him. As he himself begins to make use of these resources, he begins his own autonomous inscriptive activity; he creates the paths linking these sites through his habitual visits to them. In other words, he begins to experience these sites spatially as well as discursively, as the next section suggests.

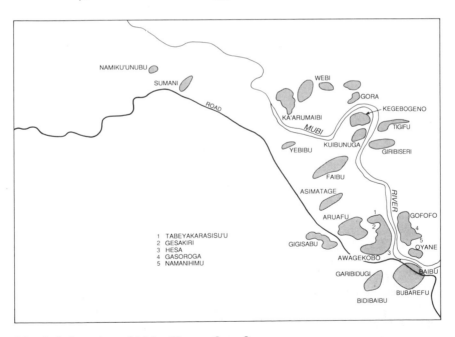

Map 2–1. Location of Major Hegeso Sago Swamps

PATHS AND WATER: THE CONDUITS OF FOI MOVEMENT

The system of paths in Hegeso, and throughout the riverine Foi region, resembles the human circulatory system—there are main arteries used by everyone, smaller paths branching off from these, and, finally, the paths to individual houses and gardens, made and used only by the current occupiers and users of that spot. These small paths tend to be referred to as "So-and-so's path." The larger ones serving a more inclusive region are usually referred to, for example, as "the Gisa Tono path" or the "Namikiribibi path."

The word for path is *iga*. It resembles the verb *iga-*, from which it differs only by the lack of a nasalized /i/. In its transitive form, *iga-* means "to make, build, create," and in its intransitive sense it also means "to turn into, to transform into." Unlike watercourses, which can only be followed, Foi paths are the graphic effect of intentional, creative movement across the earth. They transform the ground, partition the earth, and create human space. Additionally, *iga koro* means the door or entrance to a house, a conduit into highly structured space, just as a path itself eventually leads to a house or other human artifact.

Other words for paths and the use of paths partake of the imagery of points, edges, and cutting. In the 1960s the Australian colonial administration upgraded the major footpath between and through the Mubi River villages, widening it and building drains on either side. Nowadays, it has been lined with limestone and is accessible to four-wheel-drive vehicles (which have to be flown in by airplane). The Foi call this main road a *gifuri*. *Gifu* or *gifo* means "the tip or point of a knife" or "the tapered end of a bean" or "a topknot in one's hair." An *ira gifu* is the top of a tree. The turning off from a main road or a *gifuri* onto a smaller path is called *hudegeraha-* (alternately, *hugeteraha-*), which also means "to interrupt, to cut off," from the verb *degeraha-*, "1. to stop from flowing; 2. to not show up at an appointment." It is also used to describe the action of a small group of people breaking off from a larger group and going their separate way while traveling. It is important to understand that this "cutting" terminology refers not to the severing or dividing up of territory by paths but to *the cutting and channeling of people's intentions and movements*, for these are the constitutive source of places and their names in Foi.

Journeying through Hegeso territory on foot is never a matter of merely getting from one point to another. People pause to inspect trees for signs of fruiting, or for the spoor of animals. A length of good-quality rattan may be found, cut down, made into a coil, and placed in a string bag. Sometimes men will see high on a tree trunk the leathery nest of the *O. joiceyii* moth, whose larvae are edible and whose nest itself is used as a wrapping material. A dead and fallen tree trunk may be briefly attacked with axes if there is evidence that the longicorn beetle has laid eggs in it. In these and other casual "productive" acts, Foi men and women truly turn these paths into conduits of inscribed activity. Motion and movement is always exploitative, productive movement in Foi. There is no artificial distinction between "commuting" and "work."

Sometimes off to the side of a path, the remains of an old garden or a lone cordyline shrub may be glimpsed ever so faintly. Where once a path led up to that spot, the marks formerly etched onto the earth have faded; a new path, indicative of other men's concerns in other regions, now focuses travelers' attention away from those previous sites. But infrequently, a few handfuls of edible greens, the remains of previous planting, may be quickly gathered and slipped into a string bag, a terse requiem to the previous inhabitants.

Hegeso territory and the names that the Hegeso people use to identify different regions within their village area are dominated by the various watercourses. The Mubi River is, of course, the largest and virtually only navigable river in the entire region. But the numerous smaller creeks that flow into the Mubi provide the orienting and identifying landmarks. More important, they form the most common boundaries between clan territories. When Kora Midibaru undertook to conduct me on a tour of all inhabited Hegeso territory, he first divided the territory into districts centering on major streams. There were thus twenty-four such areas in Hegeso named for the streams whose courses delimit

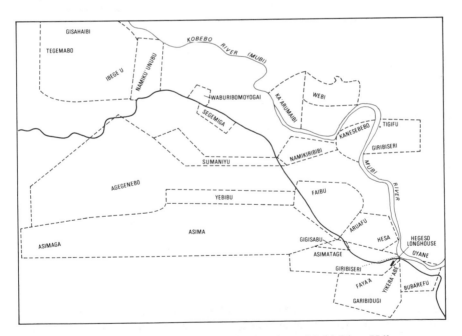

Map 2–2. District Names in Hegeso Village Territory, Mubi River Valley

them (see map 2-2)—flowing water is the dominant feature upon which the Foi focus in creating the regions of their lived space. Each district was thus oriented around the mouth (*tage*, "end") and the source (*ga*) of its identifying stream, and the place also could be named and subdivided accordingly (for example, the creek *Asima* encompassed two named areas, *Asimaga* and *Asima-tage*).

This was the way Hegeso men described where they lived: "My house is at Namanihimu," "I have a garden at Yebibu," "My father planted sago for me at Oyane," and so forth. Men usually have more than one house in different parts of the village territory. Both corporate clan and individual holdings are quite dispersed and checkerboarded. This is the result of continuous swapping of pieces of land between men and clans: men attempt to obtain access to major swamps, gardening areas, and riverine frontage along the Mubi so that they are not denied any subsistence activity or resource.

Hence, in some parts of Hegeso land—the banks of the Mubi, the major swamps at Faibu, Oyane, and Gigisabu—nearly every clan has a holding. On the other hand, land that is some distance from the longhouse or does not have significant swamp areas or riverine frontage and is otherwise without any special attributes tends to remain controlled by the original clan of possession (though the history of how the early arrivals to Hegeso obtained such holdings is no longer known).

As an aside, it seems that this approach to Foi "land use" leads to a critique of the concept of *land ownership*, so commonly and unreflectively transmitted to our host communities in the tribal world, and so preemptive and subversive of the constitutive, ontological role of land and space in tribal consciousness and perception and assessment of the person. For the Foi, at least, it is true that entitlement to land is inherited by virtue of one's membership in a clan and as the patrimony received from one's father. But unless this privileged access is "quickened" and authenticated by actual involvement with and use of the resource, one's proprietary rights over it become harder and harder to assert. Quarrels over land in Hegeso most commonly revolve precisely around this issue, especially in light of the facts that the Foi population is small relative to its large territory, and that there are often significant inequities in the amount of land controlled by local groups (see Langlas and Weiner 1988).

Men who own land in excess of their needs are always in danger of losing control of that land. They cannot find any reason to forbid other men from using it, and this use, though stipulated as temporary, often gives the borrower a basis for a future claim of ownership. Foi men repeatedly told me that for this reason, they would forbid borrowers of land from planting permanent tree crops on it—trees such as marita pandanus, *Gnetum gnemon*, breadfruit, and *kara'o* (*Campnosperma brevipetiolata*). Seen from the opposite perspective, when the owners of a piece of clan land grant this right of tree planting to a borrower, it ipso facto constitutes a conferring of clan membership on the borrower.

When Hamederaro's father, Buri, was given asylum at Hegeso after his long-house at Baruru had been decimated in a surprise attack, he was ceded a large tract of land, Oyane, which borders Hegeso and Barutage territories and is very close to both longhouses. As Buri's only son, Hamederaro inherited this land when Buri died. Over the years he has allowed Barutage men to use the land and its large sago swamps, and this has occasioned regular protests from the other Hegeso men. They have complained more than once to Hamederaro that he is in danger of losing control of that land.[3]

We might consider that Foi communally held clan land starts off as a tabula rasa, so to speak, in the absence of individual assertion of control. But when specific clan members begin to use a portion of that land, by making a garden, building a house, planting sago, tree crops, bamboo, and so forth, they give that qualityless, *anonymous*—"unnamed"—tract a human history; they ascribe to it a dimension of people's memory.

The names of places a man has occupied, upon which he has built houses, made gardens, caught fish, and so forth—these place names act as an effective mnemonic for his productive and social history within Hegeso. They encapsulate not only the specific events for which the name was first given but the lives of the succession of men who have left their mark there. Let us examine these names in more detail.

PLACE NAMES

> It is the vocabulary of a language that most clearly reflects the physical and social environment of its speakers. . . . [But] it is not merely the fauna or topographical features of the country as such that are reflected, but rather the interest of the people in such environmental features. (Sapir 1912: 228, 229)

Sapir's remarkable comments are very much in line with Merleau-Ponty's approach to language, and, indeed, with a phenomenological approach to language and human action in general. And nowhere is human interest more effectively inscribed upon the environment than in the names we give to places.

Sapir also suggested in that same article that "the transparent or untransparent character of a vocabulary may lead us to infer, if somewhat vaguely, the length of time that a group of people has been familiar with a particular concept" (ibid.: 231). For example:

> Only the student of language history is able to analyze such names as Essex, Norfolk, and Sutton into their component elements as East Saxon, North Folk, and South Town, while to the lay consciousness these names are etymological units as purely as are "butter" and "cheese." The contrast between a country inhabited

by an historically homogenous group for a long time, full of etymologically obscure place names, and a newly settled country with its Newtowns, Wildwoods, and Mill Creeks, is apparent. (Ibid.)

In the appendix to this chapter, I have listed the place names of the central Mubi area of Hegeso, that is, the area of permanent settlement. I was able to derive a lexical significance for nearly all of the names. Like the American Indian languages which Sapir briefly described in that article, the Foi language makes use of certain geographically descriptive words in its place names: *ibu*, "creek, river, water" (as in *Ibu Segemi*); *ibu karua*, "pond" (as in *Ka'arumaibi Karua*); *yeyema*, "ridge, raised ground" (as in *Daŭga Yeyema*); *tono*, "island, isolated mountain" (as in *Gisa Tono*); *merabe*, "harbor" (as in *Saboro Merabe*); *fu*, "swamp" (as in *Bubare Fu*); *kara*, "grove" (as in *Gagikara*); *ka'aga*, "small hill" (as in *Horo Ka'aga*); *geno*, "bend in river" (as in *O'oroga Geno*); *sabe*, "ridge, spur" (as in *Yagenebo Sabe*); *duma*, "mountain" (as in *Duma Yefua*); *ibu komosodi*, "waterfall" (as in *Ibu Agegenebo Komosodi*).

The place names listed, therefore, do not represent all the different *places* in Hegeso territory. They are the names of the *regions* of the Mubi Valley of Hegeso. Within each region there are probably many other tiny spots with their own names, names which they acquired only because something notable happened there in the past, not necessarily because the place itself is in some way physically distinct. The designations I listed in the preceding paragraph may inflect a number of names. The different sago swamps (*kuikara*) are named according to the streams near which they are located; there are different canoe-mooring points along the Mubi—*Segemi Merabe*, *Faya'a Merabe*, for example; each grove of bamboo is named according to the stream that lends its name to that district; and so forth. These descriptive adjuncts should not be confused with a place name itself. For example, the extensive sago swamp near the Faibu Creek (*Ibu Faibu*) is called *Faibu Kuikara*, "Faibu Sago Grove." But the place *Gagikara* is itself a name, even though it means "Thorn Grove."

Several of the place names give good evidence that, as with the English examples cited by Sapir, their original lexicality decays over time. The small creek *Hesa* was also referred to as *Hesawabo*. *Wa-* is the verb "to come," while *hesa-* is used as an auxiliary verb that modifies more basic verbs of motion. *Hesa-* means "to follow the contour of a river bank on foot," and it is always followed by *wa-* or *u-* ("to go"). In other words, the Foi usually drop the *-wabo* when referring to the place *Hesa*. Similarly, *Kubunuga* is a slightly shortened form of *Kuibunuga*, composed of three words, *kui*, "sago," *bunu*, "valley," and *ga*, "base, source." The stream *Yagikera'abe*, composed of the words *yagi*, "fish," *kera'a*, "is not," and the particle *be*, was usually shortened in favor of *Yikera'abe*.

For a few of the names, I was able to obtain a specific explanation linking the place and the name. For example, there is a place near Segemi called *Ya*, "hand" (the word *ya* in Foi also means "bird"). It is so named because in the past, a Hegeso man was killed and carried away by enemies, who dismembered his body as they fled. When other Hegeso men pursued, they came upon the severed hand of the dead man at that spot. Similarly, at *Huanobo* (*hua*, "killed"; *nobo*, "eaten"), a Hegeso man was killed and consumed by cannibal raiders from Lake Kutubu.

Yadenabo, or *Yadenabibi*, is a swift flowing creek near the head of the Sumaniyu Creek and refers to the birds that are often seen bathing in pools formed by the rocks which litter its bed (*ya*, "bird"; *dena-*, "to bathe, immerse in water"). *Yagenebo Sabe*, "Bird Dancing Ridge," on the other hand, is one of the names of the spur upon which the current Hegeso longhouse is located, and refers to the decorated men who dance within the longhouse on ceremonial occasions.

Particularly notable vegetation commonly lends its name to places, especially if the specimen is unusually large. Most of these refer to the place in terms of the base of the plant, *ga*, for example, *Bi'a'aga*, "Black Palm Base"; *Daūga Yeyema*, "Pandanus Base Hill." There are twelve examples of such place names on the list.

A lexical breakdown of several place names consists of a tree name plus *-himu*, "to chop down," indicating that at one time, the place or creek was notable for such an action having occurred nearby. Thus *Namanihimu*, *Digasohimu*, and at Ayamo, *Gagihimu*, "Thorn Cut."

Place names incorporating game-animal references are not restricted to Ayamo, the hunting area per se. In the central Mubi region there are the places *Gisa Tono*, "Cassowary Hill"; *Gisahaibi*, "Cassowary Lives"; *Horo Ka'aga*, "Bush Fowl Hill"; *Ya'onobodabikiri*, "Earth Oven Eaten Cave," referring to some incident where meat was cooked and consumed (*ya'o-*, "to cook in an earth oven"; *nobo*, "eaten"; *dabi*, "cave"; *kiri*, "is").

If places can be morally invigorated, as it were, by naming them after significant human events, then humans can also be named after such places. The Foi make a distinction between the lexical meaning of a name, which, as in the case of place names, is frequently opaque to them, and the person after whom one is named, one's *ya'o*, which is a socially significant relationship. A name could originally embody a relationship between a birth and the birthplace, but this would be irrelevant to the person upon whom the name is eventually bestowed. However, it is safe to say that most personal names that are also names of trees or other vegetation refer to a birthplace where a specimen of that name was located. This speculation is given confirmation by considering the way new names are chosen (for a variety of reasons a namesake may not be available, and new names sometimes have to be given to infants).[4] Often these refer in some way to the place where the infant was born. Of the 302 Hegeso names which I have investigated, 83 unambiguously refer to a place name or a tree or vegetable name. Some examples are *Isaka*, "Isa Woman" (*-ka* is a common ending for women's names, just as *-mena*, from the word *amena*, "man," is a common male name ending), who, as I noted in the Introduction, was named after nearby Mt. Isa, after her father perceived the name in a dream shortly after his daughter's birth; *Goraka*, "Gora Woman," who was named after the Gora Creek where she was born; and *Yorame*, who was named after the sago variety *yora*, a specimen of which was near the place she was born (*-ame* is also a common female name ending, like "-ette" or "-ina" in English).

Foi children are also named after significant deaths—these can be called "memorial names." The little girl *Ibu*'s namesake was killed by a falling sago palm, and thenceforth the girl was called *Kuiremohui*, "Sago Killed (Her)." The infant *Sese*'s namesake committed suicide by hanging himself, and people called the little boy *Yogehui*, "Killed Himself." These memorial names are passed on to new namesakes along with the original names. I suspect that in the past, when homicide and warfare were far more frequent, as were sudden deaths from sorcery, such memorial names were more common: they survive in names passed on from earlier generations, such as *Hoabo*, "Killed"; *Humofa'abo*, "Killed and Discarded"; *Gebo*, "Weep."

Along with all the names one's namesake has acquired during his or her life, a young Foi person also acquires the namesake's private or hidden name. I do not say "secret" name. These names are not secret, merely not public. A man's hidden name or names are revealed only in the song poems composed in his memory. I will return to the implications of hidden names shortly.

Keith Basso has effectively demonstrated the usefulness of phenomenological and existential approaches to language and placedness in his analysis of place names among the Western Apache (1984, 1988). The Western Apache "speak with names" during times of difficulty, confusion, or emotional stress. These names allegorically anchor a person's worries in the soothing "good thinking" that attends dwelling upon distant events in different places.

> Placenames are arguably among the most highly charged and richly evocative of all linguistic symbols. Because of their inseparable connection to specific localities, placenames may be used to summon forth an enormous range of mental and emotional associations—associations of time and space, of history and events, of persons and social activities, of oneself and stages in one's life. . . . Poets and songwriters have long understood that economy of expression may enhance the quality and force of aesthetic discourse, and that placenames stand ready to be exploited for this purpose. (1988: 103)

Basso, examining such Western Apache names as *Tsé ligaí dah sidil*, "white rocks lie above in a compact cluster," and *Tsé biká'tú yahilíí*, "water flows down on top of a regular succession of flat rocks," in words that could not be more appropriate here, noted that "Sapir's description of Algonkian words as 'tiny imagist poems' applies nicely to Western Apache place names, and there is little doubt that the practice of 'speaking with names' exhibits poetic qualities" (ibid.: 126 fn.).

Foi place names are not inert, lexical labels for places; place names have their origin in discourse, and it is within discourse—in the encompassing sense that I am using the term—that places are named. As is the case with the Apache, Foi place names act as mnemonics for the historical actions of humans that make places singular and significant. The Foi examples above indicate that is is not easy to draw a line between where "names" end and "descriptive phrases" begin, and this seems to be even more the case with Apache place names. If place names have poetic qualities, then they have *dis*placing—*ekstatic*—effects on conventional meaning: as with any construction that exerts a "trope-ic" effect on publicly attributed significance, names can hide as well as reveal the consequences of human action, a phenomenon to which I now turn.

SHOWING AND LOSTNESS: THE POETIC NEXUS WITHIN THE INSCRIBED WORLD

During my time in Hegeso, my friends and I spent much time walking along the paths throughout Hegeso territory. At these times, if we happened to be walking across land that belonged to one of the men, I would sometimes be informed that "this is the sago my father showed me," or "my father showed me this bamboo stand when I was just a small boy." Sometimes we would walk through the territory belonging to different clans, and occasionally it would be remarked, "My brother-in-law showed me this ground here so I could make a garden."

Showed, they said. Not "gave" or "lent," though the Foi language had words for these and other similar transactions. Clearly, "showed" was the appropriate idiom in this context. The Foi word used is *mitina-*, and it carries the connotation not of something "demonstrated" (as in "Show me how to do it") but of something previously hidden now being revealed. One can speculate on the etymological associations of the word: *Mi-* is a general causative prefix; it makes an intransitive verb into a transitive one. *Tina-* means "to abandon, to leave, relinquish, release," already in transitive form. Hence *mitina-*, "to cause to abandon; to make released." I can think of no other word which so perfectly translates Heidegger's own reading of the Greek *aletheia*: "*to unconceal*."[5]

For in formally "showing" a piece of ground to another, a Foi man is precisely relinquishing control over it (even if only temporarily). More important, in "showing" someone else the extent of his land and resource holdings, a Foi man is revealing the fundamental lived dimension of his "Being-there," through the attitudes of care and the actions of concernful appropriation of earthly space, the historical record of the impressions he has made on the land, the inscriptive evidence of his life. This quality of *unconcealing* characterized authentic language for Heidegger, as Kockelmans describes it:

> Within the horizon of a certain culture, which mainly in and through its language makes the world emerge from hiddenness and places it in "unconcealedness," man

and things as well as man and fellow men are concretely related. . . . [L]anguage
. . . brings about the original interwovenness of man and things in the world.
(Kockelmans 1972: 29)

Foi men "unconceal" the land to each other, furtively, reluctantly, privately.
Young men often become impatient with the slowness with which their fathers
reveal their territorial property. Men approach each other in private to arrange
a transfer of or temporary use of a piece of land, just as the initial stages
of betrothal are shrouded in the stylized, formal, and extremely private negotiations between men. With time, these transactions become known publicly:
men begin seeking donations of shell wealth for a bride payment from their
kinsmen and neighbors; a new garden or house begins to take shape under
the eyes of passersby.

People's inscriptive, productive activity is hidden, privatized, unsignified—
until men choose to reveal resources for others' use. But it is only through
language that the earth is revealed in its existential nature. Men reveal hidden
places, but it is women who, in their poetry, reveal hidden names and bring
these hidden names in relation to hidden places. And this nexus is made possible
only through death. Women's poetic creations thus constitute in Heidegger's
terms an authentic use of names and naming, because they situate the "fundamental project"[6] of death as the condition of placedness; men, by keeping productive and inscriptive relations hidden, deny the existential fact that it is
through death that places "move" from person to person through time, just
as it is through life that persons move from place to place.

For the Foi, the opposite of *mitina-*, "unconcealedness," is *berebu-*, "lostness." Men become lost through death, though places live on. The song poems
characteristically juxtapose these images of unconcealing and lostness. Among
the most obvious examples of this imagery are the following:

(Song 5):

The large cassowary which sleeps in the cave
He has gone away

The black marsupial who sleeps in the cave
He too is lost

(Song 20):

The man who sleeps by the bank of the rushing water
He is lost now

Twigs and branches clot in the swiftly flowing water
But he who sleeps there is lost

In the following song, this lostness is seen from the eyes of the deceased's
dog who survives him:

(Song 22):

The dog Awaro cries out
How will he find the way now?

The dog Kimi cries out
How will he go?

Even when the word *berebu-* is not used in the poem, the image appealed to is still one of lostness. Lostness is interpreted as a silence where once was discourse, and in this respect it invokes Heidegger's distinction between speaking and silence. This contrast is effectively utilized as a poignant device in several Foi songs:

(Song 9):

Your Little Eye myth
You can no longer tell

(Song 3):

Your weakness-causing spell
You didn't tell me before you left

(Song 30):

The airplane buzzed as it flew away
But to us you said nothing

As I have been maintaining, the relationship between motion and rest is at the heart of Foi poetic imagery. It was Heidegger who invoked the relationship between stillness and motion as a way of understanding language's dependence upon silence (1971b: 122). In silence or rest, things can be represented, they can be named and brought into relationship with each other. According to David White, the purpose of silence

> is to emphasize that the relation between language and being can be scrutinized only if we first bracket concrete speaking as such and then examine (in a state of silence, as it were) how beings are established through the actual process of naming representation. (1978: 48)

In concealing the land, in concealing magical words and political metaphors, in keeping their names private, Foi men appropriate the representational power of words. And where words can be hidden, so can the things for which they stand. Men's relations with each other become a never-ending strategy of hiding and revealing, of using names as negotiable tokens of things which are never revealed. Women, on the other hand, through poetry reveal language's ontological status: they reveal the nexus of space and time that is encapsulated in personal and place names and restore the movement of life activity to language and names.

Heidegger distinguished between these two features of language when he elaborated on the distinction between speaking and saying. Speaking employs the power of language to represent things "as if" they were factical, "ontic," "in-themselves." It gives us the illusion that we can manipulate the world, an illusion that is, after all, true. Saying, on the other hand, is the domain of poetic language in its most comprehensive sense: it is any discourse that reveals the ontological dimensions of the world, which presents things named in their spatial, temporal, and historical relation to human concerns. Insofar as Heidegger identifies all art as poetry, it is the function of poetry to reveal these existential properties of language. "That into which the work [of art] sets itself and which it causes to come forth in this setting back of itself we called the earth. . . . Upon the earth, and in it, historical man grounds his dwelling in the world" (1971a: 46).

To appreciate what Heidegger meant by this, we have to understand his earlier writings on the spatiality of *Dasein* (Being-there) in *Being and Time*. When implements are exposed to our concern, when we appropriate things in our environment and make of them *equipment*, we put such things in a spatial relationship to ourselves and hence to each other. What is inscribed by the sum total of human acts through time is a space which sets forth a world of historically constituted human being. "*Dasein*'s spatiality is a function of its commerce with the implements. *Dasein* places things. It places them by approximation and by direction" (Vycinas 1961: 40).

Relationships of "distance" and "nearness" are not primarily geometrical; that is, they are not primarily a matter of measurement of absolute units of distance. They are not ontic, in other words, but *ontological*—that is, defined with reference to human being. Those things which are ready-to-hand for us are characterized by nearness; they enjoy an intimate role in our being-in-the-world (the example that Vycinas uses is the astronomer looking through his telescope, for whom the distant star he focuses on is ready-to-hand and "nearer than the glasses on his nose" [ibid.: 39]).

Now what the work of art does, according to Heidegger, is to open the object of contemplation into its full relationship of nearness, presence, and remoteness with respect to our life projects; it situates the object within a world ontologically constituted through the continuing accretion of human concern and attention over time. It brings the object out of the seclusion of its everydayness, where its significance as a focus of human intention and attention may have been lost, forgotten, or hidden, or where its formative relationship with the earth may have simply atrophied over time as a result of our distancing neglect. Although living people's recent paths have led attention away from the abandoned, empty gardens and houses of the deceased, Foi women, through their memorial poetry, unconceal these hidden traces of former lives.

But it is through this distancing neglect that the things in our world come to have relative statuses of revealment and opacity; and they are relative and mutable because, of course, our concerns and goals change over time. Things are revealed to our scrutiny against a background of other things which recede into anonymity; we "de-circumspect" them by virtue of focusing our attention elsewhere. The work of art, however, uncovers or re-reveals this tacit ground; it allows us to see the things of our concern within the totality of their connection to a world and hence to each other. It appresents figure and ground simultaneously to us; in other words, it *obviates* the dialectic of the figure-ground bracketing. The work of art is itself a miniature version of the original "phenomenological bracketing" that Husserl postulated.

Heidegger put it this way: "The setting up of a world and the setting forth of earth are two essential features in the work-being of the work [of art]" (1971a: 48). Here, Heidegger is positing a figure-ground relationship. Our quotidian experience of things involves this ceaseless tension between what we reveal and what we at the same time hide so that it can provide a background against which the revealed object can stand forth. "What appears hides what does not and draws attention away from the entire context in which it does appear" (Kaelin 1967: 84). Foi men's historical relationship to the earth is impelled by this tension. This is not to say that Foi men are unaware of the earth as the historical ground of being, nor do they fail to contemplate the poetic dimension of their activity-on-the-earth which is the world of their being, in Heidegger's terminology. I mean only that what convention assigns to men is the possibility of transacting with land, of subordinating its functions as an arena of their historical life to their transient political maneuverings. Foi women, on the other hand, reveal hidden names and the earth as an arena of death. There can be no true historicity, no true world, without the inclusion of that finality, and this is what is missing in men's discourse about place (though, of course, it is not lacking in their *authentic relation* to place).

In Foi, the word *me* means the following:

1. "place, region, area," as in *me ti*, "this place [here]"; *Foime kasia*, "Lower Foi area [south]"; *bu'uni me*, lit. "deadfall place," i.e., a section of the bush where traps are habitually set; *guru me*, "cassowary place," a region cassowaries are known to frequent; *me wasi*, "a good place."

2. "language, speech," also used to describe the "speech" of animals, primarily birds.

3. "wild, undomesticated; the bush as opposed to the village," as in *me nami*, "wild pig"; *me dare*, "wild pitpit" (uncultivated).

4. "other, another, different," as in *amena me*, "another man"; *ma'ame mege me*, "something else, something different"; *feraga me*, "again, one more time."

This semantic unity between "place", "speech," and "wild" constitutes the most vivid Heideggerian synthesis in the Foi lifeworld. It calls to mind how the Daribi explained to Roy Wagner: " 'eat our pandanus fruit, smoke our tobacco, and you will know our language' " (Wagner 1975: 114). Language and place are a unity. The manner in which human action and purposive appropriation inscribes itself upon the earth is an iconography of human intentions. Its mirror image is speech itself, which, in the act of naming, memorializes these intentions, makes of them a history-in-dialogue. Every time the Foi make reference to a place name, they, like the Western Apache, invoke this iconographic encapsulation of a human history. For the Foi, speech, *me*—saying —creates the world, but it also brings forth the earth as a collection of human places, as the grounding of that world.

The language/place nexus in Foi percept brings us back to Merleau-Ponty. Place names create the world as a humanized, historicized space, but speech, like any other bodily activity, is conditioned and shaped by the tasks to which human interests direct it. The poetic nature of Foi song begins, not with a woman's attempts to give an aesthetic dimension to her emotion but with the everyday, unremarked-upon rhythms, melodies, and mimeses of quotidian speech itself. It is to this grounding of speech that the next three chapters are addressed.

NOTES

1. Translated by William Acker (1952).

2. This is a paraphrase of Relph's translation of the original French passage (Relph 1976: 26).

3. Charles Langlas, who lived in nearby Herebo village in 1965 and 1968, reported the following:

> Subdivisions of the local clan segment (including immigrant lineages) acquire rights to certain tracts of clan land, to the exclusion of other subdivisions, by using those tracts and particularly by planting exclusively on the tracts and thus coming to own all of the long-term crops there. Since these long-term crops are the most important resources, ownership of them is tantamount to ownership of the land in Foi eyes. This means, of course, that when a man does not use any of his inherited land or crops, his descendants lose the rights to them. (1974: 127–28)

4. A description of Foi naming practices can be found in Weiner 1988.

5. I might add that the Foi word *mowãga-*, "to clarify, to make clear, to explain," partakes of the same spatial metaphor as does our English expression: In Foi, *me wãga* means "a clearing, a cleared space in the forest."

6. This phrase is Sartre's.

APPENDIX

Major Hegeso Place Names and Some of Their Lexical Derivations

Agegenebo "Hawk Eaten"
Arua "*Arua* Tree"
Arufora'a "*Aru* Tree Cut"
Asagabe "*Asa* Tree Base"
Asahagabebo
Asima
Awagekobo "Frog Taken"
Baibu "Battle Place"
Banumafu
Bararebo "*Bare* Tree Leaf Place"
Bianetono "*Biane* Tree Mountain"
Bi'a'aga "Black Palm Base"
Bidibaibu "Blood"
Bubarefu "Tadpole"
Danimi "Near"
Daūga yeyema "Pandanus Base Hill"
Digasohimu "Tree Oil Cut"
Duma Yefua
Fabia karua
Faibu; Faibuhesaweī
Faya'a
Gagikara "Thorn Grove"
Ganedobabo "Hard Ground"
Garibidugi
Gasoroga "Seed Rattle Tree Base"
Gemasobo
Genemoboabi "Night"
Gesakiri kuikara "Dog Rope"
Gigisabu "Ripe Fruit"
Giribiseri "Banana"?
Gisahaibi "Cassowary Lives"
Gisatono "Cassowary Hill"
Gofega "*Ficus* Tree Base"
Gofofo "Black Flies"
Gora "*Gora* Snake"
Gorega "*Gore* Tree Base"
Hagenamo wasa'oga "Tall *Gnetum* Tree Base"
Hesa "Follow Bank"; *Hesawabo*
Horo ka'aga "Bush Fowl Hill"
Huanobo "Killed and Eaten"
Hubahukirahaī "Killed and Placed in a Cave"
Ībariabe Sabe "Eye Deceive Ridge" (also known as *Yagenebo Sabe*)
Ibege'u "Tree Base"

Ibuga'ana kuikara "Water Channel Sago Grove"
Igiri "Frogs' Place"
Iriwa'age "Wa'age Tree"?
Isa
Kagiri "Rain"
Kanesebebo "Kane Fruit Search"?
Kara'aga Ibu "Kara'a Tree Base Creek"
Karu'umaibi: "Sago Taken"?
Kegebe geno "Vine Whirlpool"?
Kimanihimu kuikara "Latrine Cut Sago Grove"
Kimigafera "Maggot Base Gap"
Kobebo "Swift Water"
Kosa'aga fu "Ficus Base Swamp"
Kubunuga; Kuibunuga "Sago Valley Base"
Namanihimu "Ficus Cut"
Namikiribibi "Pig Rope"? "Pigs Are"?
Namiku'unubu "Pig Viscera"
O'oroga geno "O'oro Tree Base Whirlpool"
Oyane "Hanu Grass"
Saboro merabe "White Man's Harbor"
Segemi "Mark"
Senewagoga "Small"?
Sumane "Canal, Channel"; *Sumane Isa*: "Live *Sumane*"; *Sumane Kusa*: "Dead *Sumane*"
Sumaniyu "Anus"
Surufegebo "Termite Dug"
Tabeyakarasisu'u "Ficus Grove Clearing"
Tegema'abo "Grey Clay"
Tigifu "Wasp Swamp"
Togedobabo "Cassowary Leg"
Ubiga "Ubi Tree Base"
Waburibomoyogaī "Widow's Paint Struck"
Webi "Come"
Ya "Hand"
Yadenabo/Yahadenabo/Yadenabibi "Bird Bath"
Yagenobosabe "Birds of Paradise Dance Ridge"
Ya'onobodabikiri "Earth Oven Eaten Cave"
Yebibu
Yikera'abe; Yagikera'abe "Fish Are Not"
Yumaibu Ibu "Boiling Water"

Kora's wife, Dafimi of Barutage, squeezes the starch from wet sago pith outside their house on the bank of the Mubi River.

Wa'o's house on the bank of the Mubi River.

The *doro,* temporary scaffolding erected in order to lay the sago-leaf roof thatch, are visible in this women's house under construction.

The interior of a village women's house under construction. The floor beams, the *wage* and *dufu,* have been laid.

A trap built around the *Ficus*-species *gofe* tree, whose small berrylike fruits are visible on the trunk. The entry point where the deadfall is inserted is visible toward the back.

A pig trap built on the hollowed-out trunk of a fallen sago palm.

A trap line with deadfall.

Fish dam at the mouth of Webi Mano Creek.

Abandoned bush houses: "Boy, your mountain place in the forest / Let the trees take it back."

Waterfall at the head of Agegenebo Creek: "He who sleeps near the rushing water / There he silently sleeps."

Fog on the mountainside near a gorge along the Mubi River: "The mist covering the mountain parts as you come /
Little one is that you?"

Segemi distributes tidbits of pork fat on the day of Hegeso's *dawa* in January 1988.

Egadoba removes a side of pork from the earth oven on the day of Hegeso's *dawa* in January 1988.

3 THE ICONISM OF SPACE AND TIME IN THE FOI LANGUAGE

MERLEAU-PONTY REJECTED the fundamental Cartesian dichotomy by positing the body as the privileged vantage point from which all objects are apprehended. It is our kinetic activity that orients the things in the world toward our consciousness, that creates space as a function of our *movements* through it, our accomplishments and edifices in it. The body is, in short, the origin of perception-in-the-world; it is "the third term, always tacitly understood, in the figure-background structure, and every figure stands out against the double horizon of external and bodily space" (Merleau-Ponty 1962: 101). The body is the first source of a world-scheme, as O'Neill suggests, "the source of an abstract movement or projection" (1974: xvi) which "carves out within that plenum of the world in which concrete movement takes place a zone of reflection and subjectivity: it superimposes upon physical space a potential or human space" (Merleau-Ponty 1962: 111).

When, as Merleau-Ponty suggested, we consider speech as a kinesthetic activity, as another action of the body, we move away from a concern with the purely conceptual features of language out of context, and confront language as the "subject's taking up of a position in the world of his meanings":

> The phonetic "gesture" brings about, both for the speaking subject and for his hearers, a certain structural co-ordination of experience, a certain modulation of existence, exactly as a pattern of my bodily behaviour endows the objects around me with a certain significance both for me and for others. (1962: 193)

Of course, Malinowski was the most notable anthropologist to originally advocate this approach to language, in keeping with his empirical and pragmatic orientation to human activity in general: "In order to reconstruct the meaning of sounds it is necessary to describe the bodily behaviour of . . . men, to know the purpose of their concerted action, as well as their sociology" (1965: 8).

Because speech as an activity is inseparable from the other movements of
the body, speech is always at its core spatially and temporally constituted. As
a modality of social interaction, in other words, it presents and appresents
discourse as a set of spatiotemporal relationships. Ernst Cassirer furthermore
suggested that because of this fundamental deictic grounding, language always
sought to express more abstract relationships in terms of the concretivity of
space and time:

> It would seem as though logical and ideal relations became accessible to the linguis-
> tic consciousness only when projected into space and there analogically "repro-
> duced." The relations of "together," "side by side," "separate" provide it with a
> means of representing the most diverse qualitative relations, dependencies and op-
> positions. (1953: 200)

The crucial point of departure for investigating the iconicity of Foi language
is that kinetic activity positions the body, as Malinowski insisted, and involves
the body in the construction of what Merleau-Ponty called "pseudo-presents"
(1962: 181); it reveals memory and perception as a function of the spatiotemporality of the body, and the body itself as "the medium of our communication
with time as well as with space" (ibid.).

I have suggested that we broaden our view of what "language" is. All of
our action that produces a spatial and temporal human world is "linguistic"
to the extent that it draws upon the enabling symbolic property of human
perception. When through our historical actions we create horizons of nearness
and distance on the earth, we are making the places we frequent speak as the
signifiers, as it were, of our bodily intentions and movements.

In chapter 2 I described the dimensions of the Foi macrocosm: its major
regions and named foci of significance. Here I would like to move from the
larger dimensions of inscribed territory to the smaller cosmos of the Foi house,
the exemplary venue of Foi discursive interaction. I then move to the smallest
spatial Foi microcosm, the human mouth, where sounds are also accorded distinct spatial and temporal values of distance and nearness, to show how language and existential space emerge together.

INTERIOR SPACE IN THE FOI LONGHOUSE

Let us look into the Foi men's longhouse momentarily to observe how speech
positions people and vice versa, because when I discuss the performance of
Foi song poetry, much of our understanding of its significance as an act of
discursive creativity will hinge on the intricate yet conventionalized positions
of pairs and groups of singers in the longhouse, and the manner in which
the men's shifts in position temporally construct the linear progression of song
themes. The Hegeso longhouse is 54.25 meters long and 7 meters wide. Inside,
it is bisected along its length by a central walkway of split black palmwood

slats about 2–3 meters in width. On either side of the corridor are two rows of eleven fireplaces spaced evenly along its length. Outside, on either side of the longhouse, are two rows of smaller women's houses, each approximately 8.5 meters long and 6.5 meters wide. There were twenty women's houses in Hegeso in 1985.

Two men nominally share each fireplace, one sleeping on either side (though hangers-on, casual and more long-term visitors, and young children give the appearance of a group huddled around each firepit at night). These two men, according to Foi descriptions, should be close friends, such as two brothers, or a father and son, or two brothers-in-law. They address each other, if not otherwise related, as *eresaro*, from the verb *eresaye* (*eraha-*), "to look after, to mind, to watch over," and Foi men told me that *eresaro* share food during the evening meal when in residence in the longhouse.

At this time, *eresaro* face each other across the fireplace. Their backs therefore are toward the men who share the next fireplace, and they call these men *ki'ufunage*, "back to back." When they look across the central corridor, every man is mirrored by another man in the fireplace opposite him. This man is called *erefa'asobo*, literally "look-place-over there," or "face-to-face."

When Foi men are not eating in the longhouse, they are conversing. Men generally face inwards toward their small group of sharers when eating; they turn away from the fireplace and toward the center of the longhouse during the conversation that inevitably follows food sharing. This shift is most pointed and visible: one must picture a longhouse of men, divided into small groups each around a fireplace, often single-mindedly focused on the contents of a bowl; then gradually, as the meals end, the volume of conversation increases, and the small groups break up and coalesce into a house of men.

When men engage in conversation inside the longhouse, there is little tendency to bunch up in one section, unless there are only a few people in the longhouse, because close face-to-face contact is not thought necessary for communication. Perhaps for the same reason, men prefer to occupy their own areas. Men speak from their own fireplaces; occasionally, those who wish to speak emphatically arise and pace up and down the length of the corridor as they talk. At this time, a seated man may interject a comment, or choose to dispute a point, or answer a rhetorical question. Sometimes an argument arises and voices are raised, yet the antagonists do not seek to get close to each other, as participants in a Western verbal argument invariably do.

The longhouse positions men, and thus positions discourse, even as men position themselves (their bodies) as a longhouse of men, that is, as a set of relationships spatially as well as "genealogically" conceived. Elsewhere (Weiner 1988; Langlas and Weiner 1988) I have described how the distribution of men within the longhouse is homologous with other spatial and political configurations of nominal alliance and opposition within Hegeso territory. As figures 3–3 and 3–4 show, the clustering of men in different parts of the longhouse is closely isomorphic with their residential dispersal and clustering

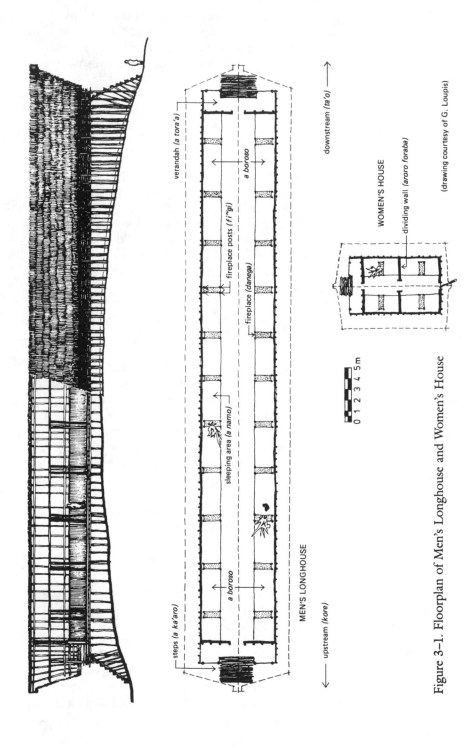

verandah (a tora'a)

a boroso

fireplace posts (fi·ngi)

fireplace (danega)

sleeping area (a namo)

MEN'S LONGHOUSE

steps (a ka'aro)

a boroso

← upstream (kore)

downstream (ta'o) →

WOMEN'S HOUSE

dividing wall (aroro foraba)

(drawing courtesy of G. Loupis)

0 1 2 3 4 5 m

Figure 3–1. Floorplan of Men's Longhouse and Women's House

through Hegeso territory: in short, men sleep in the longhouse near those men who are their neighbors. In every discursive encounter within the longhouse, Foi men thus microcosmically re-create and confirm their most encompassing territorial, political, and affinal alignments.

This is *not* to say that there is a "structure" of Foi spatial relationships which is "generated" in various different domains—territorial, architectural, and so forth. Foi men simply attempt to live near their best friends and/or closest relatives. The fact that they do so both in the longhouse and in the bush is not evidence for a "structure" of spatial relationships in Foi society (or in the

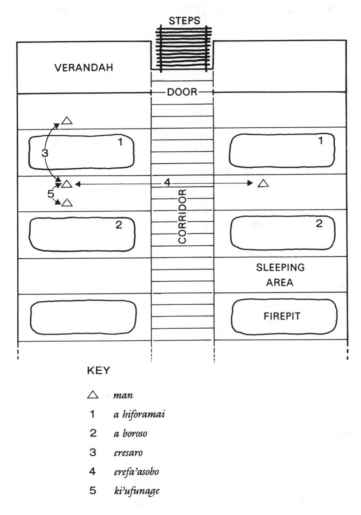

KEY

△   *man*

1   *a hiforamai*

2   *a boroso*

3   *eresaro*

4   *erefa'asobo*

5   *ki'ufunage*

Figure 3–2. Floorplan of End of Longhouse

Foi "mind"). There is a difference between the Foi longhouse and the central Gê longhouse, for example. Foi spatial arrangements emerge from a certain socio-proxemic *habitus*, as their discursive *praxis* emerges from a set of "structuring dispositions" (Bourdieu 1977) to various modes of linguistic expression. One might say that structure is created only for the anthropologist's benefit —the structure of central Gê villages is not found in the disposition of their dwellings but in the Amazonian Indians' explanation of it to the anthropologist.

I have been speaking of a microcosm of men, and indeed, events in the longhouse often proceed as if women did not exist. During men's conversational and oratorical encounters in the longhouse, women are sitting in their smaller houses which flank the men's house. Nor do they refrain from offering

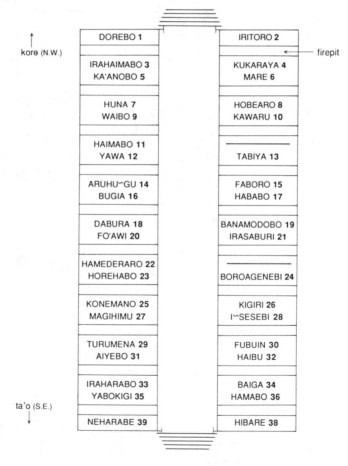

DOREBO 1	IRITORO 2
IRAHAIMABO 3 KA'ANOBO 5	KUKARAYA 4 MARE 6
HUNA 7 WAIBO 9	HOBEARO 8 KAWARU 10
HAIMABO 11 YAWA 12	TABIYA 13
ARUHU⌐GU 14 BUGIA 16	FABORO 15 HABABO 17
DABURA 18 FO'AWI 20	BANAMODOBO 19 IRASABURI 21
HAMEDERARO 22 HOREHABO 23	BOROAGENEBI 24
KONEMANO 25 MAGIHIMU 27	KIGIRI 26 I⌐SESEBI 28
TURUMENA 29 AIYEBO 31	FUBUIN 30 HAIBU 32
IRAHARABO 33 YABOKIGI 35	BAIGA 34 HAMABO 36
NEHARABE 39	HIBARE 38

kore (N.W.)

ta'o (S.E.)

firepit

Figure 3–3. Men's Sleeping Areas in Hegeso Longhouse, 1951

their opinions from time to time, especially when the men are discussing a matter that concerns them. Here, however, the face-to-face content of dialogic interaction is nonexistent. In 1980 when I was sleeping in the men's longhouse, a man named Huya'one Hira and his wife, Ama'a Irahaimabo, engaged in a continuing argument over a period of months concerning the activities of their eldest son. It occurred mainly at night after mealtimes, when they were both in their separate dwellings. Most of the time, the other Hegeso folk maintained a tactful silence, though occasionally there would be a murmured comment between men, or the somewhat more emphatically asserted opinion of another woman.

One can perceive a gradient, as it were, from the most intensely face-to-face conversations between *eresaro*, to the maximally separated conversations between men and women who, sitting in separate houses, yet manage to converse by raising their voices. The former can be made private, but the latter is necessarily a public communal discourse. *When in the longhouse,* what men and women say to each other is by definition constrained by interactional convention; it must be inspected and confirmed through public scrutiny and is subject to collective appraisal and judgment. What men say to each other, or what women say to each other within the women's houses, however, admits of selec-

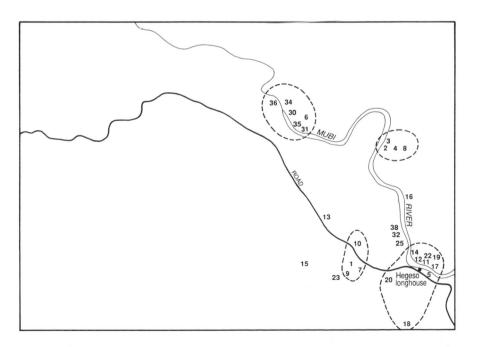

Figure 3–4. Bush House Sites of Hegeso Men, 1951

tive communication, and the contrast between intra- and intersexual dialogue depicts this conventional dichotomy in a decidedly spatial way.

Of course, when men and women as husbands and wives are alone in their nuclear-family bush houses, their conversation, though separated by the nominal dividing wall, is as intensely private as any. Single-family bush houses are ideally bisected in the interior by the *aroro foraba*, the wall that divides the dwelling into male and female sections. But many bush houses simply lack such a wall, though in such cases men and women still act as if the house were divided into two halves. In any case, men and women often sit and sleep close to each other in full view in such houses, though they are "conceptually" separated.

On the other hand, I am not saying that all intramale discourse is "private." Men's public oratorical encounters are the epitome of community interest and participation. I an *not* drawing some simple Durkheimian correlation between spatial and conceptual distantiation; I am suggesting that the *longhouse setting* positions discourse in a rather special or marked way, and that this setting both determines and comments upon the relative valuation of inter- and intra-sexual communication as communal activities.[1]

In the longhouse, men position their discourse according to other spatial relationships that have a social significance. But we can extend this social iconism inward, to its most *microcosmic* representation, since speech itself, as a series of articulatory *positions*, partakes of this same spatial isomorphism.

DEICTIC ICONISM

Ernst Cassirer's phenomenology, as did Merleau-Ponty's, accorded a fundamental constitutive centrality to bodily consciousness. This consciousness began with the awareness of movement:

> To regard movement and feeling of movement as an element and a fundamental factor in the structure of consciousness itself, is to acknowledge that here again the dynamic is not based on the static but the static on the dynamic—that all psychological "reality" consists in processes and changes, while the fixation of states is merely a subsequent work of abstraction and analysis. Thus mimetic movement is also an immediate unity of the "inward" and the "outward," the "spiritual" and the "physical," for by what it directly and sensuously is, it signifies and "says" something else, which is nonetheless present in it. (1953: 179)

"It is the intuition of *space* which most fully reveals this interpenetration of sensuous and spiritual expression in language" (ibid.: 198–99).

Cassirer also drew upon Boas's descriptions of the Klamath language: "the rigidity with which location in relation to the speaker is expressed, both in nouns and in verbs, is one of the fundamental features of the [Klamath] language" (Boas 1911: 445). He cited Codrington, who said of the Melanesian languages that "everything and everybody spoken of are viewed as coming or going, or in some relation of place, in a way which to the European is by no means accustomed or natural" (ibid.: 164f.)

More recently, and in the part of the world that concerns us here, ethnographers have attested to the critical role of spatial deixis in Papuan languages. Barth notes that the Baktaman, a Faiwol-speaking people of the West Sepik highlands, "are highly oriented towards *space* in ordering their experience. The vocabulary and grammar of their language impel a speaker constantly to specify relative location . . . of observer and actor in describing events" (1975: 18). R. D. and K. A. Shaw observed that among the Samo, a people of the West Strickland River bank, 22 percent of words counted in several short texts on different topics were locative in nature (1973: 158). Heeschen, investigating spatial deixis in the languages of the Eipo and Yale of the eastern highlands of Irian Jaya, suggests that the percentage of locatives in their speech may be 22 percent or even higher (1982: 82).

But as I have said, speech as a kinetic activity models and is modeled by such spatial and temporal configurations. As Cassirer and Merleau-Ponty both maintained, "meaning" is not distinct from "sensibility" in speech, and to the extent that speaking always involves the articulation of the position of the subject in the world, we can expect to find an isomorphism between form and sense, especially in the expression of such fundamental deictic shifters.

In other words, the actions of speaking model the significance of what we communicate, and they do so in a nonarbitrary, iconic way. Alfred Gell has provided the most comprehensive example of the iconism between articulation and meaning in his study of the sound symbolism of the Umeda of the West Sepik Province of Papua New Guinea. He first suggests that

> speaking is a physical activity, autokinetically sensed, and diversely interrelated to body imagery and motor schemas of all kinds. It does not seem fantastic that language should exploit this speaker-sensed physical substrate of speech as a source of intersubjectively communicable sense. (1979: 48)

As an example, Gell notes that words constructed around the phonetic core *mo* in Umeda center around a common cluster of meanings: *mo-tod*, "girl"; *mol*, "girl, vulva"; *mov*, "fruit"; *amov*, "termite"; *wamol*, "testicles," to take just a few. He points to the correspondence between the *mo* sound and the shape the mouth takes during the actual eating of succulent fruit:

> *Mo*, as an articulatory gesture has intrinsic functional efficacy: it "delineates its meaning" (Merleau-Ponty 1962) both as object (sketching in the rounded form of the fruit, etc.) and as *orifice* (narrow aperture bounded by lips). (Ibid.: 49)

Of course, scholars have commented on this feature of language for much of the twentieth century. Drawing upon the findings of such classical linguistic scholars as Wundt, Humboldt, and Winkler, Cassirer noted that the sounds *m* and *n* could be said to have an "inward direction," while "the explosive sounds *p* and *b*, *t* and *d*, reveal the opposite trend" (1953: 201). He also noted the tendency for the back vowels *a*, *o*, and *u* to "designate the greater distance" and frontal "*e* and *i* the lesser" (ibid.: 193). The Foi seem to make use of this articulatory isomorphism in their locative expressions, as the next section describes.

THE ICONICITY OF FOI DEICTICS

There are three basic Foi spatial markers: *ba*, "right here"; *ta*, "there" (able to be pointed to); and *sa*, "there" (distant). *Ba* and *ta* also mean "this," but the distinction between an object and its status as close-at-hand in discourse is obviously not an important one in Foi. Notice that the progression of the initial consonant from /b/ to /t/ to /s/ finds these deictics moving from abrupt, plosive sounds to continuant, sibilant ones as they express increasing degrees of removal from the speaker.

The Foi anaphoric pronoun *dera*, which can be translated as "that which has just been spoken of; that which has already been introduced in the conversation," is the ubiquitous and necessary shifter in Foi discourse. It is often paired with the spatial shifters *ba*, "this, here"; *ta* "that, there [close at hand]"; *sa*, "there [distant]," and is inflected iconically in the same manner as Foi locatives: *ba dera*, "that/here spoken of"; *bi diri*, "this thing *right here* spoken of."[2] The emphatic particle *gi* is often added to emphasize the immediacy of the event spoken about: *bi dirigi*, "this thing *right here at this very spot*."[3] Often *dera* is shortened in speech to *da*, though in this form it does not retain its spatial iconism. That is, *ba da* is correct, but **bi di* is not.

Jakobson (in Jakobson and Waugh 1979), drawing upon work by Jespersen, Chastaing, and Fonagy, noted that the front vowel /i/ is, in French and Hungarian, associated with acuteness, smallness, and also lightness, rapidity, and closeness. In Foi, the contrast between the high, unrounded /i/ and the low central-back /a/ iconically depicts spatial relations of nearness vs. distance respectively. Things immediately "ready-at-hand," in Heidegger's words, that is, things that can be literally grasped or pointed to, are inflected by the endings *bi* (this, here), *ti* (that, there [close at hand]). Note that the *si* inflection of the distant deictic *sa* is a nonspecific spatial marker that seems to be found attached to other nondeictic spatial markers, for example: *fa'o damusi*, "in the middle of the belly (i.e., one's navel)"; *ibu karuasi*, "in the water"; *ibu kege darusi*, "along the side (bank) of the river."

Foi people, in common with many other New Guinea language speakers, tend to point with their nose, mouth, and chin, rather than with their fingers or hands. In pointing to an object, a Foi speaker purses his lips and literally screws up his face, gesturing with his mouth to the object in question. The role of the tense, front vowel /i/ in this process is fundamental, as it is almost the only vowel that can be uttered when the lips and jaw are in this position.

The /i/ vs. /a/ contrast also codes the opposition between "at rest/motion toward." For example, *ara ua*, "(he) went to the house," but *ari ekera*, "(he) sat in the house." The effect of this is to transpose the near/distant dichotomy onto the *object spoken of*, and thus the iconic nature of this shifter is preserved. It is as if an object at rest is always brought *closer* to the speaking Foi subject, and indeed, in Heidegger's sense, an object at rest is always that much closer-at-hand than objects in motion.

The contrast between motion away from (*-a*) and motion toward (*-hamo*) also makes use of articulatory positions that are in a spatially complementary relation. *A* is a maximally open and lax vowel, while the use of the bilabial /m/ and the relatively closed and tense /o/ following the *-ha* particle suggests an initial openness and distance that is being constricted and brought closer. It should also be noted that the suffixes *-mo* and *-remo* or *-nemo* are suffixes of agency and possession, for example, *Gabiamo ara*, "Gabia's house"; *kanemo ma'agari*, "women's sickness (i.e., sickness caused by women)." Thus, the identification of motion toward and agency and possession, that is, objects "ready-at-hand," is preserved in Foi. This identification also extends to temporal readiness-at-hand or relationships of cotemporality, since *-mo* also means "at the time of." For example, *kone amena weiramo*, "when the white men came"; *iriyabo ū gisi haboramo*, "when the sun is straight overhead (i.e., midday)."

In every utterance, the Foi orient themselves geographically as well as subjectively. There are four cardinal directions in Foi: *kore*, "upstream" (of any flowing water, no matter what its direction); *ta'o*, "downstream"; *husa*, the direction away from water, which is by definition a point higher in altitude than the one the speaker is occupying; and *kasia*, the direction toward water, and by the same token a spot lower in altitude than the one the speaker is occupying. In other words, all water is, by definition, "below."

The geography of the Mubi Valley gives these terms a sense of absolute as well as subjective direction. The major rivers, the Mubi, Baru, and Yo'oro, and in fact most smaller, subsidiary tributaries, run from northwest to southeast, so that *kore* can often refer to any point in the distant west, and *ta'o* to any point in the distant east. Similarly, to the north of the Mubi Valley, the Central Highlands proper abruptly begins—as one moves from south to north, one moves increasingly higher in altitude, so that all regions to the north are *husa* and those to the south, in the direction of the sea, are *kasia*.

The "open vs. closed" contrast of "motion/at rest" also inflects the locative use of these cardinal deictic markers. *Kore, ta'o, husa,* and *kasia* are used only with motion verbs, to indicate movement in those directions. The locative forms of these cardinal deictics are, respectively, *kuri, ta'i, husi, kasi.* Thus, *a kuri*, "the house (that exists) upstream," vs. *yo a kore ua*, "he went upstream to his house," or "he went to his house (which is) upstream."

The Foi also inflect the cardinal deictics for relative nearness and distance.

Korobo, ta'abo, husubu, and *kasubu* indicate movement in the respective directions only a short distance away, to a spot relatively close. Thus *yo korobo ua,* "he went just a little way upstream." In this case, the frontally articulated bilabial particle *-bo* contrasts with the open, nonconsonantal *-a* to preserve the iconic features of the relative closeness/distance contrast. These terms also can be inflected as locatives: *kuribi,* "a spot a little way upstream"; and *ta'abi, husibi,* and *kasibi.* Note that they retain the immediacy of the *bi* marker of things within the speaker's immediacy, especially when paired with the shifter *dera/diri*: for example, *a kuribidiri,* "that house on that very spot just upstream," and so forth.

Foi temporal deictics—the words for "before" and "after," etc.—are built upon directional terms. *Ga* in Foi means "source, beginning, origin, font, base, root, cause," etc. *Gahae* means "before, earlier, in the beginning, a while ago" and can be broken down into the terms *ga* and *hae,* a conjugated form of the verb "to be."

The word *gamage* means "tail, end, back, latter, behind, the one following, the younger of a pair or set," and so on. *Gamagehamo* means "later on, further on, in a while, in the future." This adverb could be interpreted as the word *gamage* suffixed with the "motion from" particle *-hamo,* so that it could be literally translated as "motion away from the back [that is, the past] and toward the front [that is, the present]." This, however, would seem ambiguous, as it would lend the word a perfective connotation that it does not convey. More likely it is derived from the verb *gamageha-,* which means "to come last, to come after, to follow," and hence *gamagehamo* could be formed by the addition of the nominalizing possessive suffix *-mo,* giving a literal meaning "that which [will] come last or afterward."

The iconic contrast between /i/ and /a/ is evident in the adverbs of time, though not so clearly. The word for today is *mini,* and it also preserves a general sense of "now, at this moment." As with the spatial shifters, it can take the emphatic particle *-ge,* as in *minige,* "right now," or *mini mege,* "right now this very moment" (lit. "today only").

The other adverbs of temporal distance are not valenced with respect to past or future. Thus *hera* means "one day away, past or future," that is, either yesterday or tomorrow. In this case, the *ni/ra* distinction between *mini/hera* preserves the iconism of nearness/distance. In addition, the pronounced front-back contrast between the bilabial /m/ and the pharyngeal /h/ contributes to make the *mini/hera* distinction complementary in articulatory terms. Less clearly accommodated within this general contrast in distance are the adverbs *davi* (two days away), *dumi* (three days away), *viri* (four days away), and *soboviri* (five days away), all of which are articulated fairly frontally.

However, there is also a general front/back iconicity in Foi tense/aspect markers. Consider Murray Rule's basic list of Foi verb endings (see table 3-1). His use of the term *aspect* differs from the conventional linguistic use of the term. *Aspect* generally refers to the durative quality of the action being described:

Table 3–1: Foi Verb Endings of Time and Evidence

	Present	*Near Past*	*Distant Past*	*Future*
		Tense:		
Evidential Aspect:				
partic-ipatory	-bubege	-ge	-bi'ae	-agerege
visual	-boba'ae	-bo'oge	-bo'owa'ae	-anege
sensory	-bida'ae	-bidobo'oge	-bidobo'owa'ae	———
deduced	-ada'ae	-adobo'oge	-adobo'owa'ae	———
visual evidence	-boba'ae	-iba'ae	-biba'ae	-'aiba'ae
previous evidence	-bubege	-iyo'oge	-iyo'owa'ae	-'abege

whether it has been completed, is in process, has been completed in the past, and so on. In other words, it "refers to the inception, duration and completion of an event" (Langacker 1972: 207). Rule, on the other hand noted that Foi verb endings primarily encode the *speaker's relation* to the action being described, rather than the *agent's* or the *subject's*. In other words, these endings "reveal the particular aspect from which the speaker has viewed the event" (Rule 1977: 71). Since the Foi language does encode the orthodox notion of aspect, I will call the inflections for categories of evidence *evidentials*.

Rule described these six evidential conjugations as follows: (1) *participatory or factual*: used primarily when the speaker has actually carried out the action; (2) *visual*: the speaker is describing an action visible both to himself and to the person with whom he is speaking. Things that happened in the speaker's dreams are also described with this evidential ending; (3) *sensory*: the speaker is describing things of which he became aware with a sense other than sight, for example, smell, hearing, touch; (4) *deduced*: the speaker deduces the existence of the event he is describing based on evidence he has perceived with a sense other than sight. For example, he hears the growls and barking of dogs and deduces that the dogs are fighting among themselves. Most commonly, however, the speaker is referring to an event related to him by another person who actually witnessed or performed it; (5) *visible evidence*: the speaker is describing a recent event based on visible evidence before him at the time of speaking. For example, he sees footprints and reports that people have passed this way; (6) *previous evidence*: the speaker is describing an event, the evidence of which he has seen but which at the time of speaking no longer exists. Notice that in the present tense, the verb endings for evidentials 5 and 6 are the same as those for evidentials 2 and 1 respectively, though morphophonemically, they have different deep structures.

In general, the more immediate the event, both in time and in the degree of participation by the speaker, the more prominent are frontal consonants such as /b/ and /d/, while the more remotely situated in time and in distantiation of experience, the more marked becomes the use of the maximally back glottal stop /ʔ/, the glides or "semivowels" /y/ and /w/ (as opposed to the "hard" consonants), and the lax and rounded /o/ and /ae/ (see figure 3–5).[4]

Foi evidentials thus bespeak a fundamental concern with *subjectivity* in Foi discourse. They bring to mind Benveniste's statement: "'subjectivity,' whether it is placed in phenomenology or in psychology, is only the emergence in the being of the fundamental property of language" (1971 [1966]: 224). Benveniste went on to say that all classes of deictic markers,

> the demonstratives, adverbs, and adjectives, which organize the spatial and temporal relationships around the "subject" taken as referent . . . have in common the feature of being defined only with respect to the instances of discourse in

Figure 3–5: Phonological Iconism in Foi Space and Time Markers

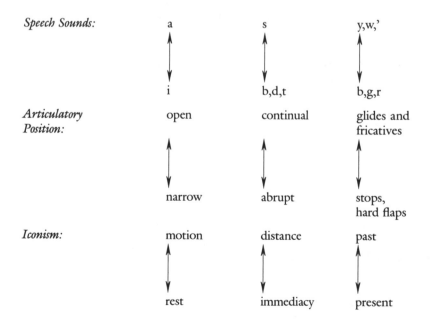

Speech Sounds:	a	s	y,w,ʼ
	↕	↕	↕
	i	b,d,t	b,g,r
Articulatory Position:	open	continual	glides and fricatives
	↕	↕	↕
	narrow	abrupt	stops, hard flaps
Iconism:	motion	distance	past
	↕	↕	↕
	rest	immediacy	present

which they occur, that is, in dependence upon the *I* which is proclaimed in discourse. (Ibid.: 226)

The effect of Foi verb endings is to make discourse a constant negotiation of perspective on events among a community of speaking subjects.

This is, of course, most exaggerated and marked in Foi litigious discourse. In disputes concerning accusations of adultery and sorcery—two of the most commonly talked about delicts in a Foi community, especially in traditional times—a great deal of discourse is spent expatiating on the qualities and categories of evidence being considered, and the comparison and evaluation of competing subjective assessments of reconstructed events and available evidence.

A good example of this was afforded by a public hearing at Hegeso in January 1988 which I attended. A young man and woman, both married to other people, were accused by the young man's wife of having had an adulterous liaison. This woman had seen the two entering the main road together from a path that leads to the women's bathing area along the Mubi River. When the two were confronted by the young man's wife, they wore what were described as unmistakably sheepish expressions of guilt and dismay. This was sufficient for the man's wife to demand a village "court."

During the ensuing discussion, various people were called forward to give testimony. (The hearing was held in the plaza of the front verandah of the longhouse. The men sat on the verandah, some four feet off the ground, while they summoned witnesses to stand before them on the ground below. Women spectators stood in a semicircle around the verandah.) It soon became clear that everything hinged on timing: When did the two emerge? How much time could they have spent together? The people who gave evidence spoke thus: "I saw the girl leave the main road, but I didn't see her arrive at the bathing place; I assume that was where she was going"; and another: "I saw the boy emerge from the bush onto the road. I assume he was coming from the bathing area, there's no other place it leads to"; and so on. The verb forms in both cases were as follows:

ba'a baramo   ibu   sa   ubiare   iyo'oge
boy that + agent water there having gone was
"It appeared he was going to the river"

ba'a bara ibu   sahamo   webigare faserabo'oge
boy that water there that way appeared arrived
                          to come
"He appeared to be coming from the direction of the river"

The *-biare* ending is a participial form of the visual evidential form *-iba'ae*: From currently visible evidence (such as the arrival of the young man), the speaker inferred an action that preceded or caused it. *-Ibigare* is a participial form of the verb *ibiga-*, "to look like, resemble, appear as." The case ended with the head-men of Hegeso concluding that there was not enough evidence to determine whether the two had been together. The witnesses could not place the previous actions of the two exactly in space and time merely from when they were subsequently sighted.

It must be kept in mind that in traditional times, before the Foi had access to the minimal health-care facilities they now have, before they were made aware of a competing Western theory of the etiology of illness, before sorcery was made illegal under Papua New Guinea customary law, *all* deaths apart from those of the very aged were considered to be caused by sorcery. Very few sorcery accusations could be proved, or were admitted to by the accused. The laments for deceased relatives always had this comprehension of the ubiquity of sorcery at their core, this understanding of death as the ultimate result of the concealed jealousies and hatreds of communal life.

The constant possibility and fear of sorcery played its role in the Foi's movement between the communal longhouse village and their individual nuclear-family–oriented bush houses. The Foi, in common with all these longhouse-based societies of the southern fringe highlands, teetered between what they perceived as the positive value of gregarious communal life and the ultimately dire consequences of prolonged coresidence with at best nominally related non-nuclear kinsmen. It is correct to phrase the traditional movement between long-house and bush house as a seasonally governed one in which the Foi responded to the cyclical availability of game, tree crops, weather patterns, and so forth, as I have done elsewhere (Weiner 1988; Weiner, ed. 1988). But it must not be overlooked that the Foi were more apt to socially evaluate this oscillating residential pattern in terms of the pragmatic consequences of rather opposed forms of sociality. The exigencies of communal tasks such as gardenmaking, raising bridewealth and other ceremonial payments, and defense during hostilities between villages demanded communal living at least temporarily. But the Foi, even today, are not apt to linger in the village once they have accomplished such a task. With relief they return to the safety and privacy of their individual houses, where the stress of managing competing viewpoints and differential subjective interpretations of often tragic events is obviated. Here women feel free to dwell upon and sing about the sad consequences of communal life.

NOTES

1. I might add that one of the problems with early descriptions of sexual segregation in New Guinea societies is that they paid too little attention to the organization of male and female spatiality per se or the way in which the ideology of male-female separation configures discursive styles.

2. Heeschen (1982: 105) reports the use of a similar anaphoric deictic particle among the Eipo and Yale.

3. Shaw and Shaw (1973: 165) report the use of a similar "locative emphasizer" among the Samo.

4. Drawing upon Maria von Tiling's work in the Somali language, Cassirer reported that

> Somali possesses three forms of the article, which are distinguished from one another by the final vowel (-a, -i, and -o [or -u]). The factor determining the use of one or the other form is the spatial relation of the person or thing in question to the speaker. The article ending in -a designates a person or thing in immediate proximity to the speaker, visible to him and actually seen by him; the article ending in -o refers to a person or thing more or less removed from the speaker but usually visible to him; while the article ending in -i indicates a person or thing known to the speaker in some way but not visibly present. (1953: 206)

It should be noted that in terms of phonetic iconism, this is exactly the reverse of the Foi system!

Chastaing (quoted in Jackobson and Waugh 1979), investigating the symbolism of French vowels, attributed the quality of "hardness" to stops, in contrast to continuants, which were "soft." The students whom he questioned felt that /r/ was "very rough, strong, violent, heavy, pungent, hard, near-by, and bitter," while /l/ seemed "light-weighted, debonair, clear, smooth, weak, sweet, and distant" (502f.)

4 THE LANGUAGE OF MOVEMENT AND FINALITY

IN THE LAST CHAPTER, I suggested that there was a real iconism between the contrast in frontally and back-articulated sounds in Foi, and a corresponding contrast in meaning pertaining to relative spatiotemporal distance from the speaker. I confined my discussion to *literal* distance in space and time—but what of "figurative" distance? Does the Foi language employ iconism to depict a contrast in, say, close and distant relatives? Are we even justified, in fact, in separating "literal" spatial and temporal dimension from such "metaphorical" extensions of it? Or, as phenomenologists such as Cassirer, Heidegger, and Ricoeur maintain, are space and time such integral foundations of perception that closeness and distance are invariably a feature of all social and moral evaluations? In this chapter I would like to discuss what Gell has called a *secondary iconism* in the Foi language and to explore the implications such iconism has for understanding Foi poetic usages.

Jakobson, in his classic article "Why 'Mama' and 'Papa'?" (1962), surveyed Murdock's sample of kin terms and pointed out that velar sounds occurred less frequently than other sounds. Leach, who expanded upon Jakobson's initial observations, suggested that in Sinhalese kin terms, velar consonants were prevalent in terms for distant relatives (1971). The idea is, as Gell notes (1979), that the difficult-to-produce, "rough" velar sounds always involve some tension, strain, and effort, and are correspondingly appropriate for depicting social relationships containing an element of distance, formality, opposition, and/or tension. By way of contrast, Gell reminds us that "bilabials seem appropriate for nutritive/gustatory contexts" (1979: 52) and would therefore occur more frequently among terms for close relatives, especially those associated with the primary nurturative roles of feeding. I will return to this observation by Gell shortly.

Now, this iconism of social distance/nearness is abundantly evident in Foi kin terms, where the velar /k/ is found only in terms for affines and male-female terms. I consider only terms of address:

ka, kae	woman, wife
kabe	man
(base)/kabusi	(sister's husband)/wife's brother
kauwa	wife's father
kena'ae	husband's sister
kumi	cross-cousin

The pattern in other Foi kin terms is less clear. It is true that in the terms for close relatives, bilabials tend to predominate:

aba	father/child
abe	father's sister/brother's child (female speaking)
abia	mother's brother/sister's child
ana	cross-sex sibling
babo	mother's sister/sister's child (female speaking)
boba	sister (female speaking)
hũa	mother/child
mai	father's brother/brother's child
wame	brother (male speaking)

Note that *base/kabusi* are the only nonreciprocal kin terms of address in Foi (except for *ka/kabe*, "wife/husband"). The asymmetry of this relationship is well represented by the velar sound in the term for wife's brother and the lack of it in the term for sister's husband: it is the sister's husband who is beholden to his wife's brother, and not the other way around. *Kabusi* literally means "wife's relative," while *busi* by itself is a general term for "relative." A Foi wishing to refer undifferentiatedly to his consanguines calls them *nomo busira*, "my kin." Sometimes they say *daro busi*. *Daro* means "side, to the side, on the side," and the meaning conveyed is of that group of relatives who are not affines but are not exactly central to a person's coresidential core.

It could be said that the cross-cousin term *kumi* blends almost perfectly an initial "affinal" *ku* with a close, bilabial *mi*, depicting quite economically the blending of affinity and consanguinity, of distance and closeness, that is at the core of the Foi cross-cousin relationship.[1]

Other Foi terms of address are somewhat more difficult to categorize: *aya*, a fairly open sound, dominated by a glide, includes a range of +/− 2 generation females, as well as certain + 1 affinal females, such as mother's brother's wife, wife's father's and mother's brother's wife, etc. *Hũa*, which is pronounced with a nasalized *u*, seems to me a fairly congested, restrictive sound, with none of the breast-feeding connotations surrounding the /p/, /b/, and /m/ sounds which are comparatively common in terms for mother. Note, however, that *abia*, the term for mother's brother, is bilabial and lax and very similar in terms of articulation to *aba*, "father/child." Foi men consider their sisters' children as much their own as those they have sired by their wives, and despite Lévi-Strauss's (1963) and Radcliffe-Brown's (1952) characterizations, in its affective and nurturative content, the Foi mother's brother/sister's child relationship, with its elements of closeness, attachment, and support, resembles the father/child relationship, if less intensely.

If the velar /k/ is associated with tenseness, difficulty, strain, and so forth, would we not expect to find that iconism preserved across the entire range of Foi words? A glance at the Foi lexicon I have maintained over the years gives the following sample of entries:

ka'a	1. rib cage; 2. arduous
ka'abe-	to be difficult, exhausting
ka'aga	slope, incline
ka'anagedi-	to be jealous
ka'anaye-	to be unwilling to do something
ka'aredi-	to threaten
kāya-	to be ashamed, to feel shame

In addition to this general sense of difficulty, jealousy, unwillingness, steepness, and so forth, *ka* and *ka'a* words also convey the sense of complete, sealed off, interior, enveloped, encompassed, held back:

karuasi	inside
kauwa'o	baling scoop made from sago frond
kawaso	plate, bowl
ka'age	this amount and no more; this distance and no farther
ka'amea	neck band of a pearl shell
ka'aneye ha-	to curl up like a ball
ka'arua	inside
ka'arubi	deep, gullylike
ka'asī-	to shrink away, to withdraw from touch
kā'i	leaf used to line earth ovens
ka'o	skin, bark
ka'uadi-	to gather, of people
ka'uiye(ma-)	to encircle, surround, as of a fence

In this case, the link is based on the idea that something contained or enveloped is something held back, a force bottled up or thwarted, congested, restrained. In this respect, the pairing of the velar /k/ with the glottal stop /'/ may be most apposite, since the glottal stop is the maximal "interrupter" of syllabic flow. If, in fact, the Foi cosmos is, as I have characterized it, a collection of ceaseless movements and vectors of motion, then any stoppage is going to imply a build-up of energy, a created potential for release, a dammed reserve held back.

Now let us examine some examples of this primary iconism of motion words in Foi poetry:

(Song 2):

ibu	*ka'ayamikiribi*	*wabo'ore*
river	waves caused by moving canoe	come

"The waves caused by a canoe in motion"

(Song 26):

ibu	*ka'asubagedia*	*yibumena*
water	crashing	sleep-man

"The man who sleeps near the rushing water"

Ka'aya-, "to ripple, of water," and *ka'asubagedi-*, "to make a crashing sound, of swiftly flowing water," are related to the following *ka'a-* words:

ka'adenedi-	to rattle, tinkle
ka'aro-(fa'a-)	to writhe, of snakes
ka'arofo'o u-	to wriggle along; to travel with difficulty
ka'arorodi-	to make a rattling noise
ka'aru-	to rumble, of pigs; to complain, grouse
ka'arubidi-	to make a humming noise, as of rushing water; to complain by muttering under one's breath
ka'arurudi-	to bang the sides of a canoe while paddling
ka'odenedi-	to grate, of broken bones

The verb constructions which make use of phonological duplication such as *-rorodi-*, *-denedi-*, *-rurudi-*, *-ninidi-*, and *-rubidi-* are used onomatopoetically; they imitate the tinkly, rattly, humming, ripply sounds they denote. In addition, they all make use of the *ka'a/ka'o* stem, which I have already associated with arduousness, difficulty, strain, tension, and the associated containment or bottling of such force or motion. In combination, they convey the sense of things banging around within a confined space, the vibration of objects moving in constant collision with each other in a closed area.

But do we have here a genuine case of iconism? The Foi words for woman, *ka*, and girl, *kabo*, partake of the tense velar /k/, indicative of separation, completeness, strain, tension. But Gell claims that the Umeda word for "girl/vulva/

gullet," *mol*, derives from the gustatory metaphor of a rounded fruit being swallowed into a constricting channel, and the general ambiguity concerning eating and copulating, and sexual-gustatory activity vs. passivity (Gell 1979). The sound in Umeda which corresponds to the Foi semantic domain /k/-/ka/of tenseness and distance is -*ag*-: as in *agwa*, "woman," *awk*, the kin category "outsiders" (*agai*). While both make use of the velar /k/ or /g/, the word *ka* in Umeda refers to ego: It is the first-person pronoun and therefore indicates a starkly opposed semantic field in Umeda in comparison with Foi.

This rediscovery of the apparent "arbitrariness" of Foi and Umeda vocal articulation leads to a consideration of what Gell has called "secondary iconism," which has been well explored by the linguist Dwight Bolinger. While "primary iconism" of the kind I have been describing so far views meaning as a literal representation of sounds and articulatory positions, secondary iconism works in the opposite fashion and sees sound and articulatory positions as literal representations of meaning. It is exemplified by the joke (which I first heard told by Michael Silverstein) about the argument between the four linguists, one French, one Italian, one English, and one German, each of whom maintains that his respective language's word for "butterfly" is the only one which faithfully depicts the lightness, delicacy, and beauty of the winged insect. When the German linguist insists that *schmetterling* is just as aesthetically appropriate as a label for the butterfly as *papillon*, he exemplifies this kind of secondary, or what Gell calls appropriately *a posteriori*, iconism. It is an iconism construed after the fact, so to speak, and it arises simply from the association that words and their meanings acquire by virtue of their ongoing use in the world. These *a posteriori* iconisms flourish and, according to Gell, "drive out" *a priori*, primary iconisms because

> it is the meaning of the word that thematizes the gesture of speech, given the context in which it is filled with a particular significance, and not the other way around, not the gesture providing the context in which the meaning of the word would become determinate by referring to a more general iconic schema. (1979: 59)

This is possible, of course, only because no matter how primarily iconic languages start out, there is always, as Roy Wagner reminds us, a scission between the sensory elicitor and its subjective constitution, a scission guaranteed by the symbolic quality of human perception itself. This discontinuity, however, does not separate the symbolic act into an ontology whereby perception precedes abstraction or symbolic formulation; rather, perception itself is fully half of the symbolic moment of human conceptualization:

> the realization that meaning *is* perception, occurring within the "natural" ground from which abstraction supposedly freed the word, indicates that "abstraction" is, rather, part of a generative and ongoing process. The invention of a microcosm by abstraction from a perceptual macrocosm is half of a highly charged dialectical

interaction, establishing a sensory continuum within which the ordering and re-figuring of meaning is accomplished. (Wagner 1986: 19)

Cassirer said much the same thing when he maintained that

> reproduction never consists in retracing, line for line, a specific content of reality; but in selecting a pregnant motif in that content and so producing a characteristic "outline" of its form. . . . To reproduce an object in this sense means not merely to compose it from its particular sensuous characteristics, but to apprehend it in its structural relations which can only be truly understood if the consciousness constructively produces them. (1953: 183–84)

The best examples of how this "second order" iconism works are to be found in Foi words for motion and motionlessness, and it is this secondary iconism that establishes them as poetic, in and of themselves, in Foi terms.

Bolinger, in his article "Word Affinities" (1965 [1940]), described this *a posteriori* iconism in English, observing

> that verbal counters have both an *x* value and a picture value, and that the two are often in conflict. . . . The *x* value is potentially variable—it decrees that *home* "might as well" be *swurish* or *locyx*. The picture value is absolute—it decrees that *home*, once embedded in the language, forms semantic alliances that make it impossible to dislodge . . . and once embedded in the mind of the speaker, becomes something more than a substitute for a thing—to a certain degree it *is* the thing, or part of it. (Ibid.: 191)[2]

Sounds and ideas become inextricably linked through use, and "nothing more is needed to cause that sound to give the cast of its idea to many words, alike in sound" (ibid: 194). Whatever was the reason that the *gl* sound, for example, became associated with things pertaining to the eye and vision, it continues "attracting other words into its system: besides *gleam, glance, glow, glare*," and so on "there are *ogle, oggle, glory*, and most recently *glamor*, which colloquially is coming to refer to visual appeal" (ibid.: 195). The *-ash* sound, so onomatopoetically suggestive of breaking, tinkling, fragments, generates "*dash, crash, trash, slash, smash* . . . (perhaps explaining why we hear mentally the clatter of small pieces when we use the word *cash*, and why *dishes* are so rattly and breakable)" (ibid.).

My Foi lexicon gives abundant examples of words with this "imitative and affinitive suggestiveness" (ibid.: 194–95). The verb *foge-* means "1. to snap a bowstring; and 2. to sharpen." The raspy, fricative /f/ followed by the hollow, velar /g/ is the Foi onomatopoetic equivalent of what could be rendered in English as *ssssssssh-pop!*—a frictiony, rough sound terminating abruptly in a dull, echoing thump. Associated with *foge-* are:

fage-	to remove pith from pandanus
fageni-	to commit adultery

fagidi-	to curve, bend, bulge
fagodi-, fofagodi-	to clap hands repetitively
fege-	to remove; to sweep
firage(di)-	to throb, pump
fofagedi-	1. to have an uneven surface; 2. to thump; to make a hollow sound
foga-	to put an axe in a loop of cane in the wall
foga e-	to sweep
fogebo	sharpening stone
fogedi-	to strike, to strike quickly
fogefoge(di)-	to throb, to pump, to thump rhythmically

The friction that causes the fricative sound of sweeping and sharpening also, apparently, brings to mind the rough surfaces that produce such sounds. The fibrous pith is removed from the interior of a pandanus fruit with a sharpened cassowary thighbone. The use of an almost identical term for adultery could bring to mind the twisty, furtive paths that people take in the bush en route to illicit assignations; or it could evoke the idea of breaking open something and removing the core. (I make these suggestions having listened to the way men discuss adultery itself, as a furtive act of breaking and entering!)

Let's continue looking at the use of the initial fricative /f/ in Foi, of all the fricatives the most compressed and vibratory. When followed by the abrupt velar /g/ it is used to describe rough-thumping, rasp-ticking, scrape-bumping, throb-pumping actions—or, to put it more abstractly, movements that involve effort and hardship which end abruptly. When it is followed by relatively more frontal consonants such as /r/, /d/, and /f/ itself, we seem to get an opposite effect—of an initial rough vibratory movement not brought to a halt but on the contrary allowed to break free and expand:

fadudi-	to shatter loudly
foforeye-	to snap off
foha-	to disembark
foraye-	to bend, fold
forayewa-	to be swiftly flowing, of rivers
fore	large, big
fo'o	1. to emigrate; 2. to uproot
fufuye- (u-)	to fly away, to scatter on wing, of birds
fura'a-	to unfold, spread out
furubu	red leaf (used as forehead decoration at ceremonies)
furudi-	to explode
fu'uwa-	to divorce
hufoforeye-	to break into small pieces

One need only listen to a Foi speaker using the word *fadu-*, with an explosive emphasis on the second syllable, and often an almost unconscious abrupt raising and spreading of the arms; or to hear the sense of a tense, contained force suddenly taking to flight, as with the word *fufuye-*, with its almost overpronounced /f/ sounds.

The examples I have been describing all have to do with qualities of *motion and space*. The phenomenological contribution to the study of language has stressed precisely the centrality of the perception of time, movement, and stasis in the constitution of a wide range of qualitative relationships, as Cassirer suggested in the passage I quoted in the last chapter. "Elementary spatial terms," he went on to say, " . . . are . . . rooted in immediate sensory impression; but on the other hand they contain the first germ from which the terms of pure relation will grow" (1953: 200–201).

More recently, linguists such as John Haiman (1980, 1985) have urged us to consider the iconic properties of *syntax*—the manner in which morpheme, word, and clause order is itself diagrammatic of the actions and relationships it describes. Combined with a sensible Boasian appreciation of language—that all languages exhibit richness and complexity in specific "areas of cultural focus" (1980: 535)—Haiman suggests that the smaller a language's basic vocabulary, the more it has to be iconic, that is, the more it will be prone to resort to some essentially extralinguistic mimesis as a means of inflection. This is most vividly exemplified in the syntax of Foi verb constructions, as the next section describes.

WORDS OF MOTION AND CONTAINMENT

One of the many insights that Ernest Fenollosa demonstrated in his essay "The Chinese Written Character as a Medium for Poetry" was his insistence on the phenomenological inseparability of things and actions:

> A true noun, an isolated thing, does not exist in nature. Things are only the terminal points, or rather the meeting points, of actions, cross-sections cut through actions, snap-shots. Neither can a pure verb, an abstract motion, be possible in nature. The eye sees noun and verb as one: things in motion, motion in things. . . . (1967: 364)

Cassirer also realized this when he distinguished between "nominal" and "verbal" languages:

> Languages of the purely "objective" or nominal type give priority to local terms over terms of direction, to the expression of rest over the expression of motion, while in verbal types the opposite relation generally prevails. . . . As man turns his attention to activity and apprehends it as such, he must transform the purely

objective, substantial unity of space into a dynamic-functional unity; he must, as it were, construct space as a totality of the directions of action. (1953: 212)

The Foi language remains faithful to this inseparability of object and action; it is quite definitely a "verbal" language in Cassirer's terms. We have already seen that through the use of the subjectively assessed verbal evidential suffixes, Foi speakers see themselves at the center of actions moving toward and away from them.

But more than this, as an SOV (Subject-Object-Verb) language, Foi grammar, syntax, and speech itself gives centrality to the verb, so much more heavily inflected than other parts of speech. Because of the syntactic juxtaposition of the direct object before the verb in Foi utterances, most verbs are inseparable from the nouns upon which the action focuses, despite the interposition of adverbial and adjectival stems between noun and verb. For example, in the sentence:

yo kui a'a   hua
she sago quickly pounded
"She hurriedly pounded the sago"

it could be said that the verb is *kuihu-*, "to pound sago," despite the interposition of the adverb *a'a*, "quickly." Another example is the way that the *ni-* stem, which by itself could be translated as "to take something in by mouth," is inflected by the various items that are orally consumed by the Foi: *kimani-*, "to eat food"; *ibuni-*, "to drink water"; *so'oni-* "to smoke tobacco."

In the next example:

yo ara   bunaye ua
he to-the-house running went
"He ran to the house"

it could just as accurately be said that *bunaye u-* is a distinct verb from *u-*. The first could be translated as "to go swiftly, to go 'runningly,'" while the second verb is the uninflected verb stem of motion away from speaker. This is the kind of syntactic iconicity we find in a language such as Foi, which does without separate words for "run," "walk," "gallop," "stagger," and so on.

Let us look at some other examples of this morphosyntactic iconicity. As one would expect among people for whom images of cutting and severing evoke such central conventional values, Foi words for cutting are highly specific. The verb *fora-* means specifically to cut something into two equal halves, such as a section of bamboo or sugar cane into two pieces. The verb *gura-*, on the other hand, means specifically to cut down a stalk of sugar cane. The verb *bo-* seems to be used in the sense of detaching a small bit from a larger whole, as in the action of cutting a leaf from a plant, or cutting hair from a head. Other words of cutting include *gua-*, "to split, chop"; *dawa-*, "to cut up meat"; and *geteraha-*, "to sever."[3]

But cutting words are easily proliferated by compounding a whole range of verbs with the verb stem *hi-* or *hu-*, which means "to strike, hit." Some of the cutting words' stems can be suffixed to *hi-/hu-* with only small change in meaning: *Hifora-* is synonymous with *fora-*, but *hiforaema-*, literally "strike-cut-take," means "to cut up and divide (meat)." *Hiboma-*, compounded from the stems "strike-cut-take," means "to amputate, to chop off, to sever." Some cutting words are compounded from even smaller stems and become correspondingly more iconic: *Himowa-* "to chop down a tree," could be broken down into *hi-*, "to strike"; *mo*, the agentive affix; and *wa-*, "to come." Others take on quite different connotations when compounded with *hi/hu-*: *Geteraha-* by itself seems to mean "to sever," but *hugeteraha-* refers to the splitting off of a small party of people from a larger traveling group, or the turning off from a main path onto a smaller one. *Dosoma-* means "to take down, to remove something from a height," but *hudosoma-* means "to cut down." Such usages preserve the iconic evocativeness of the word *hu-*, "to strike, to smite," implying that severing things, changing their course, bringing them to a halt, involves a *violent* action.

And what more violent action is there than to cause death? *Hu-* by itself means both "to strike" and "to kill," and it could be said to be the "basic" or "unmarked" form of the category that includes all the verbs which have severing, halting, or cutting-off meanings. It is the cutting off of the stream of life that death represents, the bringing to a halt all the movements through space and time of which human existence is made up, and it is in the moment of the human realization and understanding of this violent, fatal cutting off that Foi poetry is born.

But before we can turn to this theme as the constitutive moment of Foi poetic awareness, let us examine further some of the syntactic and morphological forms that cutting off takes in Foi discourse. Let us now look at what we can properly call Foi "aspect"—that which deals with the durative and completive quality of actions themselves.

Constructions with ha- *and* -kera. There are two stative verbs in Foi. *Ha-* means "to be" in a permanent or long-term sense: either of large material objects which are rooted and immovable, such as trees and houses, or when applied to people, meaning "to live, exist, subsist, reside . . . dwell." *Ha-* is also the stative verb for all things existing in an interior or internal state: *fa'o ha-*, "to be hungry" (lit. "the stomach is"); *u'ubi ha-*, "to be pregnant" (lit. "child is"); *gamu'u ua ha-*, "to be fond of" (lit. "heart-goes out to-is"). *Ha-* is also the stative of important events: *Usane ha-*, "to hold an Usane"; *soroha-*, "to hold a *soro* dance."

Kera-, by contrast, is the stative for objects that are more impermanent, transitory, and movable: *ya igi kerare ibubege*, "there are three birds"; *kuikima kerare ibubege*, "there is food (to eat)"; *nami ari kerare ibubege*, "the pig is in the house." Note the difference between the latter sentence and *nami hage hare ibubege*, "I have two pigs" (in the sense of "I own and care for two pigs"). Notice also *gamu'u [ua] ha-*, "to be fond of," but *gamu'u kera-*, "to be annoyed or angry [with]." Apparently, anger is the more transitory, fleeting, and impermanent emotion in Foi, as opposed to love and fondness, which really do "live" in the heart.

These two stative roots combine with the causative prefix *m*-* in the following ways: *Mekera-*, the far more common form, literally means "to cause to be," i.e., "to put or place." But note also *ka mekera-*, "to 'put' a woman" (i.e., to marry). *Maha-*, which I rarely heard used in its bare form, means "to place *into, under, in*," as, for example, when placing leaves in a fish dam. *Maha-*, however, at least among the Upper Mubi Foi with whom I lived, is more commonly found in conjugated form in the Foi perfective verb constructions.

Perfective Constructions. The continuative sense of actions in progress is formed around the affix *ibi*, which is also found in the verbal modifier *ibiga-*, "to resemble, to be like," as in *ya medibigabida'ae*, "It sounds just like a bird," or *bubuna ibigare fasera*, "(It) arrived appearing like a ghost," or "Something like a ghost appeared." *Ibiha-* is suffixed to verb stems to give the sense of habitual action over a long period of time, such as *ayaye nibiha-*, literally "hunting-eat-living," or "to live by hunting." *Biha-* by itself also means "to live" in the implied sense of carrying out a series of repeated habitual activities.

Ibikera-, on the other hand, denotes a repetitive, continuative activity over a shorter period of time that will realize a completion. For example, *ira kara sa hababikera-*, "to keep wandering through the bush"; kima *nibikerabubege*, "I am (in the act of) eating"; *segera dasedibikiribubiye*, "I am not lying (as I speak)."

The past perfect construction in Foi—that is, the form that indicates a habitual or repetitive action taking place over a fixed duration of time—is *ibiha- + mahare* or *ibikera- + mesere*, usually conjugated with the evidential ending *-iyo'o* indicating "previous evidence." Examples are *ayaye nibiha'iyo'o mahare*, "They lived by hunting during that period (and then ceased to)"; *kore ubikiriyo'o mahare*, "He continued upstream (for as long as it took him to get there)."

Notice how the perfect construction "cuts off" a repetitive action by switching it to the *maha-* construction; the action, as it were, is "put inside," therefore out of sight and out of evidence. I am unsure as to the derivation of the *mesere* alternative; I heard both with equal frequency and was unable to discern any semantic difference between them: Foi people maintained they were synonymous, an explanation which, as Haiman notes, is vaguely unsatisfactory to anyone who believes that, iconically, a change of form must correspond to a change in meaning.

Constructions with era-. When combined with the verb particle *era-*, both *kera-* and *ha-* apply more specifically to the active states of human beings. *Erakera-* means "to sit, to wait (a short time)"; *eraha-* means "to be alive, to be, to wait (indefinitely); to live, to stay." A Foi person leaving someone behind after a visit says, in the way of a farewell, *bi erahai*, "live here!" though I also heard it used in the more short-term sense of "wait here!" *Era-* never occurs by itself but is related to the verb *ere-*, "to see, to look," and is found in the verbs *eresaye-*, "to look after, to watch over," and the noun *eresaro*, the man with whom one shares a fireplace in the men's house.

Chaining of Sequential Verb Clauses. As I discussed previously (1988), Foi narrative discourse makes use of the past and present participial forms to enchain sequential actions. A person recounting a series of events characteristically says, for example:

yo ayaye ua	He went hunting
ayaye uare	Having gone hunting
ara vera'a wa	He returned to the house
tare vera'a ware	Then having returned
ira hisa	He lit a fire
tare hisare	Then having lit a fire
yo kima ininia dibige	He cooked and ate his food

In such cases, the chain of events is "fastened" by using a sentence-final verb with the *-a dibige* or *-bo'orege* ending, which are transcendental past-tense endings used in narrative and which are not marked by evidential conjugations.

In narrative style, the use of the *-a dibige* and *-bo'orege* phrase-final endings has the effect of "sealing off" a series of enchained, sequential actions. It introduces thematic breaks in what would otherwise be a continuous series of sequential acts, and it is a crucial diacritical in long narratives such as myths. It signals to the listener that a series of actions that have something in common, that were focused around a single summating event, is now finished, and another series is about to begin.

Of course, in Haiman's terms, no narrative device could be more syntactically iconic than one in which events are enchained one after another, in which *sequence* is foregrounded as the focus of discursive elaboration. This is easy enough to understand for enchained *actions* or verb phrases—and perhaps we can identify the iconicity in this case as a feature of narrative *style* rather than syntax.

But let us recall Cassirer's words—that logical relations grow out of spatial and temporal perceptions, and in turn dialectically remodel the former—and observe how suggestive this is of Lévi-Strauss's discussion of totemic thought. In broadening our understanding of the classificatory processes at work in totemic differentiation, Lévi-Strauss did not refuse to consider that sequential events or actions themselves could serve a speciating role. Nowhere is this more vividly exemplified, perhaps, than among certain aboriginal Australian groups, whose landscape is defined as a collection of the permanent traces of ancestral actions.

But as I noted in chapter 2, the Foi landscape is also discursively re-created as a collection of "human inscriptions," and the detotalization of this landscape is one of the major features of Foi poetry. The landscape is, in other words, iconic of human history, and it is this isomorphism that Foi women capitalize on in their compositions, as the next chapter describes.

NOTES

1. For a detailed discussion of the Foi cross-cousin relationship, see Weiner 1984; 1988.

2. Saussure himself noted that "there is no language in which nothing is motivated. . . . the mind contrives to introduce a principle of order and regularity into certain parts of the mass of signs" (1966: 133).

3. Cassirer cites Westermann's classic work on the Ewe language:

> In Ewe and certain related languages, for example, there are adverbs which describe only *one* activity, *one* state or *one* attribute, and which consequently can be accompanied only with *one* verb. . . . Westermann counts no less than thirty-three such phonetic images for the single verb "to walk," each designating a particular manner of walking: slouching or sauntering, limping or dragging the feet, shambling or waddling, energetic or weary. (1953: 180)

5 THE MOVING IMAGE IN FOI POETRY

Footprints I have made; they are broken
—Osage Corn-Planting Song
(LaFlesch 1917: 197)

I ENDED THE LAST CHAPTER by suggesting that the Foi landscape was iconic of human history; as Gaston Bachelard once remarked, "At times we think we know ourselves in time, when all we know is a sequence of fixations in the spaces of the being's stability. . . . In its countless alveoli, space contains compressed time" (1969: 8). Renato Rosaldo, in his eloquent study of Ilongot headhunting, noted that "the Ilongot sense of history [is] conceived as movement through space in which (and this is the usual analogy drawn) people walk along a trail and stop at a sequence of named resting places" (1980: 56).

Bachelard even coined the term *topoanalysis* for the "systematic psychological study of the sites of our intimate lives" (1969: 8). For people such as the Osage, the Ilongot, and the Foi, human history and intention are discursively re-created through the narration of movement between places: discourse delineates this movement and centers the core values of language around moving images.

In this chapter I begin examining the lyric content of the song poems, but I will defer consideration of their total compositional features until chapters 6 and 7. Here, using select lines and groups of lines from various songs, I want to illustrate some general features pertaining to the themes of motion that I introduced in the last two chapters.

In chapter 4, I suggested that the "verbal" nature of the Foi language and its basic SOV syntactic arrangement focused attention on the precise nature of actions and their various durative and aspectual qualities. I made passing reference to the idea that this fit into a Boasian view of language: that each language exhibits the most complexity in areas of its evaluative focus. The Foi language, in these terms, possesses a wide range of cutting and severing words which modify and alter the quality of what the Foi perceive to be the basic, constitutive motions and movements of their lifeworld.[1]

If such cutting, halting, and change-of-direction words are to the Foi what "snow" words are to the Eskimo, then it would be reasonable to assume that the most desirable of Foi poetry would capitalize on the constant tension between movement and nonmovement. In fact, this was one of the things that Ezra Pound and the imagists insisted had to be true for *all* desirable poetry. "If you can't think of Imagism or phanopoeia as including the moving image, you will have to make a really needless division of fixed image and praxis or action," Pound wrote (1951: 38). Welsh has commented on this imagist "aesthetic of movement" in a way that could be a general description of the embodiment of movement in Foi poetry:

> As soon as objects (or images, or actions or ideas) are placed side by side a relationship has been created and forces are set up among the juxtaposed elements. We see throughout modern poetry that one basic assumption of the "moving Image" is that the juxtaposition of various elements in the structure of the Image generates forces in just this way. (1978: 80)

Thus, the most salient and regular feature of Foi poetry is the way each song juxtaposes images of movement and nonmovement, or posits an action or movement and the subsequent halting or cutting off of that action. In this chapter I would like to begin describing and analyzing these forms of imagery in Foi song poetry, those that focus on the tension between the movement that is the definitive heart of life, and the stillness that constitutes the finality of death.

The core element of every Foi song poem is based on this contrast; it can be said to be as integral to Foi poetry as the "seasonal element" is to Japanese haiku (see Yasuda 1957). Let us first look at some examples:

(Song 8):

1. *duma   yefua sabe ya   erege*
   mountain Yefua ridge bird cockatoo

   auwa fore   iba'ae
   wing broken is

   ibu   sumane habo   ya   namuyu
   creek Sumane water end bird cockatoo

   vira hua   uboba'a
   shot struck gone

2. *duma   faī hesabo   ya   erege*
   mountain side following bird cockatoo

auwa forabo'owa'ae
wing broken

duma   ka'afa hesabo   ya   namuyu
mountain edge   following bird cockatoo

vira huiba'ae
shot killed

3. *ira farabo haũ   bobo   ya   namuyu*
tree farabo break off leaves bird cockatoo

auwa gefodiyo'owa'ae
wing spear pierced

ira sonane haũ   bobo   ya   namuyu
tree sonane break off leaves bird cockatoo

auwa fore   iba'ae
wing broken is

1. The ridge of Mt. Yefua, the sulphur-crested cockatoo
   Its wing is broken

   At Sumane Creek as it flows underground, the cockatoo
   Its wing is broken

2. Following the side of the mountain, the cockatoo
   Its wing broken

   Along the edge of the mountain's base, the cockatoo
   Arrow shot and killed

3. The cockatoo breaks off the leaves of the *farabo* tree as it flies
   Its wing broken

   The cockatoo breaks off the leaves of the *sonane* tree as it flies
   Its wing is broken

(Song 11):

1. *ibu barua ga   iga*
   creek Barua source path

   iga ere'e
   path look!

   kumagi iga
   Kumagi path

iga ereyiya'abe
path do you not see?

2. *ba'a na'a ibu faya'a ga iga*
boy your river Faya'a source path

iga ere'e
path look!

ba'a na'a ibu faya'a ga iga
boy your river Faya'a source path

iga ere'e
path look!

3. *kumagi tage iga*
Kumagi mouth path

iga kigiba'ae
path bush covered

sese faiyu wabu iga
marsupial faiyu coming path

iga aodiba'ae
path tree covered

1. The path to Baruaga Creek
   Look at the path!

   The path to Kumagi Creek
   Do you not see it?

2. Boy, your path at the head of the Faya'a River
   Look at it now!

   Boy, your Faya'a River source path
   Just see what it looks like now!

3. The path leading to the mouth of the Kumagi Creek
   It is covered with bush

   The path along which the *faiyu* marsupial travels
   Has been covered over with bush

These pictures of halted or cut-off movement or stillness are among the most evocative portrayals of the practical effects of death for the Foi. Of the forty-one men's ceremonial songs I transcribed, twenty-five revolve thematically

on this literal contrast between a predicated movement and its observed surcease.

In song 8, which I have already discussed in chapter 1, the deceased, a
member of the So'onedobo clan, is referred to as the sulphur-crested cockatoo,
which is one of the primary totems of that clan. The cockatoo, its wing pierced
by an arrow, drops suddenly to the ground. The meteoric quality of the cockatoo's fall from the sky represents the suddenness and rapidity with which Yabokigi himself died, allegedly "struck" by sorcery.

In song 11, we are given an image of a path through the forest as a conduit
of human movement, an inscription of regular human activity, and nothing
so starkly and sadly attests to the end of this activity and the implied death
of a human being as the sight of the bush or forest reclaiming the path after
its user ceases to maintain this inscriptive activity. The exhortative mood of
the answering line in each verse urges the listener to consider the tragic implications of these abandoned and obliterated paths.

Now, let us examine two songs in which the valence or order of movement/
stillness is reversed:

(Song 13):

1. *ba'a bamo ira huba gugu biri*
   boy this   tree huba flower here

   hūga afu   wahuge
   larvae butterfy alit

   ba'a bamo ira kabare gugu biri
   boy this   tree kabare flower here

   hūga none   wahuge
   larvae bumblebee alit

2. *ba'a na'a ira fayane gugu biri*
   boy your tree fayane flower here

   hūga afu   wahuge
   larvae butterfly alit

   ba'a na'a hefa bari gugu biri
   boy your vine bari flower here

   hūga none   wahuge
   larvae bumblebee alit

3. *ba'a na'a ira huba gugu biri*
   boy your tree huba flower here

hũga afu   wahuge
larvae butterfly alit

ba'a na'a ira fayare gugu biri
boy your tree fayare flower here

hũga none   wahuge
larvae bumblebee alit

4. *aidobo   ba'a bereromo u'ubi*
   Aidobo boy Berero's child

   ba'a howare
   boy Howare

   momahu'u ka   genemo
   Momahu'u woman Genemo

   dawa
   dawabo

5. *momahu'u   kabo genemoka*
   Momahu'u girl Genemoka

   ba'a herere
   boy Herere

   aidobo   berero
   Aidobo Berero

   kabe Howare
   man Howare

1. On the flowers of your *huba* palm
   The *afu* butterfly alights

   On the flowers of your *kabare* tree
   The *none* bumblebee alights

2. On the flowers of your *fayane* tree
   The *afu* butterfly alights

   On the flowers of your *hefa bari* vine
   The *none* bumblebee alights

3. On the flowers of your *huba* palm
   The *afu* butterfly alights

On the flowers of your *fayare* tree
The *none* bumblebee alights

4. The Aidobo clan, the man Berero
   His son Howare

   The Momahu'u clan woman Genemo
   Dawa

5. The Momahu'u clan woman Genemoka
   Her son Herere

   The man of the Aidobo clan, Berero
   His son Howare

The butterflies referred to in this and other verses of the song are spoken of by the Foi as if they were the egg-laying stage in the life cycle of the Longicorn beetle, the insect responsible for leaving larvae in the trunks of fallen trees in the bush.[2] A fallen tree is a common image of a dead man, particularly in Foi dream interpretation. The movement of the butterfly is briefly halted as it stops to lay its eggs, so that although the verse begins with a picture of the horizontal stillness of death, it yet promises regeneration from that death when the edible larvae mature and are sought after as delicacies by humans. Through the intervention of the constantly moving, flitting butterfly, the dead tree can once again become a source of edible "fruit."

In the next song, the Mubi River emerges as the most important means by which people themselves "flow":

(Song 27):

1. *ba'a na'a bare ga   burayodi   dibiri*
   boy your canoe prow rise from water curved

   na-o mihiba'ane we
   I   to embark come!

   ba'a na'a bare ga   yōdibi
   boy your canoe prow dips into water

   na-o moware   do'ane   we
   I too to embark to speak come!

2. *ba'a na'a bare ga   ya sabeyu   arumaibi*
   boy your canoe prow bird cockatoo tongue-taken

   na-o moware   do'ane   we
   I too to embark to speak come!

ba'a na'a bare ga   ya   sabeyu   arumaibi
boy your canoe prow bird cockatoo tongue-taken

na-o   moware   do'ane   we
I too to embark to speak come!

[verse 2 repeated two more times]

3. *ba'a na'a ibu   faya'a wagibu*
boy your river Faya'a mouth

ibudawabo
ibudawabo

yiya amena ibu   hesa   wagibu
we   men   creek Hesa mouth

dawabo
dawabo

4. *yiya amena ibariabe sabe   u'ubi*
we   men   Ibariabe Ridge children

dawabo
dawabo

yiya amena kana deregebo
we   men   stone cliff face

dawabo
dawabo

1. Boy, the curved prow of your canoe lifts gently from the water
   Come fetch me too

   The bow of your canoe dips gracefully back into the water
   Oh come and let me embark too!

2. Boy, your cockatoo-tongued canoe prow
   Come and get me, I say!

   Boy, your canoe prow as beautiful as the cockatoo's tongue
   I too want to get in your canoe

3. Boy, your cockatoo-tongued canoe prow
   Come and get me, I say!

   Boy, your canoe prow as beautiful as the cockatoo's tongue
   I too want to get in your canoe

4. Boy, your cockatoo-tongued canoe prow
   Come and get me, I say!

   Boy, your canoe prow as graceful as the cockatoo's tongue
   I too want to get in your canoe

5. Boy, your Faya'a Creek flowing into the Mubi
   Ibu Dawabo

   We are the men of the mouth of Hesa Creek
   Dawabo

6. We are the children of Ïbariabe Hill
   Dawabo

   We are the men of the stone-lined mountain
   Dawabo

The gentle up-and-down movement of a canoe as it moves through water is evoked in this song. The tapered bow of the canoe suggests to the singer the curved tongue of the cockatoo. And, as Kora Midibaru indicated in the interpretation of his dream in the Introduction, journeying by water is an image of the life course itself for the Foi: In this song, the deceased man is traveling in his beautiful canoe alone, and the singer implores him to let her come with him.

The centrality of movement as the initial predicate of a song poem explains why flowing water is commonly invoked: thirteen of the forty-one *sorohabora* I transcribed make use of that specific imagery. Let us look at a fragment from the following song:

(Song 7):

1. *ba'a na'a ibu   barua ga   habo   duma*
   boy your creek Barua source flow into mountain

   aodoba'aye
   let bush covered

   ba'a na'a ao   iburo'o
   boy your bush creek

   kigiba'aye
   let strong bush

1. Boy, your Baruaga Creek flowing into the mountain
   The bush has covered it over

Boy, your tiny creek
The forest has reclaimed it

In this heavily karstified limestone country, underground creeks are common; indeed, the Mubi itself flows underground at the northwestern end of Hegeso territory, and the Foi call the cave from which it emerges the "source of the Mubi." But often enough, these tiny creeks become so covered over with horizontally growing shrubs and overhanging growth that one only hears their bubbling noise without seeing them. It is only through people's efforts that such small creeks stay uncovered and swift-flowing.

In the following song, it is the sound of rushing water that constitutes what Hugh Kenner called the *peripeteia*, the "moving image" (1951: 62):

(Song 26):

2. *ibu   dufu hua   yibumena*
   creek dam planted sleep-man

   uaha   yiboba'ae
   go-live sleeps

   ibu   dufu hua   yibumena
   creek dam planted sleep-man

   uaha   yiboba'ae
   go-live sleeps

3. *ibu   dimani hua   yibumena*
   water rushing strikes sleep-man

   uaha   yiboba'ae
   go-live sleeps

   ibu   āgu   hua   yibumena
   water swiftly strikes sleep-man

   bereboba'ae
   is lost

4. *ibu   hūa   yibumena*
   water mother sleep-man

   uaha   yiboba'ae
   go-live sleeps

ibu   ka'asubagedia yibumena
water crashing   sleep-man

bereboba'ae
is lost

5. *ibu   hemomo'o hubagia yibumena*
water flotsam   remove sleep-man

uaha   yiboba'ae
go-live sleeps

ibu   āgu   hūa   yibumena
water swiftly mother sleep-man

bereboba'ae
is lost

2. Near the fish dam where you habitually slept
There you have gone to rest

Near the fish dam where you were wont to stay
There you have gone to sleep the night

3. He who sleeps near the rushing water
There he silently sleeps

Near the rushing, hissing water
Only the river's sound we hear

4. The man who sleeps near the sibilant water
He has gone to rest there

The soft crash of rushing water
But he is lost

5. He who removed the flotsam as he paddled
He has gone there to sleep

Near the splashing, rushing water
He is lost

This song makes use of the homophony between the Foi word *hua*, which means "struck" (from the verb *hu-*, "to strike, kill, hit"), "planted" (from the same verb, *mohu-*), and *hu(ˉ)a*, "mother," which tends to have a slightly more nasalized /u/. Crashing, rushing water strikes the stones in creek and river beds. Also, men must "plant" the stakes with which they construct fish dams across the mouths of small creeks. Finally, large bodies of water, such as the Mubi, Baru, and Yo'oro rivers and Lake Kutubu, are called *ibu hūa*, the "mother" of waters, as with any particularly large specimen of any category (hence *a hūa*, "mother of houses," i.e., the longhouse).

Hemomo'o is detritus and flotsam that bunches up and clots as it flows downstream. It also means "froth, scum," etc. The verb *hubagia-* (from *bagia-*, "to divide into parts" [see below]) means two things: 1. to push aside logs and flotsam as one paddles a canoe; 2. to spread fish poison in dammed water. This fine verse thus compresses the image of spreading fish poison in still water with that of the man threading a canoe through debris-laden water.

Notice in song 26 that the composer used different words to describe the moving water:[3] *ibu dimani, ibu āgu, ibu hūa, ibu ka'asubagedia, ibu hemomo'o hubagia*. Like the Eskimo and their snow vocabulary, the Foi seem to make fine distinctions between varieties of flowing water. *Dimani* apparently comes from the word *dima*, another name for women's sago song, and hence *ibu dimani* could be both "water singing like a woman's sago melody" and "water next to which women sing." *Āgu* may come from the verb *āgodi-*, "to fill up with fish, of a trap," and refers to the action of moving water pulling fish into weirs and manmade dams.

Some other examples are:

(Song 2):

1. *ibu   ira   ma   yibi   wabo'ore*
water   stick   carrying   sleep   if-gone

   "The man who sleeps near the fast-flowing river"
   (lit. "water which carries twigs along")

   ibu   ka'ayamikiribi   wabo'ore
   river   waves caused by moving canoe   come

   "The waves caused by a canoe in motion"

(Song 20):

1. *ibu   hekoro   yibumena*
river   bank   sleep-man
   "The man who sleeps by the bank of the river"

   ibu   hekoro   bagia   yibumena
   river   bank   debris island   sleep-man

   "Twigs and branches clot in the flowing river"

Bagia- means "to divide into parts" and is another one of the ubiquitous "cutting" and "dividing" words of the Foi vocabulary. Anything that is caused to branch or fan out into several strands is described by this verb: the branching roots of a tree are called *bagi'u*. In this case, a clot of debris in the middle of a river causes the water to divide into two or more separate streams.

3. *ibu   hefofore   hua   yibumena*
   river bank   strikes   sleep-man

"The man who sleeps by the crumbling bank of the rushing water"

Hefofore was mentioned in the last chapter in connection with "*fufu*" words which convey a sense of held movement suddenly released in a rising, flying way. *Hefofore*, from the verb meaning "to break into small pieces," refers to the action of a rushing river crumbling its banks into pieces and carrying them away.

This use of the many synonyms for moving water more than anything else attests to the role of what Lévi-Strauss called *detotalization* in the poetic and discursive creation of an icon of motion. In this case, not only is a picture of moving water ostensively invoked, but the serial listing of different varieties of rushing, hissing, crashing water itself causes the verse to flow in the same way. In the next section I examine in more detail the thoroughgoing use of detotalization in the constitution of the moving image in Foi poetry.

THE POETRY OF DETOTALIZATION

Let's return momentarily to song 11 and look at a common theme of Foi song poetry:

1. The path to Baruaga Creek . . .
   The path to Kumagi Creek . . .

2. Boy, the head of the Faya'a River . . .
   Boy, your Faya'a River source land . . .

3. The path leading to the mouth of the Kumagi Creek . . .
   The path along which the *faiyu* marsupial travels . . .

Like Ilongot narratives, the Foi song unfolds a sequence of places; its impact is ostensively spatial, and, as Schieffelin has noted for the very similar Kaluli songs, "it is possible with any song to construct a map of the region concerned, including hills, streams, gardens, sago stands, and other resources, and . . .

trace a history of the area" (1976: 184). The sequence of places of course also constitutes a temporal sequence—as the singer moves from place to place in the song, she iconically images the movement of the deceased between those places during his lifetime. As I mentioned earlier, such chaining of place names in song discursively re-creates a person's life in spatial and temporal terms and preserves the sense of life's encompassing *flow*.

The following song is one of the few that focus on Mubi River garden and sago areas in memorializing the life of Kabosa of the Orodobo clan:

(Song 40)

1. *ba'a na'a yebibu ibu*
   boy your Yebibu creek

   aginoba'aye
   let another steal it

   ba'a na'a yefua duma
   boy your Yefua mountain

   aodoba'aye
   let bush cover it

2. *ba'a na'a yebibu ibu*
   boy your Yebibu creek

   aginoba'aye
   let another steal it

   ba'a na'a yefua duma
   boy your Yefua mountain

   aodoba'aye
   let bush cover it

3. *na'a hũamo   ibu   sumaniyu*
   your mother's creek Sumaniyu

   ibu   aginoboba'ae
   creek stolen eaten

   ba'a bamo yahadenabo
   boy that Yahadenabo

   ibu   aodoba'aye
   water let bush cover it

4. *ba'a na'a ibu   agegenebo*
   boy your creek Agegenebo

   ibu   aodoba'aye
   creek let bush cover it

   ba'a na'a yebibu ibu
   boy your Yebibu creek

   ira   waba'aye
   tree let come

5. *ba'a na'a sonobo   duma*
   boy your Sonobo mountain

   aodoboba'ae
   bush covered

   ba'a na'a yefua duma
   boy your Yefua mountain

   kigiboba'ae
   tree covered

1. Boy, your Yebibu Creek
   Let another man eat it

   Boy, your Yefua Ridge
   Let the bush cover it over

2. Boy, your Yebibu Creek
   Let another man eat it

   Boy, your Yefua Ridge
   Let the bush cover it over

3. Your Sumaniyu Creek
   This creek, let another man steal it

   This boy's Yahadenabo Creek
   Let the bush cover it over

4. Boy, your Agegenebo Creek
   Let the forest reclaim it

   Boy, your Yebibu Creek
   Let the trees cover it up

5. Boy, your Sonobo Ridge
   Let the bush cover it

   Boy, your Yefua Ridge
   Tree covered

The -*ba'aye* ending is an exhortative ending indicating "to let someone do
x." "Let another man claim your territory," the composer exhorts, and there
is the underlying note of contempt for those of the deceased's kinsmen who
would so immediately and unfeelingly appropriate a dead man's property. It
is true that the forest itself obliterates the traces of people's productive lives,
but people grimly know that it is the dead person's kinsmen who far more
efficiently and quickly avail themselves of the dead man's land and resources.

    These serial listings of place names are only one instance of the pervasive
use of detotalization as a poetic device, and Lévi-Strauss himself was aware
of how easily detotalization could embody a temporal, as well as a spatial and
categorical, speciation when he chose the example of the Osage Bear and Beaver
chant. In that song, the bear enumerates the signs of age visible on his body:
"my toes that are folded together . . . the wrinkles of my ankles . . . the muscles
of my thigh, loosened with age . . . the muscles of my abdomen, loosened
with age . . . my ribs that lie in ridges along my side" (LaFlesch 1917: 160–61),
and so forth. And with each refrain, the bear sings that of these signs of old
age, "when the little ones make of me their bodies, they shall be free from
all causes of death, as they travel the path of life" (ibid.).

    Notice now how the Foi make use of quite a similar theme to evoke a tem-
poral imagery, though here we have only the inevitability of death rather than
the promise of reversible regeneration, as in the Osage song:

(Song 3):

1. *ba'a na'a ĩ   hone ubu kusa do'ane   dobo'owua*
   boy your eye dizzy go   spell to speak recited

   dia ubo'oriye
   said did not go

   ba'a na'a kigi wara'obo kusa do'ane   dobo'owua
   boy your bone weakness spell to speak recited

   dia ubo'oriye
   said did not go

1. Boy, your sleep-causing spell you used to recite
   You never told me before you left

   Boy, your weakness-causing spell you used to recite
   You never instructed me before you left

(Song 16):

1. *ba'a na'a ira   nabi tera'a bunubidobo'ore*
   boy your tree nabi bark   if emaciated

   ai na   do'oyo'o
   ai! to me do not speak

   ba'a na'a ira   tera'a yafubidobo'ore
   boy your tree bark   if loose

   ai na   do'oyo'o
   ai! to me do not speak

2. *ba'a na'a ira   bodo   yafusoabidobo'ore*
   boy your tree bodo   loose-if-descends

   ai nane wae dibubege
   ai! I   no   saying

   ira   kaema bunu soabidobo'ore
   tree burnt black if descends

   tare na'a kabe ibu   do'obege
   then you man who are speaking

1. Boy, your *nabi* tree-bark belt has grown loose around your waist
   But do not tell me about it

   Boy, your bark belt hangs loose around your thin waist
   But why tell me about it?

2. Boy, your *bodo* tree-bark belt slips down your waist
   But it is not me

   Boy, your dreadlocks have become dirty and scanty
   But who is it you are accusing?

During a man's lifetime, little by little he imparts his fund of secret lore to those younger men who have rendered services to him, especially those who undertook to care for him if he passed through a period of infirmity. A man will teach these younger men his magic and sorcery techniques, and in pre-Mission times, he would have passed on whatever knowledge of cult life he had managed to gain during his lifetime. In song 3, a man comments regretfully that his patron's death "cut off" this flow of knowledge from elder to younger man.

In song 16, the deceased, who died from sorcery and was characteristically emaciated upon death, is described in terms of his now ill-fitting clothing, hanging loose upon his frame, and his dirty, matted hair. The song also refers to the accusations of sorcery that invariably occur at these times: In this case, a Banimahu'u clan man was accused of complicity in the man's death.

In a more figurative sense, sudden deaths from illness cause accusations to "flow" between members of a longhouse community. Foi sorcery is an inevitable consequence of coresidence and communality; it is not practiced on strangers and "enemy" villages and people. Here, then, is the paradox of Foi sociality: that in plain terms, it is lethal, because man is a hunter, and his lethality affects all living things, including other people. Perhaps that is why in singing of death, the songs focus on men's hunting activities.

The last feature of this temporal moving image concerns the invocation of seasonal contrasts, as the next section details.

THE MOVING HUNTER

In chapter 2 I described the alternating rhythms of the yearly cycle of contrastive social arrangements of the Foi. The place names of Ayamo are disproportionately featured in Foi song poetry: men are memorialized or idealized by reference to their *hunting* activities more commonly than in relation to their "dry season" gardening activities. Seventeen of the forty-one men's *sorohabora* I transcribed explicitly focus upon place names, and of these seventeen, nine mention place names at Ayamo, three mention places only near the Mubi, two mention both, one describes hunting territories that are not at Ayamo, and two make use of landscape images without specifying their location.

Why, then, are Ayamo place names the more common theme of memorial song poetry? Ayamo is of course the venue for men's hunting and foraging activities, and as I mentioned earlier, such activities are precisely the exemplary activity of men. It is hunting, not gardening, that creates the most compelling image of male virility and aggressive vitality. And because hunting requires a constant movement over the land—whether it is the regular checking of widely spaced traps or the actual stalking of animals with dog and axe—no other activity is so starkly opposed to the stillness of death. The following song makes use of this contrast:

(Song 5):

1. *se'*   *duma*   *yibu kunuga*
   marsupial mountain sleep cave

   sebe'o'oyo'o
   do not search

   sese   *baro yibu kunuga*
   marsupial baro sleep cave

sia   o'oyo'o
search do not go

2. *sigina   daba yibu kunuga*
cassowary large sleep cave

   uaha   yiboba'ae
   go-live sleeps

   sese   budu yibu kunuga
   marsupial black sleep cave

   bereboba'ae
   is lost

3. *ya   dabura hūa   yibu   kunuga*
bird red   mother sleep cave

   sia   ubihamone
   search do not keep going

   ya   gibi   hūa   kunuga
   bird bush fowl mother cave

   sia   o'oyo'o
   search do not go

4. *kuiyare yibu   kunuga*
python sleep cave

   sia   o'oyo'o
   search do not go

   tuba   budu yibu kunuga
   tree kangaroo black sleep cave

   sebe'o'oyo'o
   do not search

1. The *duma* marsupial which sleeps in the limestone caves
   Do not search for it

   The *baro* marsupial which sleeps in the caves
   Do not attempt to seek it

2. The large cassowary which sleeps in the caves of stone
   He has gone away

The black marsupial of the stone caves
He too is lost

3. The bush-fowl mother who sleeps in the cave
   Do not go looking for her

   The red bush-fowl mother who sleeps in the cave
   Do not seek her

4. The python who sleeps in the stone cave
   Do not go looking for it

   The black tree kangaroo who sleeps in the cave
   Do not try and find it

There is an ambiguity in this song—it is actually Mare, the deceased, who is spoken of as different game animals which can no longer be found: they no longer sleep in their accustomed shelters. At the same time it is as if the deceased himself is being commanded not to find game animals.

Men's hunting is inextricably associated with the time of year in which, in its ideal form, it is most frequently conducted—the wet months of the *kagi hũa hase,* the "mother of rain time." Thus, when Foi sing about the creeks, caves, and mountains of Ayamo, they invoke the drizzly, cool primary forests of winter. The following song may be taken as a homage to the tree kangaroo:

(Song 4):

1. *kagi aũwa hubiwe'iya'are*[4]
   rain softly falling-come

   ba'a na'a igebe
   boy you is it?

   kunu   kunuga hubiwe'iya'are
   palmwood floor   rattling-come

   ba'a na'a igebe
   boy you is it?

2. *kana togebiwe'iya'are*
   stone overturn-come

   ba'a na'a iyo'oge
   boy you is

   ira waru sina   irari hubiwe'iya'are
   tree waru shoots dew brushing-come

ba'a na'a iyo'oge
boy you is

3. *kunuga hubiwei'iya'are*
floor   striking-come

   ba'a na'a iyo'oge
   boy you is

   ira bai̅ sina   irari hubiwe'iya'are
   tree bai̅ saplings dew brushing-come

   ba'a na'a iyo'oge
   boy you is

4. *oro   sina   ireri hubiwe'iya'are*
bamboo shoots dew brushing-come

   ba'a na'a iyo'oge
   boy you is

   ira bai̅ sina   ireri hubiwe'iya'are
   tree bai̅ saplings dew brushing-come

   ba'a na'a iyo'oge
   boy you is

5. *duma   haro   sese   sone*
mountain climbing marsupial Sone

   dawabo
   dawabo

   duma   hau sese   sawa
   mountain side marsupial Sawa

   ibudawabo
   ibudawabo

6. *duma   oro sese   sawa*
mountain top marsupial Sawa

   dawabo
   dawabo

   duma   fai sese   sone
   mountain side marsupial Sone

   dawabo
   dawabo

1. The sound of rain falling softly while someone approaches
   Boy, is that you?

   A sound like palmwood floor beams rattling as someone comes
   Boy, could that be you?

2. You overturn the stones as you approach
   Boy, is that you?

   Your legs are wet like dew on the *waru* tree saplings
   Boy, could that be you?

3. The sound of rattling as someone approaches
   Boy, is that you?

   Your legs are as wet as the *baĩ* saplings covered with dew
   Boy, could that be you?

4. You brush the dew off the bamboo shoots as you come
   Boy, is that you?

   You are wet from the dew of the *baĩ* tree saplings
   Boy, could that be you?

5. Along the hillside, the tree kangaroo named Sone walks
   Dawabo

   Along the side of the mountain, the tree kangaroo named Sawa wanders
   Ibu Dawabo

6. At the crest of the mountain, Sawa wanders
   Dawabo

   Along the mountainsides, Sone travels
   Dawabo

The patter of rain, the tinkle of water on rocks, the rattling of the palmwood slats of a house floor as people walk—these are the soggy, fluid, moving, liquid sounds of the rainy season at Ayamo. Every tiny patter makes people imagine the silent padding of the marsupials as they roam through the bush seeking fruit by night, evading hunters by day in their treetops. And of course, Ayamo itself is the "high" place, the place of mountainsides and peaks. Its name literally translates as "sky + *possessive*," "the sky's realm," one might say.

Although the hunting season and Ayamo place names are favored settings for the memorialization of men, it is in sago making, the exemplary *women's* subsistence task of the village-based gardening season, that the songs themselves originate. The next chapter examines the process of women's composition and points out the analogy between the seasonal dimorphism of men's and women's subsistence tasks and their contrastive roles in poetic creativity.

NOTES

1. Witherspoon (1977: chap. 2) reports that the processes of motion and stoppage are central to the Navajo cosmos. He cites the following passage of Hoijer's:

> in three broad speech patterns, illustrated by the conjugation of active verbs, the reporting of actions and events, and the framing of substantive concepts, Navajo emphasizes movement and specifies the nature, direction, and status of such movement in considerable detail. Even the neuter category is relatable to the dominant conception of a universe in motion: for, just as someone is reported to have described architecture as frozen music, so the Navajo define position as a resultant of the withdrawal of motion. (Hoijer 1964: 146)

2. I can hardly resist pointing out that *gikoba* is the generic Foi word for butterfly; the Foi do not differentiate between the dozens of species found in the Mubi area. From this point of view, a hypothetical Foi linguist would possibly identify closely with the plight of our previously introduced German linguist.

3. The invocation of different qualities of flowing water was also a poetic device employed by the Wind River Shoshone in their shamanic Ghost Dance song (Shimkin 1964: 349).

4. *hubiwe'iya'are*: The ending *-iya'are* is a nominalized form of the *-iyo'o* ending which indicates knowledge gained of a past action from present, sensible evidence. The ending *-iyo'oge* can be translated as "was that you? (based on the evidence I see myself as I walk through the bush)."

6

WOMEN'S SONG, MEN'S DREAM

The beginning of all art:
  a song when planting a rice field
    in the country's inmost part
—*Matsuo Basho (trans. H. G. Henderson)*

LET ME BRIEFLY REVIEW what I have discussed so far. In chapter 1 I introduced the notion of the fundamentally *embodied* and *spatial* nature of trope itself: that distant things—both spatially and conceptually, if we can separate the two—become closer "at hand" through their embodiment in metaphor. I also suggested that to approach the socially meaningful nexus of Foi poetic discourse, we had to distinguish between the static nature of trope as cultural fiat and its dynamic imagery that constitutes its effect as a spatiotemporally situated, perceptual activity. I then elaborated upon the spatial constitution of Foi discourse at all its linguistic levels—phonological, morphological, syntactic, semantic, and poetic. Finally, in the last chapter I demonstrated that the most ubiquitous and evocative images of Foi poetry elaborate upon the contrast between movement and stasis, or between motion and its surcease, as the fundamental qualitative dimension of persons and objects in their spatial and temporal constitution.

However, I momentarily cautioned against a too literal Durkheimian extension of this central Foi aesthetic—I suggested that its role in the constitution of social and sexual categorizations was not determinate or structural but rather interpretive, or analogical, encompassing simultaneously both a "model of" and "model for" the roles that the Foi see as constituting their social universe. Like any trope, the contrasts between distance and nearness, and between motion and stillness, demand an interpretive realization rather than a static predication in terms of structural homologies.

In this chapter I would like to describe the conditions under which the song poems are composed, to note their major compositional features, and to inspect the different themes that women articulate. I want to suggest that at the core of the dynamic of Foi tropic and poetic discourse lies the realization and confirmation of contrastive male and female discursive modalities—*providing* we realize right from the start that the Foi demarcation of this contrast is as much a *comment upon* or *interpretation of* as it is a *normative summation of* behavioral tendencies. Through song, women simultaneously comment upon the feminine life condition and evaluate the tragic dimensions of life both with and without men. It is women's prerogative, in a sense, to aesthetically constitute men's and women's discursive subjectivity.

I would like to begin with a distinction that Gaston Bachelard once drew between female *reverie* and male *dream*. It is true that Bachelard was more interested in what he saw to be a pattern in male and female words in the French language than in an *analysis* of different states of imaginative free consciousness; he was more concerned with both glorifying the feminine qualities of image, reverie, and poetry and denigrating the harder, harsher male virtues of critique and concept. Within every man and woman there is a ceaseless struggle, a dialectical tension between the evening, tranquil stillness of feminine reverie and the daytime striving of the masculine dream. It is suggestive that among all the ways he presented this contrast, he should also say that

> the dialectic of the masculine and the feminine . . . goes from the less deep, ever less deep (the masculine) to the ever deep, ever deeper (the feminine). It is in reverie . . . that we find the feminine deployed in all its breadth, reposing in simple tranquility. Then, as it must be reborn with the coming of the day, the clock of the intimate being rings in the masculine—in the masculine for everyone, men and women. Then, for everyone, the times of social activity return, an activity which is essentially masculine. (1971: 61)

Let me rephrase this in terms that might have more general application: Bachelard is suggesting a distinction between *the atemporality of human being* and the *temporality of human striving*. For him, feminine values transcend the pragmatic world; they exist in an interstice of human attainment wherein reside the timeless values of nurture, tenderness, and maternal comfort. Masculine values belong to a conscious, more superficial world of realized and realizable dreams, a world governed by the periods of human timepieces and the rhythms of time itself, which image our urgings and strivings in a world of law, concept, and analysis.

But a Heideggerian appreciation of human being must necessarily *invert* this dialectic. It is precisely the temporal nature of being which is its core feature, while striving, the attainment of goals, brings continuity to an end; it signals a turning away from a concernful attitude toward the world.[1]

In the Foi world of space and time, it is men who strive to bring temporal continuity to a halt. They seek to artificially harness it and channel it for their own inauthentic purposes. By *inauthentic* Heidegger meant, among other things, all those acts that are impelled by reference to an authoritative "they," a contrived and artificially transcendent moral authority which is deferred to for the purposes of construing goals for action. In Heidegger's terms, Foi men's cutting of spatial and temporal flows embodies a turning away from what he called being-toward-death: the authentic, concernful being which encompasses its own finality as an integral part of its temporality. When image is directed toward an end, when Foi men harness its moving properties to the atemporal goals of their own striving, image loses the living aspect which grounds it and degenerates into the static, two-dimensional metaphor which enables all that is representational in Foi discourse.

But as much as men are concerned with bringing continuity to a halt, it is women who, in their reveries while making sago, concern themselves with the most critical act of finality, the death of humans. While women are engaged in the monotonous, rhythmic work of making sago, they dwell on the deaths of their husbands and male kinsmen. Men are concerned only with ghosts, which are the volitional residue or precipitate of power that remains after men die, and which can be tricked, connived, cajoled, or threatened into acting on behalf of living men. Women, on the other hand, immortalize men themselves as they lived. They sing of men in terms of their temporal being, rather than in terms of their atemporal spiritual striving and influence.

As I mentioned in the Introduction, for the Foi dreams are sources of power. They are one of the primary avenues of meaningful communication between ghosts and humans. During sleep, a person's animating spirit, the $\bar{\imath}\,h\bar{o}$, leaves the body and wanders around, encountering other such spirits, including those which have become permanently detached from bodies after death. In this way, these spirits or ghosts can impart information to the living. One who can interpret the symbolism of dreams effectively can gain access to the knowledge of ghosts: knowledge, primarily, of magical formulae. But, as I have already noted, what ghosts do and say can never be taken literally; their motives and purposes are concealed from the society of the living. A man must possess skill in construing appropriate interpretations of the events symbolically perceived in dreams.

In order to expose himself to the possibility of contact with ghosts, a man seeks out those places to which ghosts are thought to be attracted: certain pools of still water, the whirlpools that form near sharp bends in the river, the bases of certain flowering trees which attract many birds, places where powerful magical spells were once performed. A man prepares for dreaming by fasting and avoiding sexual contact with women. He then sleeps alone near one of these spots until he dreams vividly, at which time he will conclude that a ghost has made contact with him.

I have suggested that the interpretations of dreams for the Foi involves the manipulation of metaphoric creativity. Men say that certain events and objects perceived in dreams "stand for" other things. Any red-colored bird seen in a dream represents pearl shells; any white-colored bird represents pigs; a dream of a large tree falling down or fallen portends the imminent death of a man; a dream of sexual intercourse with a woman portends the future capture of a game animal. These equivalences, though they embody a real cultural significance and are metaphorical in their effect and constitution, are, however, standardized. They are part of a repertoire of conventional interpretations which are known to all men. Other dreams demand more particular and idiosyncratic interpretations, and these allow for the creativity and skill of individual dreamers. The skill that men display in interpreting dreams effectively is coterminous with the discursive skill they display when speaking oratorically, that is, when employing the metaphors of "tree leaf talk" which conceal their true meaning at the same time that they reveal embodied cultural and political significance.

Through dreams men gain access to metaphor; women, in their reverie over dead kinsmen, create images. Metaphor embodies the striving of men in a static, atemporal formula; poetic image embodies the historical nexus of human attachment and loss. Metaphor is detachable, anonymous, secret, hoarded, transactable. Poetic image is performative, evocative, intrinsic to women's authorship, publicly displayed and celebrated, valuable only insofar as it cannot be cashed in for the negotiable finalities that valuate the currencies of men's power. Men's dreaming is a silent world of elusive contact with detemporalized spirits; women's poetry is a sung message of love, loss, and grief, proclaiming the temporal ascendancy of human relationship.

Of course, the poetry that women compose depends upon the innovation of tropic juxtaposition, just as the contextual effectiveness of men's oratory and dream interpretation depends upon their accurately and insightfully depicting real-life people and events in allegorical terms that enhance their meaningful historicity. Image and metaphor are, as I have been stressing, both grounded in what Roy Wagner calls the dynamic trope of perception. Speech is incomplete without both trope and image, and men and women can no more do without one than they can do without discourse itself. What I am suggesting is that men and women use the contrast as a way of evaluating their relationship to a world of discursive being. It is not only that image and metaphor have different semiotic or tropic foundations; more important, *they embody the contrast in the way discourse is situated with respect to the other temporal processes of the lifeworld*, and it is this contrast that is given a gender marking in Foi conceptualization.

Charles Keil, in his fascinating analysis of Tiv song, recalls Bruno Snell's analysis of Greek philosophical language: that the word *melody* comes from *melea*, "the limbs in their muscular strength" (1979: 197). Song originates in the body in motion, only initially in the movement of the vocal organs but more completely in the motion of the entire body. It would seem likely that if song were a female creation for the Foi, it would arise in the most vivid and exemplary of feminine activities.

Sago processing begins when a man determines that a sago palm is mature—in the Foi area, between fifteen and twenty-one years after the sucker first appeared. He then fells the palm and strips the outer bark from it, at which point his role in the process is over. His wife and any female helper accompanying her then construct a bench from the discarded bark, arranged so that she may sit perpendicularly to the palm. With her knees drawn up slightly, she begins to scrape the exposed pith with a piece of obsidian, hafted into a wooden mallet. The woman lifts her arms and strikes, lifts and strikes, and as she scrapes the pith, she sings.

When a quantity of shredded pith has been accumulated, the woman carries it to a trough, constructed from two triangular-shaped mid-ribs of sago placed so that the wide bases are attached to each other. This forms a basin with narrow ends and a wide, deep middle. The trough is raised at one end, and at the other, a palm-spathe vessel catches the liquid that flows down it. The woman places the pith in the center of the trough, pours water over it, and then loosens the starch granules by beating the pith with a four-foot-long hard-wood stick. Then, kneading and squeezing the moistened pith, she causes the white, starchy liquid to run down the trough, through a woven basket fastened along the bottom end, where the pith fibers can be caught. The starch in suspension accumulates at the bottom of the spathe vessel. The woman then removes the starch from the vessel and either packs it into a woven basket or wraps it in a cylindrical bundle of sago leaves and carries it back to the village. It must then be allowed to dry before it can be cooked.

Sago songs, *obedobora*, start out as work songs. One of the most common refrains I heard was the following: *abu biri-o, obe-u!* "sago mallet, oh, *obe-u!*"; *a'a mae, obe-u*, "make sago quickly, *obe-u*." Commonly, women sing to urge themselves and the task to finish quickly, as in the following song which Mu'-ubia sang for me:

(Sago Song 1):

1. *ira   abu-o*
   wood mallet

2. *biri huie*
   here strike

3. *ira   ka   wasa*
   wood woman mallet

4. *biri huma'ae*
   here strike

5. *duma   haro   hubu kaboneo owa*
   mountain climbing struck Miss   owa

6. *meye   wa'ayo'o   owa*
   not yet do not come owa

7. *duma   oro hubu kabonere owa*
   mountain top struck Miss   owa

8. *meye   wa'ayo'o   owa*
   not yet do not come owa

9. *meye   wamone   owa*
   not yet do not come owa

10. *ibu busu   humekerabo kabonere owa*
    river dappled light strike + put Miss   owa

11. *meye   wa'ayo'o   owa*
    not yet do not come owa

12. *ibu   hohotogabo kabo na-o owa*
    river mirror   girl I too owa

13. *meye   wamone   owa*
    not yet do not come owa

14. *duma   humegenemodobo kabonere owa*
    mountain to make dark   Miss   owa

15. *meye   wa'ayo'o   owa*
    not yet do not come owa

16. *ibu anogo hamayibu   kabonereo owa*
    river fish net to have gaps Miss   owa

17. *meya   wamona   owa*
    not yet do not come owa

18. *ibu gikoba   humogoreye ubu kabonera owa*
    river butterflies to scatter go Miss   owa

19. *meye   wa'ayo'o   owa*
    not yet do not come owa

20. *duma   haro   hubu kabo na'a owa*
    mountain climbing struck girl you owa

21. *meye   wamone   owa*
    not yet do not come owa

22. *meyere eya*
    not yet eya

23. *nomo ira kabiri   ma'oyo'o eya*
    my   tree kabiri mallet to take eya

24. *meya'are eya*
    not yet eya

25. *gi   soboye owa*
    ground there owa

26. *duma   haru huaye eya*
    mountain hill   to leave eya

27. *meya'a umone   eya*
    not yet do not go eya

28. *ibu danimi fufae eya*
    river Danimi to fly eya

29. *meya'a o'oyo'o   eya*
    not yet do not go eya

30. *duma   sonobo kigiri hesae   eya*
    mountain Sonobo base to follow eya

31. *meya'a o'oyo'o   eya*
    not yet do not go eya

32. *duma   kanawebi hesae   eya*
    mountain Kanawebi to follow eya

33. *meya   umona   eya*
    not yet do not go eya

34. *duma   gara   u'ubi kigiri hesae   eya*
    mountain orphan child base to follow eya

35. *meya   o'oyo'o   eya*
    not yet do not go eya

36. *ibu   webiga   fufae eya*
    river Webi source to fly eya

37. *meye   umona   eya*
    not yet do not go eya

38. *ira   tegare gifubi-e eya*
    tree tegare canopy eya

39. *meya   degamone eye*
    not yet to hide   eye

40. *oro   yiyebi oro huae eye*
    bamboo small top strike eye

41. *meye   o'oyo'o   dobo'o eya*
    not yet do not go spoken eya

42. *bi   yebihamone   eya*
    here do not leave eya

43. *kui   tuba foraye   ma'ayo'o eye*
    sago hand broken to take   eye

44. *meya   o'oyo'o   eye*
    not yet do not go eye

45. *kui   hufuruwa   ma'ayo'o eye*
    sago to break apart to take   eye

46. *ai   meya'are eye*
    ai! not yet   eye

47. *kui   ka'abe   ma'ayo'o eye*
    sago difficult to take   eye

48. *meya'a o'oyo'o   eye*
    not yet do not go eye

49. *kui   tirarudia ma'ayo'o eye*
    sago to bundle to take   eye

50. *meya'a o'oyo'o   eye*
    not yet do not go eye

51. *kui   ka'abe   ma'oyo'o eye*
    sago difficult to take   eye

52. *meye   umona   eye*
    not yet do not go eye

53. *ibu   kosega   hubagiae eye*
    river phlegm to spread eye

54. *meye   umona   eye*
    not yet do not go eye

55. *ibu   hemomo'o bagiae   eye*
    river flotsam   to spread eye

56. *meye   yebihamone eye*
    not yet to leave   eye

  1. Oh, sago mallet
  2. Strike this sago quickly
  3. Miss Sago Mallet
  4. Beat this sago quickly
  5. You strike the mountainside as you set, Miss, *owa*
  6. Do not fall so quickly, *owa*
  7. You strike the top of the mountain as you sink . . .
  8. Do not fall yet . . .
  9. Do not come yet
10. You reflect in dappled sparkle off the river
11. Do not fall so quickly
12. You reflect off the river like my image, girl
13. Do not come yet
14. The mountain turns dark as you set, girl
15. Do not come yet
16. You shine through the holes in the fishing nets
17. Do not come yet
18. You scatter the butterflies on the river, Miss
19. Do not fall yet
20. You strike the side of the mountain as you fall
21. Do not come so quickly
22. Do not come yet
23. I still have to hold my mallet, girl
24. Not yet, girl!
25. Don't make this ground dark yet, girl
26. Don't leave this mountain yet, girl
27. Don't go yet
28. You fly down the Danimi Creek

29. Don't go yet
30. You fall toward the bottom of Mt. Sonobo
31. Don't leave me yet!
32. You follow the bottom of Mt. Kanawebi
33. Do not go yet
34. You follow the bottom of Mt. Kagiri
35. Don't go yet
36. You fly toward the head of Webi Creek
37. Don't go yet
38. You shine through the top of the *ko'oya* tree
39. Don't hide from me yet
40. Shining through the bamboo on the mountaintop
41. Don't go, I say
42. Don't leave me here
43. I still have to beat sago
44. Do not go yet
45. I have to bundle up my sago
46. Ai! Do not go yet
47. I have to wrap my sago
48. Do not go yet
49. I have to wrap up my sago
50. Do not go yet
51. I have much work to do
52. Do not go yet
53. You spread along the river surface like froth
54. Do not go yet
55. You sparkle off the river flotsam
56. Do not leave me yet

Here the rhythm of the woman's sago-processing activities is compared with the linear movement of the sun across the sky. The sun is a girl for the Foi: to her belongs all the daytime work, especially sago making. The moon is a man: to him and his dogs, who are the stars, belongs the nighttime activity of hunting.[2] As the sun descends, its rays reach toward Mu'ubia as she works at her sago camp along the bank of the Mubi. She notices how the surrounding vegetation changes color, how the sunlight reflects in different ways off the surface of the water and the debris floating in it. These are the changes in the landscape with which one can measure the passage of time.

The sun reaches one mountain after another; like a light-footed young girl, like an aimless orphan wandering through the bush (line 34), she skips along the paths that people use, across one stream after another, and as she races toward the west, the source of water, Mu'ubia urges her to slow down: don't sink so fast, I still need light to work by! She shines dappled through the top leaves of the forest canopy, and through the stalks of bamboo on the mountaintop, and as she flickers through the branches, Mu'ubia knows that the mountainside will soon hide her completely.

Note some of the images of movement that are both explicitly and implicitly compared in the song: as the sun scatters (*humogoreye*, lit. "strike-causative prefix-scatter") the butterflies as they flit along the water surface (line 18), Mu'ubia is breaking the dried sago into smaller lumps that she can wrap up and carry home (lines 43 and 45). At the same time, she is bundling and wrapping up her sago (line 49), contrasting the inevitable movement of the sun, which cannot be halted, with the end of a day's work and its product, which always stops and starts again. The sun shines through the gaps in women's nets (line 16) and spreads frothlike along the river surface (line 53), just as the white, frothlike liquid suspension of sago flows through the sievelike straining bag (not explicitly mentioned in the song).

But by far the most commonly composed song consists of a repetitive listing of the singer's teknonyms. Foi men and women commonly address each other teknonymically, and as Lévi-Strauss perceptively noted, teknonyms are not about birth but about death:

> the reason why parents may no longer be called by their name when a child is born is that they are "dead." ... procreation is conceived not as the addition of a new being to those who exist already but as the substitution of the one for the others. (1966: 194–95)

The Foi seek to give an infant a name as soon as possible, and ideally, it should be the name of a person already dead. If no names of recently deceased people are available, infants are given the names of elderly people. A person who feels that he is too young to have his name bestowed upon an infant becomes angry, thinking that his death is being hastened.[3] This point is given a wry evaluation in the following passage from a song performed by Gebo:

1. *yarogemo hŭare   owe*
   Yaroge's mother *owe*

2. *meya'a wae owe*
   not yet no   owe

3. *gofofomo hŭare   owe*
   Gofofo's mother . . .

4. *meya'a wae owe*
   not yet no   *owe*

5. *tamanimo hŭara   owe*
   Tamani's   mother . . .

6. *meya'a wae owe*
   not yet no *owe*

7. *yogomaĩ   hŭara   owe*
   Yogomaĩ's mother . . .

8. *meya'a wae owe*
   not yet no *owe*

Gebo's children, in order of their birth, were the four men Yaroge, Gofofo, Tamani, and Yogomaĩ, the eldest a man of almost forty in 1988, the youngest a slightly physically and mentally retarded boy of about sixteen. Gebo, as do many women when they make sago, repeats these teknonyms in the order of her children's birth. What is interesting is that Gebo began this song as did Mu'ubia, with an exhortation to the sun girl not to sink so quickly. The refrain of that song, which we also heard in Mu'ubia's sago song, now has the double meaning of "Don't let the sun go down yet!" and "Don't let these children replace me too soon!" The "flow" of children from eldest to youngest is not conceived in terms distinct from the other movements by which the Foi measure the passage of time. And, in common with other peoples of this southern interior region of Papua New Guinea (for example, the Etoro [Kelly 1976]), the Foi tend to view the birth and growth of their children as coincident with the decline of their own life force and vigor.

In other words, the sago songs are not only about women singing passively about the deaths of men; it is *death* itself, as a temporally construed end product of life, that informs this singing, and it can as easily take the form, as we have just seen, of a woman singing of her own impending death. In the last chapter we learned of the often bitter feelings of abandonment and betrayal with which the living react to the deaths of their loved ones; here we also encounter the fear of one's death and the grim irony of its being linked to the growth and development of one's children.

Death, of course, is not the only way that people lose their loved ones. It is more often the case, especially in modern Papua New Guinea, that people leave the Foi area, often for long periods of time. Usually they seek wage labor, education, or merely the excitement of seeing the more developed and urbanized regions of the country. This traffic is primarily by airplane these days, though stalwart young men still walk back and forth to the highlands. At least once a week in the Mubi Valley in 1979–81 (more often these days, I think), we would hear the distant drone of an airplane engine and search the top of the mountain range to the north, waiting for the small aircraft to appear over the ridges.

Some of the men awaiting these airplanes are departing almost permanently, some are departing under strange circumstances, and some are departing ill to Mendi hospital; of these, very few return alive to their village. It is with great trepidation that mothers watch their sons climb aboard these craft, not knowing whether the future will reunite them. The following songs focus on this role of the airplane as the sinister disrupter of the bonds of nurturance and attachment.

Kunuhuaka, whose love for her eldest son, Bebe, was fierce, possessive, and prideful, saw him board one of these planes on his way to take up his enlistment in the Papua New Guinea Defense Force. Afterward, back in her sago camp, she sang the following song:

(Sago Song 6):

1. *humotorohahaibi   weya'a*
   to break through comes

2. *na'a ibiba'ae*
   you is

3. *eye*
   eye

4. *iri fagi   siabi   weya'a*
   tree branches to search for comes

5. *ne   ibiba'ae*
   you is

6. *eye*
   eye

7. *ira so'oboro sebe   weya'a*
   tree canopy search for comes

8. *na'a ibiba'ae*
   you is

9. *eye*
   eye

10. *humeseseregaibi weya'a*
    to shine   comes

11. *ne   ibiba'ae*
    you is

12. *eye*
    eye

13. *kui   gaboba'ae foraye   weya'a*
    sago base-is   break through comes

14. *na'a ibiba'ae*
    you is

15. *eye*
    eye

16. *ũgi   abotu'u kama'uri meya'a*
    breadfruit *abotu'u* top   not yet

17. *na'a ibiba'ae*
    you is

18. *eye*
    eye

19. *humeseseregaibi weya'a*
    to shine   comes

20. *na'a ibiba'ae*
    you is

21. *eye*
    eye

22. *kaubi   weya'a*
    region-here comes

23. *ne   ibiba'ae*
    you is

24. *eye*
    eye

25. *eresaibi   weya'a*
    to look after comes

26. *na'a ibiba'ae*
    you is

27. *eye*
    eye

28. *humotorohahaibi weya'a*
    to break through comes

29. *ne   ibiba'ae*
    you is

30. *eye*
    eye

31. *ira so'oboro sebe   weya'a*
    tree canopy search for comes

32. *na'a ibiba'ae*
    you is

33. *eye*
    eye

34. *kui gaboba'a kamu'uri meya'a*
    sago base-is top   not yet

35. *ne   ibiba'ae*
    you is

36. *eye*
    eye

37. *sibi arori hiba'ane   uba'a*
    ship prow to embark gone

38. *na'a ibiba'ae*
    you is

39. *eye*
    eye

40. *gagaruri hiba'ane   uba'a*
    to carry to embark gone

41. *na'a ibiba'ae*
    you is

42. *eye*
    eye

43. *awa'a bareri hiba'ane   uba'a*
    sky   vessel to embark gone

44. *ne   ibiba'ae*
    you is

45. *eye*
    eye

46. *borowame   humogore'ane uba'ae*
    aquatic bird to scatter   gone

47. *na'a ibiba'ae*
    you is

48. *eye*
    eye

49. *bagua   humogoreye uba'a*
    aquatic bird scattered   gone

50. *na'a ibiba'ae*
    you is

51. *eye*
    eye

52. *e   kabo sere-o*
    eh girl sun-o

53. *na'abo dibu-o*
    to you I speak

54. *eye*
    eye

55. *e   kabo wāga-o*
    eh girl Clear-oh

56. *nebo   dibu-o*
    you alone I speak

57. *eye*
    eye

58. *e   kabo yuri-o*
    eh girl Yuri-oh

59. *na'abo iba'ae*
    to you is

60. *eye*
    eye

 1. You break through the clouds as you come
 2. It is you
 3. *eye*
 4. You peek through the tree branches as you come
 5. It is you
 6. *eye*
 7. You break through the tree canopy as you come
 8. It is you
 9. *eye*
10. You shine as you come
11. It is you
12. *eye*
13. You break through the sago palms as you come
14. It is you
15. *eye*
16. Don't peek through the top of the *abotu'u* breadfruit
17. It is you
18. *eye*
19. You shine as you come
20. It is you
21. *eye*
22. You look out over the whole land as you come
23. It is you
24. *eye*
25. You watch over the whole land as you come
26. It is you
27. *eye*
28. You break through the clouds as you come

29. It is you
30. *eye*
31. You peek through the top branches as you come
32. It is you
33. *eye*
34. Don't you light up the sago palms yet
35. It is you
36. *eye*
37. You light up the prow of his departing ship
38. It is you
39. *eye*
40. You light up the guns carried by his departing ship
41. It is you
42. *eye*
43. You light up the airplane as he embarked and left
44. It is you
45. *eye*
46. You cause the egrets to scatter over the lake
47. It is you
48. *eye*
49. You cause the *bagua* birds to scatter over the lake
50. It is you
51. *eye*
52. Oh, Miss Daytime
53. It is to you I am speaking
54. *eye*
55. Oh, Miss Clear Light
56. To you alone I speak
57. *eye*
58. Oh, Miss Yuri
59. It is to you I speak
60. *eye*

Like the other songs, this one is built around the theme of the fleeing sun maiden. "You break through the branches of the treetops; it is you, girl," Kunuhuaka sings. These two lines are punctuated by a drawn-out *"eye"* of four syllables. Kunuhuaka sings of the sun shining through the clouds and the fronds of the sago palms, illuminating the bases of the palms, shining over the land. But it also shines upon the airplane that took Bebe away from Hegeso, and the prow of the ship that he would thenceforth call his home—he was taking up a post on a patrol boat at Lombrom patrol base in Manus Province. Notice that she uses the English word *sibi* for "ship," though in referring to the boat's guns, described to her by Bebe before he left, she calls them "that which is carried" (*gagaruri*). As the airplane "scatters" to the north, so does the sun scatter the aquatic birds that are found on Lake Kutubu. It is the rising sun, the dawn of a new day, that is taking Bebe away from home.

Kunuhuaka is also the only composer I encountered who made use of rhyme, in this case, between *meya'a* and *weya'a*. Not only do these words rhyme, but they emphasize the contrastive movements that make this song so poignant: "don't arrive yet, Miss Sun, you only bring with you the departure of my son," she is saying.

Although Kunuhuaka composed this song, she sang it with another woman, Siyame. Siyame merely echoed each of Kunuhuaka's lines three beats behind her. This is why they chose to use the drawn-out, four-beat *eye* in every third line, which they were able to sing in unison, before returning to the echolike singing of the theme lines.

Some time after Bebe had left to take up his enlistment, he sent back several Polaroid photos of himself taken at Lombrom. One of them showed a clothesline with his and his mates' uniforms hanging up after washing; another showed Bebe in uniform and beret, holding his rifle. Still another was of the patrol boat on which he served as private. Kunuhuaka brought these photographs to my house shortly after I arrived in Hegeso for my third field trip in 1984. She showed me the photos, by then slightly crumbled and yellowed with much handling. "See him in his uniform? See his gun?" she asked me, as if it were a litany she recited to herself every time she looked at the pictures. As she spoke she began to cry, the resigned, stoic tears that mothers everywhere cry for their missing children. It wasn't until 1988 that I heard the following song, which made me think of those photographs in a different way:

(Sago Song 7):

  1. *yengi banima ba*
     nettles banima that

  2. *ba'a na'a hame   wae*
     boy your brother not

  3. *eye*
     eye

  4. *yengi boro ba*
     nettles boro that

  5. *ba'a na'a wame   wae*
     boy your brother not

6. *eye*
   eye

7. *yengi   gugabe   ba*
   nettles flying fox that

8. *ba'a na'a base   wae*
   boy your sister's husband not

9. *eye*
   eye

10. *ganuga boge aba   ba*
    hat   club father that

11. *ba'a na'a kabe wame   wae*
    boy your man brother not

12. *eye*
    eye

13. *ganuga boge aba   ba*
    hat   club father that

14. *ba'a na'a base   wae*
    boy your sister's husband not

15. *eye*
    eye

16. *bi'a fore   aba   ba*
    rifle large father that

17. *ba'a na'a aba   wae*
    boy your father not

18. *eye*
    eye

19. *bare   sibi ba*
    canoe ship that

20. *ba'a na'a hūa   wae*
    boy your mother not

21. *eye*
    eye

22. *sabe   sode*
    knife sheath

23. *ba'a na'a ana   wae*
    boy your sister not

24. *eye*
    eye

25. *oro   yerebi ba'a terewaro*
    bamboo yerebi boy Terewaro

26. *na'abo dibu-o*
    to you I speak

27. *eye*
    eye

28. *kui   kenege ba'a bebe*
    sago mid-rib boy Bebe

29. *na'abo dibu-o*
    to you I speak

30. *eye*
    eye

 1. Your *banima* nettles hanging there
 2. It's not your brother
 3. *eye*
 4. Your *boro* nettles there
 5. It's not your brother
 6. *eye*
 7. Your nettles hanging like flying foxes
 8. It's not your brother-in-law
 9. *eye*
10. The owner of the club-shaped army hat
11. It's not your Mister brother
12. *eye*
13. The owner of the club-shaped army hat
14. It's not your sister's husband

15. *eye*
16. The owner of your big rifle
17. It's not your father
18. *eye*
19. The seagoing ship
20. It's not your mother
21. *eye*
22. Your bayonet sheath
23. It's not your sister
24. *eye*
25. The *yerebi* bamboo clan boy Terewaro
26. It is to you I am speaking
27. *eye*
28. The Sago mid-rib clan boy Bebe
29. It is to you I am speaking
30. *eye*

To Kunuhuaka, the olive-drab uniforms hanging on the line resembled the color of the different varieties (*banima, boro*) of stinging nettles (*yengi*) commonly encountered in secondary-growth areas in the Mubi Valley. But she also was drawing upon the association between warriors and nettles, because they are both "stinging, fighting" things and because of the way men rub their skin with nettles as an all-purpose palliative and stimulant, particularly before battle. In line 7 she compares the dark-colored uniforms to flying foxes as they hang from the branches of trees during the day.

"These things are not your brother, your brother-in-law, your father, your mother, . . . " she sings. Bebe's gun, uniform, and ship may be the adjuncts of his newly acquired status and importance as a public servant and a wage earner, and they mark him as a modern warrior in the new national sense. But can they take the place of his relatives who care for him and who are now unable to see to it that no one sorcerizes him while he is living by himself?

With line 25 begins the part of a song the Foi call the *dawa*. It is the point at which the subject of the song is named and identified, and this ends the song. *Dawa* is the Foi verb meaning "to cut (and distribute)." These lines "cut" the song, that is, bring it to an end.[4]

The use of the word *dawa* itself, and a number of associated variations on it, figures very prominently in men's reformulations of the songs, their *soroha-bora* performances, and I will discuss them in more detail in chapter 8. Women rarely mention the word *dawa* in the final section of their sago songs, and most sago songs do not even have a final name-revealing section at all. Hence, I will defer a full discussion of the role of the *dawa* in Foi song until I come to the men's songs themselves. Let me note only that it is in these songs that a man's nonpublic, "hidden" (though rarely secret) name is revealed publicly (in this case, Bebe's nonpublic name is Terewaro). In the *dawa*, the clans of the subject's mother and father are also identified (Bebe's father is of the Orodobo [bamboo] clan; his mother, Kunuhuaka, is of the Kuidobo [sago] clan). These are invariant features of the *dawa,* which in the men's performance emerges as the most highly structured part of the song.

The next song, which I heard in 1980, was the result of perhaps the most sensationally tragic death that occurred during all my time with the Foi. Early one morning that year, we awoke to hear that the wife of a Hegeso man, Nelson Kigiri, had hanged herself. Nelson, whose Foi name was Yaroge, was then a schoolteacher at nearby Tanuga Community School and was one of the few tertiary-educated Foi at that time. His wife, Sahabo of Damayu village, was rare not only for being high-school-educated but for having gone on to nursing school. A fluent pidgin speaker, of course, she had lived extensively outside the Foi area and at the time of her death worked at the health center at Pimaga. They were both highly intelligent and, by Foi standards, urbane.

Later in the morning after Sahabo's body was found, Nelson boarded an airplane for Mendi. Most people interpreted this as, if not an admission of complicity in Sahabo's death, at the least a pusillanimous refusal to answer questions and face his and his wife's relatives.

Shortly after this, the chief of police of the Southern Highlands Province himself flew down to Pimaga with Nelson and made a short speech to those assembled people eager to hear someone in authority say something. Through an interpreter, he told those gathered that Sahabo's death was definitely a suicide, and that they should remain calm and follow their own custom about arranging compensation. For whatever reason, the police had handcuffed Nelson, probably as a demonstration of their power and authority, and all of us there remember the utterly downcast and tortured expression on his lowered face as the police led him out from the airplane. His mother, Gebo, wailed loudly in mourning fashion as he approached the crowd, full of fear, shame, and despair.

That night, while Sahabo's body lay in Gebo's women's house with her female relatives wailing over it, the men of Sahabo's village, Damayu, gathered in the Hegeso men's longhouse, along with men from Hegeso's allied neighbor villages, Barutage and Herebo. It would be these three villages' responsibility to raise the compensation payment of shell wealth and currency that would be presented to Sahabo's father's and mother's clans. The men argued about the amount of wealth that would have to be given; every aspect of the couple's relationship was examined, discussed, and analyzed: Did Nelson mistreat Sahabo? Did he beat her? Why did he appropriate her paycheck and not give her any money? Had he paid the entire bridewealth, or were her relatives angry about not having received all of it? Was Nelson dallying with another woman, and did he sorcerize Sahabo? As is the case with all violent or precipitous deaths, the community discursively re-created the events and conditions that surrounded it, weighing evidence, suggesting and discarding hypotheses, confirming and rationalizing the death to everyone's satisfaction.

This is men's re-creation of death. They control and reshape it as a politically significant event. Its final outcome determines avenues of indebtedness between clans that might shape intervillage relationships far into the future. But the women's re-creation of death takes an entirely different form. Some months later, when I visited Gebo at her sago camp, she sang the following song for me:

(Sago Song 5):

1. *ba'a na'a bare   awa hua   ubo'ora eya*
   boy your airplane up   struck gone   eya

2. *do'oyera   owe*
   did not tell owe

3. *ba'a na'a bare   kuabogabo'ore eya*
   boy your airplane hummed   eya

4. *dia   o'abibi-o   eya*
   saying wanted to eya

5. *ba'a na'a kabe ensu ababo hibabo'ore owe*
   boy your man shoes walk   embark   owe

6. *nabo do'oyere   owe*
   to me did not say owe

7. *do'abibidobo   owe*
   could not tell owe

8. *ba'a na'a kosa'a fabo   hibabo'ore eya*
   boy your shirt   white embark   eya

9. *do'oyera   owe*
   did not tell owe

10. *ba'a na'a kosa'a namuyu   ababo hibabo'ore eya*
    boy your shirt   cockatoo walk   embark   eya

11. *dia   o'oyera   owe*
    saying did not go owe

12. *ba'a na'a duma   a'o   hugoreye ubo'ore eya*
    boy your mountain cloud pierced gone   eya

13. *dia   o'abibi-o   owe*
    saying wanted to owe

14. *fufu masibu hūa   owe*
    neck necklace mother owe

15. *do'oyera   owe*
    did not tell owe

16. *ya   masibu hūa   owe*
    arm necklace mother owe

17. *dia   u'abibio   owe*
    saying should have owe

18. *gō   hage hagikabo'ore owe*
    string bag two carried   owe

19. *dia   o'abibi-o   owe*
    saying wanted to owe

20. *awa masibu hūa   owe*
    hand necklace mother owe

21. *dia   o'oyera   owe*
    saying did not go owe

22. *orodobo   ka   gebo ma'ame eya*
    Orodobo woman Gebo thing   eya

23. *yaroge-o owe*
    Yaroge owe

24. *so'onedobo   kigirimone owe*
    So'onedobo Kigiri   owe

25. *ka'ariba owe*
    Ka'ariba owe

  1. Boy, you have ascended in your airplane, *eya*
  2. But you didn't tell me, *owe*
  3. Boy, we heard your airplane hum as it flew away . . .
  4. You wanted to tell me but you didn't . . .
  5. You put on your shoes and embarked . . .

6. But to me you said nothing
7. You wanted to tell me, but you could not
8. You put on your white shirt and embarked
9. But you did not tell me
10. You put on your shirt, white as a cockatoo, and left
11. But you didn't tell me before you left
12. You pierced the clouds as you flew away
13. You wanted to tell me but you couldn't
14. The widow's *kamora* necklace
15. You didn't tell me
16. The *kamora* wristband
17. You should have told me before you left
18. You took your two suitcases
19. You wanted to tell me but you couldn't
20. The widow's *kamora*
21. You didn't tell me before you left
22. The Orodobo clan woman, Gebo
23. Yaroge
24. The So'onedobo man, Kigiri
25. Ka'ariba

Like Kunuhuaka, Gebo associates flight in airplanes with all the other accessories of life in the European's world: shoes, white shirts (the standard item of attire for public servants in Papua New Guinea), and suitcases. But the interesting part of the song occurs when Gebo refers to herself as the "widow's necklace" and the "widow's bracelet" (lines 14 and 16). This refers to what the Foi also called the *kamora*, the decorations a widow traditionally wore during her mourning period. But in this case, the necklace also suggests the noose found around Sahabo's neck, and the bracelet likewise suggests the handcuffs Nelson wore as he was taken aboard the airplane.

I have been speaking as if death and abandonment were the invariant themes of all these songs. The next two songs indicate that they in fact can originate in the contemplation of any dimension of human suffering.

As perhaps one might expect in a society in which men were traditionally accorded respect and admiration for their assertiveness, bravery, prowess in battle, aggressiveness, and lethality (though the Foi did not place nearly as high a value on these characteristics as, for example, do the Enga or Chimbu), there is a certain amount of mistreatment of women. Men berate their wives verbally and occasionally beat them for a variety of sins of omission and commission—failure to provide food, failure to work diligently, real or imagined coquetries with other men. Nor do women passively accept this mistreatment; it is no way "in the nature of things" for Foi women to submit to their husbands. A man who strikes his wife hears about it loudly, publicly, and in no uncertain terms, and men can undergo a great deal of humiliation if their treatment of their wives is judged to be cavalier in any sense. Those rare men who make a habit of such domestic violence (I knew of two, one at Hegeso and one at Barutage) are treated with a certain amount of neutral contempt by other men. They are seen as pusillanimous, poltroons.

Such mistreatment is a common theme of women's poetry. My field assistant, Kora Midibaru, heard his wife's mother singing this next song. She had married Waria as an aged widow, and he used to beat her repeatedly, claiming that because she was old, she was good for nothing. In the song, the woman refers to the nettles she must rub against her bruised skin and the walking stick she must use because of her sore limbs. The following version was recorded as a men's *sorohabora* during a practice session (see next chapter) in March 1988:

(Song 39):

1. *nane yengi baya'a dogo   hūa   iyo'o*
   I   nettles baya'a bundle mother am

   ba'a na'a dibuyebe
   boy   you   not saying?

   nane yengi fagena dogo   hūa   iyo'o
   I   nettles fagena bundle mother am

   dibuyebe
   not saying?

2. *nane ira   waru tābu hūa   iyo'o*
   I   tree waru stick mother am

   ba'a na'a ka'arubidibuyebe
   boy   you   not complaining?

   nane ira   mono tābu hūa   iyo'o
   I   tree mono stick mother am

   ba'a na'a tenewanedibuyebe
   boy   you   not muttering?

3. *budu kirari ma'aboya'ayo'o*
   black rope   should take

   ba'a na'a ho'obuyebe
   boy   you   not dislike?

   kare   kui ino'oya'ayo'o
   women's sago should cook

   ba'a na'a tenewanedibuyebe
   boy   you   not muttering?

4. *abu   biri mayiye   diburo*
   mallet here haven't taken talk

   ba'a na'a dibuyebe
   boy you not saying?

   abu wasa mayiye   dibure
   abu wasa haven't taken said

   ba'a na'a dibuyebe
   boy you not saying?

5. *yo hūa   kabo keborame*
   his mother girl Keborame

   kabe waria
   man Waria

   yo hūa   ka   mege bamo
   his mother woman only that

   kabe waria
   man Waria

6. *kibudobo   kabe tonebo*
   Kibudobo man Tonebo

   kabe waria
   man Waria

   yo hūa   kabo keborame
   his mother girl Keborame

   kabe yamagi
   man Yamagi

1. My parcel of stinging nettles I carry
   Now what do you say to me?

   I carry my little package of *fagena* nettles
   Boy, what do you say about me now?

2. I am the mother of the *waru* wood walking stick
   Boy, are you criticizing me now?

   I am the mother of the *mono* wood walking stick
   Are you muttering under your breath about me?

3. So, I am not taking the rope of the black pig
   Is that what you dislike about me?

   Evening sago I am unable to cook
   Is that what you are swearing about under your breath?

4. I haven't taken my sago mallet
   Come now, boy, is that what you are saying?

   I haven't taken my sago hammer
   Is that what you are saying?

5. His mother, the woman Keborame
   The man Waria

   His mother, the only woman
   The man Waria

6. The Kibudobo man, Tonebo
   His son Waria

   His mother, the woman Keborame
   Her son, Yamagi

The Foi interrogative particle is -*be*: for example, *na ububege*, "I am going"; *na'a ububegebe*, "Are you going?" The -*yebe* and -*somoyebe* interrogative endings, however, have an angry, aggressive, sarcastic dimension to them: for example, *na'a ma'ame noma dibusomoyebe* could perhaps best be translated as "Just what is it you are saying to me?" (i.e., "Go ahead, make yourself perfectly clear!").

In verse 3, the woman refers to *kari kui*, literally, "woman sago," which is what the Foi call sago cooked for the evening meal. By contrast, they refer to any sago cooked during the day as *wana'ari kui*, literally, "carrying-pole sago," to indicate, perhaps, that it is cooked and eaten while one is working.

Notice in verse 2 the word *ka'arubidibuyebe*. In chapter 4 we learned that it partakes of the same range of meanings we found attached to *ka'a-* words: things that vibrate, rattle, hum, or tinkle, especially within a confined space. This verb and its synonym, *tenewanedi-*, refer to the humming muttering of complaints under one's breath.[5] Such words maintain the "moving image," although the depiction of an imputed halted motion—the man is claiming that his wife is *not* carrying out her appointed tasks—also preserves this central feature in the song.

Another problem that wives have to deal with is their husbands' jealousy. In the sago swamp, women are surrounded by dense jungle and often by themselves; thinking of this, men express anxiety that their wives may arrange to be visited by their lovers. The following song was composed by a woman who became exasperated at her husband's accusations.

(Women's Song 4):

1. *ī   huni   mabo kabore*
   eye beckons steals girl

   na wae
   I   not

2. *ya   huni   mabo kabore*
   hand beckons steals girl

   na wae
   I   not

3. *fufuruforabo kabori*
   wander   girl

   na iyo'oyebe
   I   is not me?

4. *iri   irikaro gō   hagibu   kabore*
   tree twigs   string bag carrying girl

   na wae
   I   not

5. *amena oro   yerebi dobo*
   men   bamboo yerebi clan

   dawa-o
   dawabo

6. *amena ira   ma'aru dobo*
   men   tree ma'aru clan

   dawa-o
   dawabo

1. The kind of girl who looks around furtively
   I'm not that type

2. The kind of girl who beckons toward men with her hand
   That's not me

3. The kind of girl that wanders around searching for men
   Am I that type, do you say?

4. The kind of girl who carries twigs in her string bag
   That's not me

5. The men of the *yerebi* bamboo clan
   Dawa

6. The men of the *ma'arua* tree clan
   Dawa

I heard this song performed as a woman's *sorohabora* in 1984, though it was an impromptu performance arranged on the spot for my benefit and did not occur in ceremonial context. Kunuhuaka and some of the other Hegeso women told me that women performed their own songs in the women's houses while men were singing in the longhouse, but I never witnessed this during any of the actual ceremonial performances I attended.

Nevertheless, in such cases, the *dawa* verses in their complete form become part of the performance. The seven songs I recorded that one night were all performed by pairs of women singing in a one-beat delay, similar to that used by Kunuhuaka and Siyame during their recital of Kunuhuaka's sago song: that is, the first woman begins the verse, and her partner joins in with the same line one beat later, providing a roundlike echo effect. In these women's *sorohabora*, the *owe* and *eye* refrains of the sago songs are also dropped.

Adultery in the Mubi Valley seems to be a recreational pastime that everyone from the very young to the nearly postsexual tries to participate in, despite the dangers of discovery (more salient in people's decision making than any moral approbation), the embarrassing and wearisome public litigation, and the inevitably expensive compensation payment. Married women aggressively seek out younger, unmarried men as sexual partners; men similarly show interest in younger women. A host of conventional signals, in which even the youngest child seems to be well versed, are available for those who wish to make their intentions known. A man—so I was told—can stealthily approach a woman at her sago camp and, from hiding, throw twigs in her direction. If she ignores them, it means she is not interested. But if she stops work and ostentatiously searches around for the source of the disturbance, it means she wants to know who threw the twig, and for the same reason. My male informants, warming to the topic, always reminded me that one runs a high risk in these endeavors—there is always the possibility that a virtuous (or at least disinclined) woman will simply scream blue murder, bringing anyone in the vicinity around to investigate. The would-be seductor would have little recourse but flight at that point. Indeed, it seems that virtually every personable young man in Hegeso has spent at least some months or years roaming around the New Guinea highlands waiting for the tempers of cuckolded husbands and enraged clansmen to cool off.

Women, in singing about the deaths and departures of their husbands and male relatives and the mistreatment they bear at the hands of men, contrive to represent the terms of their own feminine alienation from what must often strike them as the fatuity of men's striving. When men appropriate these songs for their own ceremonial purposes, then, they not only give expression to their own feelings of loss and abandonment, they confirm the importance of women's representation of their own male world. The next chapter discusses how women's songs are transformed into men's performances.

NOTES

1. I am extremely grateful to Michael Jackson for first bringing to my attention this dialectic between being and striving.

2. A version of the myth which details the origin of the sun, moon, and stars is found in Williams 1977.

3. I apologize for the use of the generic male pronoun. These points apply to women, too, of course.

4. The use of *kireji* or "cutting words" in Japanese haiku has been described by Henderson, for example, "*kana,* which usually marks the end of a haiku, and *ya,* which divides a haiku into two parts that are to be equated or compared" (1958: 8).

5. *Tenewanedi-,* by the way, is associated with the following other words:

tegeneni- to peck (of birds, and of people at their food)
(hu)tenane- 1. to hear a buzzing sound in one's head; 2. to bounce back; to get up unhurt after a fall
tenanedi- to grow up, develop, mature
tene- borer; *a tene:* mosquito net
tenemia- termite (which makes a thin, high-pitched boring sound in the house as it eats)

APPENDIX

The Musicological Structure of Women's Sago Melody

The sago melody is rhythmically dominated by the steady beat of the women's sago mallets. In the following simple melody, the woman Yefua is singing at around 1.2 beats per second. There are 7 beats per phrase, and the song proceeds in a fairly steady ⅝ time. The theme is identical to the sago song of Gebo's discussed in the chapter.

abu biri-e oba-i	sago mallet, oh!
a'a mae-e oba-i	quickly take it
abu biri-e oba-i	sago mallet, oh!
a'a mae-e oba-i	quickly take it
abu wasa oba-i	sago mallet, oh
a'a mae-e oba-i	quickly take it
ira abu-e oba-u	mallet stick, oh
a'a mae-e oba-u	quickly take it
kaburi oba-u	Miss sago mallet, oh
a'a mae-e oba-u	quickly take it
abu biri-e oba-u	sago mallet, oh
a'a mae-e oba-u	quickly take it
ira abu-e oba-u	mallet stick, oh
a'a mae-e oba-u	quickly take it
abu wasa oba-u	sago mallet, oh
a'a mae-e oba-u	quickly take it
ye-e ye oba-u	ye-e, ye, oh!
ye-e ye oba-u	ye-e, ye, oh!
ye-e ye oba-u	ye-e, ye, oh!
[pause]	
abu biri-e oba-u	sago mallet, oh
e-ye oba-u	e-ye, oh!
abu wasa oba-u	sago mallet, oh
e-ye oba-u	e-ye, oh
waibomo hūara oba-u	Waibo's mother, oh
meye wae oba-u	not yet, oh!
garibimo hūara oba-u	Garibi's mother, oh
meye wae oba-u	not yet, oh
viraremo hūara oba-u	Virare's mother, oh
meya'a wae oba-u	not yet, oh
arasemo hūara oba-u	Arase's mother, oh
meya'a wae oba-u	not yet, oh
ama'amo hūara oba-u	Ama'a's mother, oh
meye wae oba-u	not yet, oh
tabiyamo hūara oba-u	Tabiya's mother, oh
meye wae oba-u	not yet, oh
kigirimo hūara oba-u	Kigiri's mother, oh
meye wae oba-u	not yet, oh

MEN'S SONG, WOMEN'S FIRE

. . . poetry begins to atrophy when it gets too far from music.
—*Ezra Pound, The ABC of Reading*

THE MOST VIVID TABLEAU that men construct to describe the scene at the ceremonial performance of men's *sorohabora* is that of a young man, beautifully decorated, being handed a bamboo tube of drinking water by an admiring young woman during a break in his all-night singing and dancing. Women, so Foi men told me, keep water on hand for those men to whom they have become attracted by virtue of the beauty of their performance. These women also hold bamboo flares to illuminate the skin and decorations of the men, and as the men move up and down the corridor of the men's house during the night, the women follow them with their torches.

There is a most compelling dialectic here, for around their most profound experiences of alienation, sorrow, and abandonment, the Foi have constructed the life-affirming conventions of sexual attractiveness and enticement. Men and women characteristically seek each other out as marriage partners during and after *sorohabora* performances, so that while the existential centrality of death is socially valued poetically at this time, yet it ultimately results in the reaffirmation of the valued life-giving aspects of sexual longing.

What it involves is a reversal of the placedness of death and sexuality in their quotidian constitution. Sexual activity takes place rather furtively in the bush. Husbands and wives are supposed to meet for this purpose near the women's sago camp or near a garden. During the *sorohabora*, however, the longhouse becomes the venue for the initial stages of sexual flirtation and attraction. It represents a marked reversal of the central place in the longhouse normally accorded to the dead body during mourning. The corpse lies in the center of the longhouse corridor, surrounded by seated women huddled over it, caressing it, slowly bending over the corpse and then withdrawing from it in a rhythm of back-and-forth swaying, wailing, and shaking rattles, but all within that confined circle of death.

During the men's songs, however, the corridor is filled with proudly upright men, standing stiff with weapons held rigidly at their sides, yet bobbing up and down slightly in time to their own singing. These men engage in a continuous *pavane* of moving and stopping, marching and singing. Their skins are "bright like fire" from the *kara'o* oil and facial paint they have applied. The torches glint off their bodies in flashes of oily red-orange light, and there is a vibration of white cockatoo feathers as they march up and down the corridor. Nothing could be so starkly opposed to the stillness and silence and dullness of death as this shining movement of singing young men.

When we consider the men's songs performed in the longhouse in relationship to their origin in the sago camps, it is not just a matter of opposed spatial zones in some abstract, objectively conceived domain of Cartesian coordinates. We must consider the way in which these songs actually construct and *embody* space and movement: the manner in which the sago songs embody the rhythms and motions of female work, and the way in which the dancing that accompanies men's singing fashions a kinesthetic dimension out of acoustic and poetic space.

I invoke such writers as Heidegger (1962), Merleau-Ponty (1962), Sartre (1956), and the phenomenological psychologist Erwin Straus (1966), all of whom sought to counter the Cartesian bias which separates human thought and perception from human activity and the human body from its surroundings, the bias which makes of our lived environment some neutral, inert, and static set of spatial and material resources. I noted earlier that Heidegger located the origin of being in the concernful attitudes we bring to objects and situations that we encounter in-the-world.

> In other words it is on the basis of our original active pursuit of projects in a world—which world in consequence reveals itself either as an "instrumental-complex" offering assistance, or conversely, objects displaying a "coefficient-of-adversity" to our project—that we become aware of ourselves, not as we might suspect, as centres of cognition or *spectators* but as the embodied centres of activity or *participators* indicated by this world of instruments and adversity. (Glynn 1982: 214)

Ihde has suggested in this vein that dance is the way we experience a direct participation with song. "Music *amplifies* a participative sense of bodily involvement in its call to dance," he writes (1976: 159). If poetry is the most condensed, concentrated form of language, dance is certainly the most "concentrated" expression of what Bourdieu calls bodily *hexis* (1977).

In this chapter I describe men's ceremonial performance of the *sorohabora* and examine specifically masculine themes dealt with in Foi poetry. Let us first set the stage by considering how the moving image of Foi song is embodied by men's danced ceremonial performance: that is, how they turn women's poems into a total kinesthetic image.

"When did you first hear the sago song upon which this *sorohabora* is based?" I always asked the men. Their answer was highly stylized. "When we go to tap *kara'o* oil, we hear our wives singing in the nearby sago groves as they work." Foi men commented frequently on the fact that sago and *Campnosperma* trees were found in the same swamps next to each other; it was one instance where a marked dichotomy in exemplary male and female tasks was not accompanied by a marked *spatial* or *zonal* dichotomy as well. In the swamp, men and women come together for opposite reasons: women to process the most quotidian, mundane food staple; men to produce their most authentic, autochthonous wealth item.

"Nothing pleases us more than hearing the sweet sound of the women singing as we walk through the swamp," men would characteristically add when imagining this setting. Yet there was a definite—and conscious—note of anxiety and tension underneath these characterizations. For men would also explain that they prefer that their women sing continuously while making sago, so that the men will not suspect that they are meeting lovers. Silence in this context is definitely viewed with suspicion, as potentially antisocial. It is not unusual for a man to creep furtively up to his woman's sago camp to keep an eye on her—and the women know well that this happens.

When I recorded the women's sago songs, the singers were obliged by the situation itself (the fact that a tape recorder is first turned on and then turned off) to provide a start and a finish to their songs. Of course, just because the word *dawa* doesn't always enter into the recitation of the names and teknonyms in the final lines of a woman's song poem doesn't mean that it does not end the song as effectively as the chanting of the last *dawa* line does in the men's song (as we shall see). But still it seemed to me that women's sago songs frequently began and ended somewhat arbitrarily. Linked as they are to the rhythms and timing of sago scraping, a woman starts and stops singing as she scrapes pith, gets up to carry the pith to the washing trough, then returns to the palm to resume scraping. And of course, mothers have infants and small children to care for who periodically require attention. A more accurate aural image of women's singing can be obtained by walking through the swamps and pausing to listen to nearby women without actually approaching their sago camps. There, you hear snatches of a refrain, then perhaps a fragment of a wordless falsetto croon, a silence and the strong breathing of heavy exertion, the sound of a baby crying, sometimes the laughing and chatter of two women talking and gossiping as they work together, and through it all, the stop and start of the dull thud of the sago mallet and the wet *thwack!* of the pith-beating stick.

No setting could be more drastically opposed to the sago camp during the day than the inside of the men's longhouse on the night of a ceremonial performance. There, everyone in the village—men, women, and children—is crouched, talking, smoking, eating, tending fires, preparing bamboo tubes of water, holding bamboo flares. It is as far removed from the quotidian concerns of everyday life as a Foi activity can be. By elaborately decorating themselves, men are removing themselves from the mundane inscriptive activities of everyday life. By choosing the longhouse as the venue of their performance, by dancing as well as singing the poems, men are "condensing" and "compressing" the enabling moving images that ground their poetry, as poetry itself does to discourse, Pound reminds us. Men dance in the longhouse, and dance itself is the poetic rendition of everyday movement. Poetry, song, and dance are but different facets of what we can call the aesthetic embodiment of discourse in its most encompassing, inscriptive sense.

THE STRUCTURE OF MEN'S *SOROHABORA*

While women's songs begin as individual compositions and performances, men's renditions of them are always a group affair. There are two units of ceremonial performance. The first is the *soro ira* or "song tree." This is a pair of men who habitually sing together. They learn each other's rhythm, timing, and idiosyncrasies of melody through repeated sessions together, and they practice their songs together prior to a ceremonial performance.

The *soro ira* take the woman's original verses and sing them as a pair of matched lines. For example, a woman's song which is rendered as follows:

wana'ari kui   migi'orebo'o   owe
mid-day sago have not given owe

dibuyebe   eye
are you saying eye!

kare   kui   migi'orebo'o   owe
evening sago have not given owe

tawadibuyebe   eye
are you complaining eye!

is sung in the following manner by a *soro ira:*

1st man: *wana'ari kui migi'orebo'o*
2nd man: *kare kui migi'orebo'o*
1st man: *dibuyebe*
2nd man: *tawadibuyebe*

Each of the men's first lines ends with a drawn-out ululation or bleat produced by a rapid vibration of a glottal stop. As it fades out, the other man of the pair begins his line. The second pair of lines end with both men droning out the last vowel in a nonululating low tone, and as they in turn fade out, the next pair begin the recital of their verse.

Most commonly, each pair of men sing five verses, consisting of four lines as illustrated above (two matched pairs). The first three verses, as Foi men told me, "are about places: we call the names of the mountains, the streams, the sago swamps." The last two verses constitute the *dawa* or *dawadobora*. This is the part of the song where the name of the subject, the owner of the places mentioned in the first half of the song, is revealed. It is, as the Foi singers told me, the finish or ending of the song.

Dawa means "to cut up (and distribute)" and usually refers to the cutting up and distributing of meat. The Foi also call the recently imported *Sa* or *Ya* pork-exchange festival of the southern highlanders by the name *Dawa*. The cutting up and giving away of meat marks the end of the ceremonial exchange, just as the *dawadobora* in the men's songs "cuts off" the song from the one that succeeds it, and "gives away" the names of the deceased to public apprehension. Once again, we find at the core of Foi men's song structure the ubiquitous imagery of severing and restarting, the chopping up into discrete bits of a continuous flow of vital energy and human signification.

The structure of men's performances is dominated by the couplet format, which itself is a function of the fact that the songs are sung by a pair of men. The first line of the male-produced couplet describes an image of life: an animal trap in the bush, a spell or myth habitually recited, a canoe moving along the river. It identifies a previous condition of active, moving "life-lihood." The second line offers a contrasting assertion of what has happened to that previously vital condition: an abandoned bush track, a spell forgotten and not passed on to other men, a fallen tree. It offers a view of life's finality. The couplet form thus quite elementarily juxtaposes the most incisive Foi images of motion and the end of motion, itself the most encompassing image of the transition between vitality and mortality. Through their focus on movement and landscape, they assert the true spatiotemporal dimensions of human death, that is, that death is the cessation of life movement over the earth.

During an actual *sorohabora,* between three and six *soro ira* sing as a group. This is the second unit of *sorohabora* performance, and the Foi call it the *soro ga* or "song base." The alternating structure of the *soro ira's* recital of verses is replicated at this level also: each pair sings one verse at a time in turn, going from one end of the group to the other and then returning to the original pair. When each pair has sung its first verse, the first pair then sings its second verse, and so on. The final two verses with their chanting of the *dawa* lines in turn make for a pleasing synchronic repetition, so I was told.

Erwin Straus suggested that in dance, the center of motor activity shifts to the trunk:

> Corresponding to the dominant position of the trunk in motor activity, there is
> a transposition of the ego relative to the body schema. The "I" of the awake,
> active person is centered in the region at the base of the nose, between the eyes;
> in the dance it descends into the trunk. (1966: 26)

While the men sing, and as they stand waiting their turn to recite their verses,
they bob up and down in time to the music in a bent-kneed fashion. Each
man holds a bundle of arrows and a bow, or a spear in one hand. These are
rhythmically struck on the floor in time to the bobbing. Often, each man begins
his line by vigorously stamping his heel down on the floor to coincide with
his first syllable. Finally, one or two men in each *soro ga* hold a seedpod rattle
which is shaken in the same rhythm as the other percussive accompaniments.

In general, men's public postures are standing up, opening up the chest
and upper torso area. In singing and oratorical encounters, the arms are used
to emphasize one's discourse: they provide the percussive rhythm during performance of the *sorohabora,* and they enact and underline the speech of men.
Women's characteristic positions, on the other hand, are sitting, with an emphasis on closing up the central body area, the assumption of close-in crouches.
The women's use of a full-length cape, which conceals the entire body except
for the face, and the chest cloth, emphasizes this closing off of the mid-body
in public. Women's singing and formal wailing also take place in the sitting
position, with legs bent upward toward the body (as while making sago) or
folded underneath the buttocks (as when sitting cross-legged next to the corpse
in the longhouse). Women's positions emphasize stasis, compactness, motionlessness; men's postures emphasize a dynamic, charged motion, an openness
and potential for vigorous, rhythmic movement.

THE MOVING SONG

The musicological phrasing of the men's performances varies considerably in
comparison with the phrasing of women's sago songs. I noted in the appendix
to chapter 6 that the sago melody is dominated by the 7-beat-per-phrase rhythm
of the sago mallet. There were about 1.2 beats per second in a steady 5/8
time. The men's songs, by contrast, were more than twice as fast: the thumping
accompaniment of the weapons struck on the floor occurs at 2.8 beats per
second. There were between 7 and 10 beats in the first and third lines (the
opening lines of each man's couplet) and between 5 and 7 beats in the second
and fourth lines. While both men and women are getting roughly the same
number of beats in per phrase (7 for women, 7–10 for men), the men are
completing their opening lines in under four seconds and their second lines
in less, while the women are taking over six seconds to sing their phrases.

Not only do the men move their bodies and percussively accompany themselves with the rhythmic striking of feet and weapons while singing, they also

move as groups within the longhouse during the course of the night's singing. This movement comes at the end of every round of songs completed by each *soro ga,* and it serves to punctuate the performances and give men the opportunity to drop out and rest and let others take their places.

Theoretically, the different *soro ga* are supposed to be synchronized so that each group finishes its round of five verses at the same time. After every other group of five verses, upon the recitation of the last *dawa* verse, the two lines of men in each *soro ga* form a single line and move to the position that was occupied by the *soro ga* adjacent to them. The *soro ga* at one end of the longhouse must file all the way down to the other end. At Hegeso longhouse, the groups move first in one direction (from the front end to the back) and then back again.

The reason why the *soro ga* move after every other group of five verses is that each *soro ga* must sing its five verses *twice* when they reach the end. This is because each *soro ga* begins a new round of songs after it has reached the end position. In addition, at this time each man changes position with his *soro ira* partner. Each pair does this after the first recitation of the last *dawa* verse of their song and before they begin the second and last recitation of that round. When they have finished this final recitation of their round, each man stamps vigorously with his feet to mark its completion.

During the *sorohabora* performance, many men may be performing. The *soro*

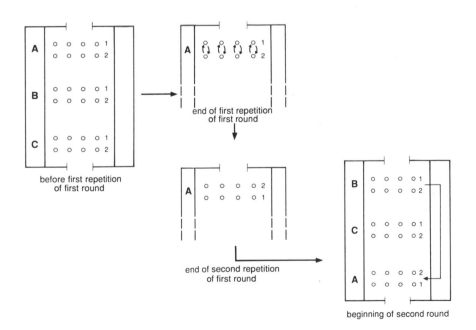

Figure 7–1. Movement of Male Singers between Song Rounds

ga may have to include six or even seven pairs of men (more could not fit along the width of the central corridor). In such cases, the pairs reduce their songs to four, three, or even two verses each, in the interest of completing all the songs in their repertoire during the course of the night. As many as ten or twelve *soro ga* can participate simultaneously during an evening's performance in the larger longhouses such as Hegeso.

When dawn approaches, one of the *soro ira* will assume the leadership of all the performers in the longhouse. The identity of this pair may have been agreed upon beforehand, or it may be tacitly decided during the night as one pair of men is seen to stand out from the rest in terms of the beauty of their decorations and the effectiveness and poignancy of their singing. At this time, the men consider themselves one single *sora ga*, and each pair will sing one pair of lines as the men finally leave the longhouse and descend into the plaza with the breaking of the day.

The movement of men back and forth through the longhouse is an integral part of the presentation of the songs, for it is clear that this movement is mimetic of the various movements and flows that are the recurrent subject matter of the songs themselves. It is as if the men, by moving, changing position and direction, halting, and marching again, are deliberately playing upon the themes of movement and stillness in the most iconic manner possible. The poem is the moving image, and the manner in which it is simultaneously "danced" is the most dramatic moving image performed by the Foi.

In Erwin Straus's brilliant essay "The Forms of Spatiality," he suggested that unlike instrumental, purposive, goal-oriented movement, which takes place in visual or *optical* space, dance takes place in *acoustic* space (1966: 20). Because song is nonlinear and repetitive, the motion it images is nonlinear. Like the whirlpool in the flowing river (*geno*), dance (*gene-*) moves around and around a center, counterfeiting a linear movement within a more encompassing periodicity and recursiveness. Optical space is the space of distances, horizons, tracks. Acoustic space is nongeometric, nonlinear; it images a *movement without dimension,* as we saw in chapter 4 when we examined the iconism of motion words in the Foi language. Victor Zuckerkandl, in his masterful work *Sound and Symbol,* argues that music exists solely and completely in the spaces *between* tones and suggests that

> *all* motion, seen as well as heard, motion of things as well as motion of tones, is, in the last analysis, "of one flesh and blood." Not unjustifiably may we say that musical motion is at the core of every motion; that every experience of motion is, finally, a musical experience. (1956: 138)

I suggested that in its original form as the women's *obedobora,* Foi song poetry was intimately related to the rhythms of women's sago making. What, then, is the *spatially inscribed activity that models men's performance* in the way that sago making shapes women's song?

It might be profitable to comment on the fact that the Foi word *ira* means "tree" but is also used to denote a grouping which for lack of a better term we might call "lineage." A man's *ira* is he and his sons (and in appropriate cases, his sons' sons) considered as a discrete grouping within a local clan. It is emphatically *not* a category. It is spoken of only in terms of living men and their offspring; there are no preexisting lineage positions within a clan that have to be filled. It is the unit of territorial contiguity and of resource management, the group of men who exert effective control over the marital destinies of their sisters and daughters; while the local clan shares the responsibility of contributing to the bridewealth funds for its male members and sharing in the payments received for its women, the clan as such does not arrange marriages.

The *soro ira* is to the *soro ga* what the lineage is to the clan, in other words. Men may drop out and others take their place during the ceremonial singing, but the integrity of the song is unaffected, just as the territorial integrity of lineage and clan is unaffected by the death of their individual members. The *soro ga* is a miniature version of men's most important social identity—but it is not a "reflection" of it: the men who become *soro ira* to each other have no necessary "relationship" to each other, and any *soro ira* can make up a *soro ga*. The *soro ira* and *soro ga* are just poetic "images" of Foi social identities, as the dance itself is an image of movement through space.

POETIC IMAGES OF MASCULINE VITALITY

We have learned that no women's song is considered inappropriate for performance by men at the *sorohabora* nighttime ceremony. But for the purposes of this chapter, with its focus on the nature of men's ceremonial display and themes, I will restrict myself to those songs that women composed on the topic of male attributes themselves—the prideful, competitive, sexually assertive qualities of men that define the fullness of their life and which are so tragically brought to an end upon death.

Prior to the ceremonial slaughter of pigs, the villages involved consider themselves in competition with each other. Each one wants to be the first to assemble its animals, to ready its vegetables and firewood and earth ovens. During the weeks that precede the pig kill, men visit the other longhouses to inspect other men's preparations, and perhaps to comment mordantly on the quality of their progress.

The following song depicts the competition between the men of Hegeso and Barutage villages prior to their *dawa* held in January 1985. The men of Hegeso, Herebo, and Barutage longhouses were coordinating their pig kills and had made many arrangements for the loan and purchase of pigs to meet their obligations to men from distant villages. Before the pig kill, some men found they could not provide what they had promised. There were arguments concerning who would meet the defaulters' obligations, piquant comments on the untrustworthiness of certain clan head-men, accusations of pig theft and other foul play.

(Song 1):

1. *ba'a na'a ē   siri   hubu   kegere*
   boy your garden large struck disparage

   dibihamone
   do not speak (disparage)

   ba'a na'a a   siri   hare   tegebu kegere
   boy your house large doing built   disparage

   dibihamone
   do not speak (disparage)

2. *ba'a na'a buru kirari mabo kegere*
   boy your black rope   taken disparage

   dibihamone
   do not say (disparage)

   ba'a na'a ya'o   kirari mabo kegere
   boy your many-colored rope   taken disparage

   dia   o'oyo'o
   saying do not go

3. *ba'a na'a ē   siri   hubu   kegere*
   boy your garden large planted disparage

   dia   o'oyo'o
   saying do not go

   ba'a na'a musu'uni kamabo kegere
   boy your smoke   rising disparage

   dibiha'oyo'o
   do not keep saying

4. *ya'a amena ībariabe sabe   u'ubi*
   we   men   Ībariabe Ridge children

dawabo
dawabo

ya'a amena ibu   faya'a wabo
we men   river Faya'a coming

dawabo
dawabo

5. *yiya amena ibu   faya'a kege*
we men   river Faya'a bank

dawabo
dawabo

yiya amena yagenebo sabe   u'ubi
we men   Yagenebo Ridge children

ibu   dawabo
river Dawabo

1. Boy, you have made a big garden
   But don't disparage me

   Boy, you have built a great house
   But don't denigrate me

2. You hold the rope of the black pig
   But don't disparage me

   You hold the rope of the piebald pig
   But don't speak disrespectfully of me

3. You clear the bush to make a big garden
   But don't hold me cheaply

   The smoke rises from your new garden
   But don't disparage me

4. We are the men of Ïbariabe Ridge
   Dawabo

   We are the men of the Faya'a Creek flowing
   Dawabo

5. We are the men of the banks of Faya'a Creek
   Dawabo

We are the men of Yagenebo Ridge
Ibu Dawabo

Just as men's hidden names are revealed in the poetic songs, so are the villages themselves referred to by alternate poetic designations. Hegeso village is located on a small spur known as Ībariabe ("Eye Deceive") Sabe (*sabe* = "ridge, nose, knife, edge"), or Yagenebo ("Birds Dance") Sabe. *Tono* is the word for an island or an isolated mountain or hill. Most Foi longhouses are located on such spurs or ridges, where in traditional times they could be more effectively palisaded and defended.

Myth telling can be said to exist in a complementary relationship to the performance of *sorohabora* in the longhouse. After the evening meal, some men occasionally gather children, young and old, around them and recite one or more myths. The setting is relaxed; everyone is sitting down and digesting dinner, some men light bamboo pipes, and men and boys all participate in listening to the narrator and asking questions about the story from time to time. As the evening progresses, the younger members of the audience drift off to sleep one by one, and finally the men themselves return to their sleeping places for the night.

Discourse of this sort complements the communal activity of food sharing in the evening. It emerges from the intensified conviviality of this time of the day, when people are gathered together under one roof to eat, relax, and contemplate and comment on the day's activities. In stark contrast to these situations are the highly electric, crowded, noisy occasions of ceremonial *sorohabora* performance.

This song for Hibare, a So'onedobo man of Hegeso, appeared in abbreviated form in *The Heart of the Pearl Shell*.

(Song 9):

1. *ba'a na'a ī   mano tuniro'o*
   boy your eye small myth

   dibiha'adiye
   cannot recite

   ba'a na'a ya   karo   tuniro'o
   boy your arm upper myth

   do'odiye
   cannot say

2. *ba'a na'a ī   mano tuniro'o*
   boy your eye small myth

dibihamone
do not recite

ba'a na'a ya   karo   tuniro'o
boy your arm upper myth

dibihamone
do not recite

3. *ba'a na'a ī   mano tuniro'o*
boy your eye small myth

dibihamone
do not recite

ba'a na'a ya   karo   tuniro'o
boy your arm upper myth

dibihamone
do not recite

4. *oro   yerebi dobo ka   fumarewamemo*
bamboo yerebi clan woman Fumarewame

kabe hibare
man Hibare

ira   namani dobo bugimenamo
tree namani clan Bugimena

kabe dabiyayo
man Dabiyayo

5. *ira   namani dobo bugimenamo*
tree namani clan Bugimena

ba'a dabiyayo
boy Dabiyayo

oro   yerebi dobo ka   fumarewamemo
bamboo yerebi clan woman Fumarewame

ba'a Hibare
boy Hibare

1. Boy, your "Little Eye" myth
You can no longer tell

Boy, your "Upper Arm" myth
How can you tell it

2. Boy, your "Little Eye" myth
   Do not recite it

   Boy, your "Upper Arm" myth
   Do not recite it

3. Boy, your "Little Eye" myth
   Do not recite it

   Boy, your "Upper Arm" myth
   Do not recite it

4. The clan of the *yerebi* bamboo, the woman Fumarewame
   Her son, Hibare

   The clan of the *namani* tree, the man Bugimena
   His son, Dabiyayo

5. The *namani* tree clan, the man Bugimena
   The boy Dabiyayo

   The *yerebi* bamboo clan, the woman Fumarewame
   The boy Hibare

In chapter 5 I examined the memorial song for Dosabo (song 3), in which the singer made use of the image of a man whose death has prevented him from teaching another man his magical lore. Here in song 9 we find the life of a man similarly depicted in terms of the temporality of discursive activity. But in this case it is not the private, hidden transfer of secret formulae that is referred to but the publicly recited myths that the deceased was known to have recounted.

In *The Heart of the Pearl Shell*, I noted that Foi myths often contain the veiled charters for important magic spells, and that these "hidden" charters are evident only to those men who have been taught the spells. Men's lived discourse always has a hidden component. But because the effect of women's song is to *unconceal*, to reveal hidden names and discourse, each of these facets of men's dialogue is separately identified and memorialized.

As I noted earlier, men of the component longhouses of an extended community usually plan their pig kills together. Because such events are attended by Foi from all villages, and many other non-Foi from distant places, men attempt to coordinate their efforts to achieve as grand a scale as possible. They spend the preceding years before a pig kill soliciting pledges of shell wealth from men outside the extended community. These men will be repaid with portions of cooked pork on the day of the pig kill.

Obviously, men must compete with each other to obtain enough pledges so that all their pigs will be accounted for, and conversely, they must obtain enough animals to meet their promises. A good deal of bickering, accusations of pig theft and sharp practices, and so on invariably accompanies this process. Women at this time come under a certain amount of pressure to maintain gardens in good order so that there will be enough vegetables for the feast, and of course they are not kept in the dark concerning their menfolk's difficulties at this time. They hear men of different villages taunting each other concerning the quality of their preparations, and, as it seems is women's lot everywhere, they know that a certain amount of the irritability of men generated at this time will be redirected to them.

The woman's original message is "You ask me why I have not finished making sago and preparing food—but you haven't even obtained the pearl shells and pigs that you owe other men!" But when sung by two young Barutage men, it mocks the Hegeso men's insults directed toward Barutage. "Are we women that you should tell us to make gardens and cook sago?!" the men's version is saying.

(Song 14):

1. *ē   siri   hubu   kegere*
   garden large planted disparage

   dia   ubuyebe
   saying is it going?

   kare   kui   meke'abo   kegere
   women's sago ought to cook disparage

   dia   ubu   korobore
   saying going close upstream

2. *ē   siri   hubu   kegere*
   garden large planted disparage

   dia   uboba'ae
   saying is going

   kare   kui   meke'abo   kegere
   women's sago ought to cook disparage

   dia   ubu   korobore
   saying going close upstream

3. *yiya amena ibu   faya'a wagibu*
   we   men   river Faya'a mouth

   dawabo
   dawabo

yiya amena igiri sabe   na'abo
we men   Igiri Ridge to you

dawabo
dawabo

4. *amena yagenebo sabe*
   men   Yagenebo Ridge

   dawabo
   dawabo

   amena igiri sabe
   men   Igiri Ridge

   ibudawabo
   dawabo

1. You should plant a big garden, you jeer at me
   Is this what you are saying?

   You should be cooking first sago, you insult me
   People pass this talk as they go upstream

2. I should plant a big garden, you derogate me
   This is what you are saying

   I ought to cook first sago, you insult me
   People are talking about me as they go upstream

3. We sing of you men of the Faya'a Creek mouth
   Dawabo

   You men of Sorofigitono
   Dawabo

4. We sing of you men of Yagenebo Ridge
   Dawabo

   You men of Igiri Ridge
   Ibu Dawabo

Here is a novel twist to the "moving image." *Dia ubu korobore*, "talking as they go upstream," refers to people spreading a story as they paddle back to their bush houses upon leaving the longhouses. The upstream direction applies not only to Hegeso and Barutage villages, whose bush houses are mostly upstream of their respective longhouses, but to the relative positions of the two longhouses themselves: Hegeso is upstream of Barutage.

"First" sago refers to what the Foi call *kare kui*, "woman's sago," the sago that a woman cooks first when she is preparing the evening meal, and which she eats first. *Wana'ari kui*, literally "carrying-pole sago," by contrast, was described to me both as sago eaten during the day, as I mentioned earlier, and as "evening sago"—that which a woman cooks for her husband.

In *The Heart of the Pearl Shell*, I analyzed a myth[1] in which I observed that a man's ceremonial drum, beaten only during the *Usane habora* ceremonial dancing, is an adjunct of his ability to speak assertively. Like the elongated bamboo smoking pipe which is an indispensable adjunct to Foi male conversation, the likewise phallic long, tubular drum draws an unmistakable equivalence between a man's public discursive assertiveness and his privately implemented genital reproductive powers. It is held at the hip (rather than in front of the chest like the highlanders' drums) and struck forceably in front of the groin with sweeping strokes of the stiffened arm. The small seedpod rattle that men use as rhythmic accompaniment during the *sorohabora* singing, by contrast, seems a minuscule and attenuated version of the explicitly phallic display of the drum beating at the *Usane habora*.

When men beat the drums during the *Usane habora* nighttime dancing, women are supposed to be irresistibly drawn sexually to the male performers. As women make sago, they very commonly sing to their husbands, "Don't come around with your sweet-talking drum and try to entice me away from work!"

(Song 15):

1. *ira tengo sa'o   nomo*
   tree tengo drum to me

   odibihamone
   do not call out

   ira sugu sa'o   nomo
   tree sugu drum to me

   odobobareo
   shouldn't call out

2. *ira sugu sa'o   nomo*
   tree sugu drum to me

   odibihamone
   do not call out

   ira suabo sa'o   nomo
   tree suabo drum to me

odobobarebe
shouldn't call out

3. *yiya amena sorofigi   tono*
   we men   Sorofigi Ridge

   dawabo
   dawabo

   yiya amena yabagamu
   we men   Yabagamu

   ibudawabo
   ibudawabo

4. *amena yabagamu*
   men   Yabagamu

   dawabo
   dawabo

   amena kana derege
   men   stone side

   dawabo
   dawabo

1. Your *tengo* tree drum
   Don't call out to me

   Your *sugu* tree drum
   You shouldn't call to me

2. Your *sugu* tree drum
   Don't cry out to me

   Your *suabo* tree drum
   Don't call out my name

3. We are the men of Sorofigitono
   Dawabo

   We are the men of Yabagamu
   Ibu Dawabo

4. We are the men of Yabagamu
   Dawabo

We are the men of the mountainside
Dawabo

Again, as is the case in song 3 (chapter 5) and song 9 considered above, the private and communal aspects of male discourse are contrasted and evaluated. Because the public drum is so ostensively related to a man's "private parts," it readily serves as an image for the "secret serenading" that men engage in when attempting to woo their women.

The next song neatly summarizes the characteristics of a head-man: he who helps others get married, raises many pigs, etc.

(Song 18):

1. *ka   sabora tabeyabo ya   dibige*
woman maiden head-man hand stated

   ya   wāyoiba'ae
hand limp, pliant

   ba'a bamo kirari mabuya mege'ame
boy this rope held only perhaps

   ya   kinayo'o dibige
hand stale stated

2. *ē   siri   hubu ya   dibige*
garden large planted hand stated

   ya   derege
hand stonelike

   ba'a na'a kui ka'amea kiginimabo ya   dibige
boy your sago ka'amea scraps hand stated

   ya   kinage
hand stiff

3. *yadobo kabo āyabo*
Yadobo girl Āyabo

   ba'a deya
boy Deya

   yiya amena kui inibi   dibige
we men sago cooked-eaten stated

   yiya hedawa dibige
we dawabo stated

4. *kui   kenege   dobo kabe fasu'u'ubi*
   sago mid-rib clan man Fasu'u'ubi

   kabe deya   dibubega
   man Deya speaking

   yiya amena kui   kenege
   we men   sago mid-rib

   dawa   dibubega
   dawabo speaking

1. The man who fastens a wife for others with his own hand
   That hand is now weak

   The man who holds the rope of the black pig
   His hand is limp and weak

2. The man who cleared a great garden
   His hand is stiff and lifeless

   The man who gathered *ka'amea* sago scraps for his many pigs
   His hand is weak now

3. The Yadobo woman Āyabo
   Her son Deya

   We are the men of Cooked Sago clan
   Hedawa we say

4. The man of the Sago Mid-Rib clan, Fasu'u'ubi
   Deya, we say

   We are the men of the Sago Rib clan
   Dawa

In the Foi language, a *kabe tabeyabo* is a man who habitually raises the wealth for many men's bridewealth payments, i.e., a head-man. In the Foi idiom, a head-man is he who "fastens" or "ties" one's wife. But its use here is significant. *Tabeya* refers to the large wooden tongs used to handle wood and food on a fire. But the *ira tabeya* is a large, straight tree associated with head-man status because of its great height. Perhaps a head-man plucks women as easily as men pluck food from a fire; perhaps it takes skill to extract a bride from a situation where one can easily get burned.

There is a significant use made of iconism in this song. In the second verse, there is rhyme between *kinage*, "stiff" (in the sense of stale, withered), and *derege*, "stonelike" (as in *kana derege*, "stone cliff face"). But this image also resonates with the alliterative phrase *kui ka'amea kiginimabo*, the "stale scraps of *ka'amea* sago" fed to pigs. It is also echoed in the last verse when the Kuidobo clan is referred to as the "clan of the sago mid-rib," *kui kenege*. Like a stale or stiff hand, *kinage*, the *kenege* is the stiff part of an otherwise pliant, limp frond of sago leaves.

It is during the performance of the *sorohabora*, when men, women, and children all are crowded into the longhouse, that it presents itself in its most vivacious, life-filling capacity. The inscriptive movements of men at this time, however, have to be seen together with the "poetic" formulae that accompanied the construction of the longhouse, as the next chapter details.

NOTE

1. The story "Fonomo and Kunuware," pp. 181–88.

APPENDIX

Transcript of Men's Song

On January 6, 1985, at a ceremonial performance of *sorohabora* at Hegeso longhouse, six Hegeso men formed one *soro ga*. The following is a transcription of one round of their performance—that is, a set of three complete songs of five verses each. The transcript gives the lines in the actual order in which they were sung. The musical transcription, however, instead of alternating each man's lines within the *soro ira*, has given each man's pair of lines as a unit.

Verse 1

1. Abeabo:
   Ba'a na'a ĩ hone ubu kusa do'ane dobo'owua

3. Memene:
   Ba'a na'a kigi wara'obo kusa do'ane dobo'owua

2. Abeabo:
   Dibi ubo'oriye

4. Memene:
   Dia ubo'oriye

Verse 2

1. Wa'o:
   Duma Yefua sabe ya erege

3. Midibaru:
Duma Yefua habo ya namuyu erege

2. Wa'o:
Auwa fore iba'ae

4. Midibaru:
Vira hua uboba'a

Verse 3

1. Kora:
Ba'a na'a kō tegeri ma'aya dera

3. Garibi:
Ba'a na'a wagebo [kegebe] ma'aya dera

2. Kora:
(a)Foraboba'ae

4. Garibi:
Debe ma uboba'ae

Verse 4

1. Abeabo:
Ba'a na'a ī hone ubu kusa (do'ane dobo'owua)

3. Memene:
Ba'a na'a ya karo kusa (do'ane dobo'owua)

2. Abeabo:
Dobo'oriye

4. Memene:
Dibiwa (ubo'oriye)

Verse 5

1. Wa'o:
Duma fai hesabo ya erege

3. Midibaru:
Duma ka'afa hesabo ya erege

2. Wa'o:
Auwa forabo'owa'ae

4. Midibaru:
Vira huiba'ae

Verse 6

1. Kora:
Kō kegebe debe ma'aya dera

3. Garibi:
Kō kegebe ma'aya dera

2. Kora:
   Foreye ma ubihabora-o

4. Garibi:
   Debeya ubihabora-o

Verse 7

1. Abeabo:
   Ba'a na'a kō tugame kusa . . .

3. Memene:
   Ba'a na'a ya karo kusa . . .

2. Abeabo:
   Dobo'oriye

4. Memene:
   Dia ubo'oriye

Verse 8

1. Wa'o:
   Ira farabo haũ bobo ya erege

3. Midibaru:
   . . . Haũ bobo ya namuyu

2. Wa'o:
   Auwa gefo diyo'oware

4. Midibaru:
   Auwa fore iba'ae

Verse 9

1. Kora:
   Ba'a na'a ira waru ma'aya dera

3. Garibi:
   . . . ira bai ma'aya dera

2. Kora:
   Forabo'owa'ae

4. Garibi:
   Forebiba'ae

Verse 10

1. Abeabo:
   Yiya amena bi'a [h]uba

3. Memene:
   Yiya amena gesa Moma

2. Abeabo:
   Ibu dawabo

4. Memene:
Dawa dibihabora-o

Verse 11

1. Wa'o:
Yiya amena ira so'one

3. Midibaru:
. . . amena ira namani

2. Wa'o:
He dawabo

4. Midibaru:
Hedawarabo

Verse 12

1. Kora:
Momahu'u ka Fofo

3. Garibi:
Oro Yerebidobo kabe Waria

2. Kora:
Ba'a Kawaru

4. Garibi:
Kabe Baya

Verse 13

1. Abeabo:
Momahu'u Isa'ibu

3. Memene:
Momahu'u Ka'ibu

2. Abeabo:
Kabe Dosabo

4. Memene:
Iba Kabe Bo

Verse 14

1. Wa'o:
Yo hūa ka (mege) bamo

3. Midibaru:
Yo hūa ka mege bamo

2. Wa'o:
Ba'a Suibo

4. Midibaru:
Dawa'abo

Verse 15

1. Kora:
   Oro Yerebidobo Wariamo

3. Garibi:
   Yo hũa ka Fofomo

2. Kora:
   (Kabe) Ira Baya

4. Garibi:
   Kabe Kawaru

bl = bleating sound with voice   x = beat established by pounding of spears

Verse 6.

1. ko~ ke-ge-be de-be ma'a-ya de-ra - a - o
2. fo - re-ye ma u-bi-ha-bo-ra - o
3. ko~ ke-ge-be ma'a-ya de-ra-a - o
4. de-be-ya u-bi-ha-bo-ra - o

Verse 7.

1. ba'a na'a ko~ tu-ga-me ku-sa - a - a
2. ao-bo'o - ri-ye - e - o
3. ba'a na'a ya ka-ro ku-sa-a-'d - o
4. di-a u-bo'o-ri - ye - o

Verse 8.

1. i-ra fa-ra-bo hau~ bo-bo ya e-re-ge-e
2. au-wa ge-fo di-yo'o-wa-re-e - e - o
3. hau~ bo-bo ya na-mu-yu a-a-a - o
4. au-wa fo-re i-ba'a-e - o

Verse 12.

Verse 13.

Verse 14.

Verse 15.

8   "... POETICALLY THE FOI DWELL ..."

The Mythopoesis of Men's Longhouse Construction

Let us think for a while of a farmhouse in the Black Forest, which was built some two hundred years ago by the dwelling of peasants. Here the self-sufficiency of the power to let earth and heaven, divinities and mortals enter in simple oneness into things, ordered the house. It placed the farm on the wind-sheltered mountain slope looking south, among the meadows close to the spring. It gave it the wide overhanging shingle roof whose proper slope bears up under the burden of snow, and which, reaching deep down, shields the chambers against the storms of the long winter nights. It did not forget the altar behind the community table; it made room in its chamber for the hallowed places of childbed and the "tree of the dead"—for that is what they call the coffin there: the Totenbaum—*and in this way it designed for the different generations under one roof the character of their dwelling through time.*

—*Heidegger, "Building Dwelling Thinking"*

HEIDEGGER SEEMED TO HAVE one advantage over anthropologists: he did not think it was necessary or desirable to separate a consideration of man's relationship with his gods from a consideration of his relationship with the earth and his world of *matériel* and activities. Our tendency to see architecture as either wholly utilitarian or wholly symbolic but never both at once often prevents us from understanding dwellings as "total aesthetic facts."

I began with a perspective that did not separate our speech and signification from the rest of our body's activities. I also suggested that, as Ezra Pound said, we can consider poetry the most compact, condensed form of speech. Now what poetry is to other speech and dance is to movement, building is to all purposive activity. When we build our houses, our tools, our edifices, we condense all of our world movement into a microcosm.

We have nearly arrived at the end of this book, but one task remains, and that is to obliterate the contrast between metaphor and image that I have been at pains to establish. For I have also maintained from the beginning that both are *spatially* and *temporally* constituted in terms of the nearness and remoteness with which we distance the varying concerns of our life. What we do with our words is what we do with our space and time; what we do when we build is what we do when we create the tracks and paths of our cognized landscape. "Building accomplishes its nature in the raising of locations by the joining of their spaces," Heidegger wrote (1971a: 160).

When Heidegger quoted Hölderlin's phrase ". . . poetically, man dwells . . ." he wanted to say that both poetry and dwelling belong to the center of man's being. The Foi poem affirms the spatiality of life and death, the fact that *location* is humanized space which itself dies in the absence of human concern. The memorial poem re-creates the spatiality of Foi being. But "building" does the same thing: it creates a space within which the center of people's movements can exist and around which their inscriptive sojourning can be anchored.

Heidegger invoked the ontic/ontological distinction in his discussion of the construction of lived space in his essay "Building Dwelling Thinking." "Spaces receive their being from locations and not from 'space,'" he wrote (1971a: 154). Locations crystallize out of a qualityless environment as a result of our recognition of meaningful things that happen in them. Such locations then become linked in the existential manner I discussed in chapter 2. Only within such humanized locations can space be properly apprehended. That is why the idea of a clearing, *raum* in German, which also means "space," was seized upon by Heidegger: Human space is a clearing within which our intentions build things.

I have been saying that for the Foi, movement creates space. In poetry, the "moving image" emerges as a result of the serial juxtaposition of linked place names, species, and so forth. I suggested that in this manner, the life course of the deceased is "detotalized" into a temporal series of locations that he inhabited during his life.

In this chapter I want to discuss the manner in which detotalization is the basic format of both magical and poetic discourse among the Foi. But further, I want to confirm that detotalization is not just an intellectual operation of the Cartesian mind but a function of the *embodiment* of discursive signification, as Merleau-Ponty, Cassirer, and indeed Lévi-Strauss himself have shown us: *detotalization is basically a spatial and temporal process.*

Finally, I want to portray the Foi longhouse as embodied space. The longhouse is constructed as a series of linked locations, and these locations correspond to a different part of the body of certain mythical culture heroes. The power of these heroes is their status as hunters; they are thought to "draw" animals to the longhouse, into which their essence has been fixed by means of a series of spells.

Let us first consider the day of a pig kill where hundreds of pigs are slaughtered by their owners. These men distribute the portions of freshly butchered pork as payback to those men from whom they solicited pledges of shell wealth and money. Insofar as a community's public reputation for generosity and success in obtaining animal wealth is at stake on these occasions, it is of great importance for Foi men to use whatever means are at their disposal to ensure their continual acquisition of animals.

The recipients of meat gifts characteristically are the men who have ceded their daughters and sisters as wives to the pig killers. Like the bridewealth payments which first effect the transfer of women from their natal groups to those of their husbands, periodic gifts of meat from a man to his wife's male relatives offset the supernatural influence that these men can exert on the off-spring of that marriage: they maintain the good rapport between wife givers and wife takers that is necessary to the growth and continued health of children. If these gifts are not forthcoming, or if the bridewealth is deemed to be insufficient in some manner, the resulting anger and frustration of the children's maternal relatives can lead to the ghost-induced sickness and even death of the children.

The Foi thus dismember and distribute animals to their affines to maintain the "flow" of women and children; to ensure that this flow continues they also, during the construction of the longhouse, symbolically "dismember" a deity so as to safeguard the flow of animals to a community of male hunters. In Foi longhouse magic, the "ghosts" of the magical formulae employed are fixed into the actual architecture of the house—they are made real, concrete, "mundane," so that a real flow of animals to the men of that house can be promoted.

But in more general terms, wherever the Foi chop something up into bits, detotalize something, they effect a flow, a movement; they release the moving image. The imagist aesthetic I have made use of in this book is not merely a lyrical device, in other words; it is a core apperception of how space and motion are articulated for the Foi. One can speak of the "paratactic" aesthetic of Foi life: wherever two things are placed side by side, a flow between them results. Of course, this also works in reverse: wherever a single entity is decomposed into constituent parts, a potential for motion is set loose.

As I have suggested, Foi cosmology centers around the distinction between what is perceived to be the natural and unending flow of vital forces and energies, and the contrasting realm of human action whose intent is to halt, redirect, and contain such forces into socially and morally appropriate channels. Included in this natural flow of vital forces is the movement of pearl shells, cowry shells, and meat between men. Rather than seeing themselves only as initiators and "end-users" of such flows, Foi men often perceive their more important role as that of "switchyard operators" whose goal is to channel the direction of these items for their own purposes.

FOI LONGHOUSE CONSTRUCTION

Foi longhouses are rebuilt every twenty to twenty-five years. The first act in building consists of planting the support posts, the *a debe gese* (literally, "house underneath"), which are made from certain hardwood trees. Because this wood has an extremely long life, these posts are simply transferred from the old house site after the longhouse has been dismantled and resited. The support posts are planted in four rows, two on each side of the house. Each outer pair of rows is separated by the length of the sleeping areas (approx. five feet), and the two pairs are themselves separated by the four-foot width of the central corridor. Men place them two feet apart for the length of the longhouse. Where the fireplaces are to be located, at six-foot intervals along the length, special longer house supports are planted, the *figi*. These provide the structural support for the roof itself and the fireplace racks *(bani)* to be built subsequently.

At each end of the longhouse, the two fireplaces which are one in from the end—four in all—are called the *a boroso*. The structural posts supporting the roof at these fireplaces are called the *a boroso ira*. The sleeping areas associated with these fireplaces are reserved for the head-men and cult leaders (sometimes but not always one and the same) of that longhouse community. They are said to "support" the community through their ritual acumen, knowledge of magic, leadership in warfare and exchange, and wealth, as the *a boroso ira* themselves support the longhouse.

The more perishable wood used for the floor beams, interior, and roof, in contrast, must be fashioned again. After men plant the house posts, they lay the cross-hatched joists *(dufu)* and bearers *(wage)*, leaving spaces for the firepits. The roof frame is then constructed, first by laying its four main purlins *(karu)*. The lower two on either side are supported by the back firepit posts *(figi)*, while the higher ones, midway between the roof peak and the gables, are supported by the front firepit posts. Then, men tie the vertical battens, the *saria*, between the two sets of purlins. Across these are placed one-inch strips of pandanus wood, the *kamabe*, at two-inch intervals. The sago thatch is hung from these pandanus wood strips.

After everything has been completed on the roof except the sago thatch *(bora'a)*, work resumes on the interior. The builders lay sections of trunks from the black palm (limbum) across the central walkway *(kunuhua)*. Each pair of men who are to share a fireplace then complete their own firepit *(danega)*, fireplace rack *(bani)*, and sleeping area *(a namo)*, as well as the section of sago mid-rib wall *(kau kaga or kāga)* around their sleeping areas. The sleeping areas are floored with thinner, more flexible strips of bark. The pairs of men construct their firepits by stringing loops of cane between the gaps left for this purpose and then criss-crossing them with more cane strips to form a basin-shaped framework. A mixture of clay and earth is used to fill in the basin, making the firepit. The two-tiered fireplace racks are then constructed on the *figi*. Long beams of three-inch diameter, the *anu ira*, are laid along the back of each side—these serve as headrests for the men when they sleep.

The current Hegeso longhouse has eleven fireplaces on each side, the most that any Foi longhouse contains. It should be recalled that the sequence of men from the back to the front parallels the sequence of men's bush houses from the upstream to the downstream end of Hegeso territory. In other words, the men of Hegeso orient themselves with respect to the territory they occupy and replicate this orientation in their sleeping arrangements within the longhouse.

When the interior has been completed, the sago thatch is hung from the *kamabe*. Temporary scaffolds called *doro* are built to facilitate this. Finally, the outer walls are erected from pieces of sago mid-rib lashed together with cane.

LONGHOUSE CONSTRUCTION MAGIC

While I was resident in Hegeso village between 1979 and 1988, two men were responsible for reciting the spells needed to complete a longhouse. One was a head-man of Orodobo clan; the other was a former cult leader of the Momahu'u clan. These two men told me they were each responsible for one end of the longhouse, the ends at which their *a boroso* were located respectively. The Orodobo man's spells were designed to attract animal wealth to the house, while the Momahu'u man's spells concentrated on attracting shell wealth.

I begin with the spells for shell wealth. The following spell is recited when the front overhanging roof gable, the *sabe geso*, or "nose" of the longhouse, is completed. This spell is also recited when the new longhouse is swept for the first time:

> With the man Haï's heart
> With the woman Kiri's heart[1]
> With the point of the twisted pearl shell
> With the rope of *Sō* cowry
> With the *Ka'amea* pearl shell
> With the short, straight cowry necklace
> With the heart of the *sore* bird
> With the heart of the *arabe* bird
> With the *furubu* tree
> With the *fefe* tree
> With the *kegebe amu* vine
> With the *kegebe arabo* vine
> With the heart of the *ga'are* bird
> With the heart of the *ware* bird
> With the heart of the cross-cousin
> With the heart of the second cross-cousin
> With the heart of the distant female relative
> The Damayu longhouse
> The Kutubu longhouse
> The Fasu longhouse
> The Ifigi longhouse
> The highlander's house above
> The Barutage longhouse

The Herebo longhouse
The Hegeso longhouse
With the heart of the:

> *ware* bird
> *kegere* bird[2]
> *sore* bird
> *bia* bird
> *tu'u* tree
> *furubu* tree
> *yu'uri* cordyline
> *ama* cordyline
> *hiname* grass
> *foroboro* grass
> *sawayo* taro

The girl Heyame and the boy Hanemene, this married couple, these two have sown the seeds of the red *yu'uri* cordyline, *ma'aweyabo*.

Heyame and Hanemene are a married couple who plant the seeds of the red cordyline around the longhouse. The leaves of these cordylines, specifically the bright red and yellow varieties, are employed in a variety of pearl-shell–acquisition spells and are always associated with shell wealth (see Weiner 1984, 1986). As is the case with most highlands societies, Foi houses of all sorts are surrounded by dense groves of cordyline and croton shrubs.

The Momahu'u man who related this spell to me explained that he calls out the names of all the other Foi longhouses—Ifigi, Damayu, and so forth —"because our sisters are married there and the bridewealth for them must come here." The highlanders' and Fasu longhouses are mentioned "so that they will bring wealth with them when they come to eat pork at our pig kills."

The terms *kumi* ("cross-cousin") and *māya* ("second cross-cousin") are used to describe descendants of out-married sisters. They are mentioned in the spell because they have obligations to bring wealth with them when they come to eat pork at Hegeso on ceremonial occasions.

Let me briefly review the structure of Foi "spell talk." Foi magic spells have two main formats. The first is exemplified by the preceding spell, in which desired objects and other objects which resemble and symbolize them are repeated one after the other in a long list. The second format is given by the following formula:

> I am not doing x;
> I am doing y.

or:

> This is not an x;
> This is a y.

The following spells make use of this format as they "detotalize" the body of Hanemene, a mythical hunter.

When the *arere dufu*, the strip of wood laid across the entrance to the front door, is being fastened, one gathers *furu* vine leaves and wraps them around the *dufu* with *tiraribu* vine and recites the following spells:

> I am not tying these leaves to the *dufu*;
> I am tying them to Hanemene's backbone.
>
> I am not using this *tiraribu* vine;
> I am using the veins of Hanemene.

When men plant the *a debe gese*, the posts supporting the longhouse floor, the following spell is spoken:

> I am not planting these *debe gese* posts;
> I am planting the toes of Hanemene.

When the *agikobo menamosabo*, the sides of the front door, are being constructed, the following spell is recited:

> I am not planting these door sides;
> I am planting the femurs of Hanemene.

When men place and fasten the battens of the roof framework, the *saria*, the following spell is recited:

> I am not laying the battens;
> I am laying the rib cage of Hanemene.

Upon the laying of the sago thatch on the roof:

> I am not putting down this sago thatch;
> I am putting down the two outspread wings of the *aiyabe* eagle.[3]

When the floor planking of split black palm, the *kunu*, is being tied down, the following spell is recited when the plank between the door posts is fastened:

> I am not putting down this *kunu*;
> I am putting down the chest of Hanemene.

When men are constructing their fireplaces and laying the clay foundation on the cane frame, this spell is recited, now invoking Hanemene's wife, Heyame:

> I am not putting down this clay;
> I am putting down the woman Heyame's menstrual blood.

When men light their fires for the first time, they sweep the floor and once more recite the *sabe geso* spell.

These are the nine spells that the Momahu'u man recites for the front end of the longhouse. These nine spells "reside" in the *agikobo menamosabo*, the two sides of the door. That is, the "ghosts" of these spells reside there, I was told. Men tell children not to play near the door for fear that the ghosts might harm them. The Momahu'u man also added that when men hear a tapping noise in the longhouse, it means these ghosts are moving about.

The Momahu'u man further noted that young men seeking to become men of high status would sleep near the door of the longhouse after the spells had been recited, hoping that the ghost of Hanemene which had been "planted" there would reveal the spell to them in a dream. This event would be interpreted as a portent that the young man would indeed become a head-man later in life. Foi men regularly sought to sleep at places where ghosts were thought to reside, as I said earlier—the Momahu'u man himself, Dabura Guni, learned the longhouse magic when he slept near such a whirlpool and was visited by a ghost while he dreamt.

The spells for the other half of the longhouse involve the detotalizing of the body of a certain Yibumena. They begin with the spell recited when the *wage* floor bearers are being laid:

> I am not laying straight these *wage*;
> I am laying Yibumena's femur.

When men are tying the *wage* to the four main corner support posts with cane, the following spell is recited:

> I am not taking this cane;
> I am taking Yibumena's veins.

When the house posts, the *a debe gese*, are being planted, this spell is recited:

> I am not planting these house posts;
> I am planting the severed leg and foot of Yibumena.

When men are laying the floor joists, the *dufu*, the following is recited:

> I am not straightening out these *dufu*;
> I am straightening the backbone of Yibumena.

Yibumena's backbone is also referred to in a spell that attends the planting of the *boroso ira* at the back end of the house:

> I am not causing these *boroso ira* to stand up;
> I am causing Yibumena's backbone to stand up.

The spell for fastening the *arere dufu* is identical to that recited at the door at the other end, with the exception that reference is made to Yibumena and not Hanemene.

Similarly, the spell attending the fastening of the *sabe geso* contains the same repeated phrases as the Momahu'u man's *sabe geso* spell for the other end. The same kinds of leaves are chewed and spit onto the *sabe geso*. The Orodobo man added at the end of his otherwise identical spell, "I am fastening the heart and lungs of Yibumena to this *sabe geso*."

When men are building their fireplaces, they may or may not know the magic associated with the following procedure: The various red and yellow cordyline leaves, other red-colored leaves, and the feathers of various birds associated with pearl shells or hunting, such as the Pesquet's parrot and the harpy eagle, are gathered by each man and buried in the clay of their fireplaces, and the following is recited:

> Yibumena is sleeping with his arms and legs spread out.

The longhouse becomes embodied space through these procedures.[4] At each end of the longhouse, each of the two principal spell reciters makes use of the primordial Foi human images: the married couple (sexual intercourse) and the hunter (death). Hunting and marriage image each other and provide the experiential ground for one another. Hunting and sexual intercourse are interchangeable activities for men; their equivalence surfaces regularly in myth, magic, and dream interpretation (see Weiner 1986, 1988). The provisioning of meat to one's wife's relatives certifies filial relationships in the community: men's control of their wives' children is contingent on their giving periodic gifts of meat to their wives' male relatives. The flow of meat, in other words, parallels the flow of semen (see also Wagner 1977; Weiner 1988).

This is the life-giving side of hunting. But because hunting is enabled within the domain of ghosts, it retains an existential ambiguity, as I suggested in the Introduction. Thus there is its other side, the side that makes hunting appropriate as an adjunct of death and funeral ritual rather than life and bridewealth, as the next section details.

LONGHOUSE MAGIC AND THE MEN'S HUNTING CULT

In the period before the Christian Mission began to exert an effect on Foi religious beliefs, after the men had been sleeping in the new longhouse for about two months, the *bi'a'a guabora* rites (literally, "black palm split," or as Williams translated it, the cult of the "Arrowhead") were held. They were performed in order to promote fertility in general, and specifically to ensure success in the hunt. *Bi'a'a guabora* was primarily associated with funeral ritual,[5] but men also performed the rites on a variety of other important occasions, such as the completion of the longhouse and the remarriage of a widow.

Bi'a'a guabora began quite simply when the men of the longhouse prepared for a hunting expedition in the bush. There they stayed between ten and twelve

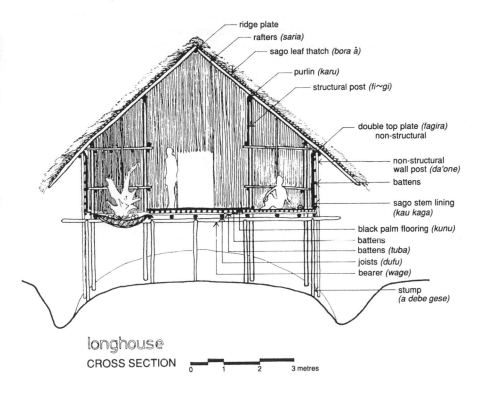

longhouse
CROSS SECTION   0   1   2   3 metres

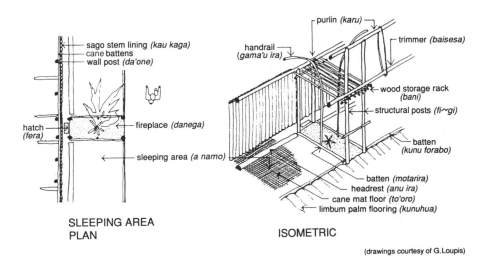

SLEEPING AREA
PLAN

ISOMETRIC

(drawings courtesy of G.Loupis)

Figure 8–1. Details of Foi Longhouse

days in a special house called the *bi'a'a a*, the arrowhead house, and returned with as much game as they could find: marsupials, fish, bush-fowl eggs, and so forth (all of which are referred to generically as *aso*, "wild animal flesh").

Half of the men then returned at night, so that the women and children would not see them, and hid the meat they had caught. The next day they began to ready bamboo, firewood, sago, vegetables, and all the other things they would need for cooking the meat. The other men, meanwhile, had remained in the bush and had decorated themselves with different varieties of cordyline. When they returned to the longhouse decorated in this way, they too carried their meat with them. Several of the men carried the entire catch in large string bags. The men approached the longhouse in single file, very quietly. When they entered the house, the first man began to dance, and each man entering after him did the same thing until they had lined up along the length of the central corridor. They silently marched up and down in the heavy-footed, stamping rhythmic dance that men perform while singing the *sorohabora* in the longhouse.

After they had marched back and forth several times, the first man took a branch of the *Piper betel* (Foi: *gisu'u*). He walked down the line of men as they continued to march in place with their string bags of meat and, striking each bag five times with the branch, he announced, "Hey! This man has killed animals!" The dancing then ceased, according to my informants.

When the first man had struck each man's bag, the last man then took another branch of *Piper betel* and offered it to the first man, who took a bite, as did all the other men in their turn. The men then put their string bags of meat on the floor. The meat was distributed to all present, cooked in the bamboo tubes, and eaten.

After the meal, the men arose again. Each man counted every plank in the central corridor of black palm and said, "I will kill this many wild pigs in *kagi* traps." Each man counted the sago mid-rib slats in the side walls, each one standing for an *aso bohabo*, the spotted phalanger, that would be found in his traps. Each man then counted the slats in the end walls, each one standing for the *sese fore* marsupials (species unknown) that would be found in his traps. One by one they then counted the number of purlins in the roof, and each stood for a python that would be obtained. After that, the fireplaces were counted, each one standing for the hedgehoglike *aso hãga*, the "spiked" marsupial. The fireplace racks, the *bani*, were counted next, and each one stood for the *yarainobo*, a goanna species.

After this, one of the men took a leaf of the yellow *foreyabe* cordyline. He climbed up the wall and inserted it between the sago thatching in the roof. He called out, "*Weyo!* I am going to kill a man!" And for every enemy that would be slain in battle, men planted *foreyabe* leaves in the roof thatching.

A pig kill was held upon the completion of the *bi'a'a guabora* ceremony, and people from all other longhouses were invited to bring shell wealth to exchange for pork. Of course, the night of the pig kill is the time when men decorate themselves and perform the *sorohabora* in the longhouse.

Each of the steps in the longhouse ceremonial can stand by itself—the magic spells have a beginning and end to themselves; the *bi'a'a guabora* rites are performed in identical fashion on a number of different occasions; the memorial songs, too, are sung at night following most large-scale pig kills. Each has a logic in and of itself; each can be analyzed separately.

Yet their sequence within the framework of longhouse construction as a single event is also significant and determinate—each of the three motifs builds upon the previous one, extending and preempting it. As is the sequence of images in a myth, the sequence of ceremonies associated with the construction and lived constitution of a longhouse is dialectically structured. In short, the building of a longhouse is a mythical event.

The series of magic spells serve to depict the longhouse anthropomorphically as the detotalized bodies of the mythical heroes Yibumena, Hanemcne, and Heyame. These heroes are considered to have been incorporated into the architecture of the house itself. The longhouse becomes the avatar of the Mythical Hunter. In the *bi'a'a guabora* rites, the house parts—its planks, wall slats, and individual sago thatches—were said to stand first for whole animals and then for individual men, the enemies of the community who would be slain in battle. A community of hunters, in other words, were represented as a community of warriors (hunters of men). Finally, in the *sorohabora* songs, the deceased members of the longhouse are detotalized into the series of place names they morally invigorated through the hunting activity they pursued there.

There is a recursive, embodied metonymy at play here: In constituting the longhouse parts as a "counting tally" for game animals to be obtained, an equivalence or "exchange" is established between meat types and the body parts of the mythical heroes denumerated in the building spells. This is closely followed in terms of ritual sequence by the actual pig kill, in which whole men come to receive the body parts of slain (domestic) animals as exchange items. This, in turn, is paralleled by the longhouse's own elicitation of whole enemies to be killed—a "return" of constituted human body parts for slain animals—which itself mirrors the detotalization of geographical sites in the poetic invocation of the house's dead members, an animation of the house by way of its replacement of lost lives.

One could say that the success of this last commemorated activity was a direct result of the magic originally performed. Each sleeping place is associated with its owner and his territory, and the sequence of sleeping areas from one end to the other reflects the actual sequence of men's houses as one goes from upstream down the Mubi River. The longhouse is first and foremost an encapsulated representation of spatial relationships among men. Within the longhouse, landscape and body become fused as images of one another. As such, the sequence of magical procedures that constitute the architecture of

Foi built space is thoroughly and wholly poetic. But more than this, it is men's hunting which is depicted as having an efficacy of itself—it is the most thoroughly "ghost-related" productive activity in which Foi men engage. By fixing the mythical hunters into the architecture, the Foi bring the remoteness and distance of hunting into the proximity of their most immediate spatial microcosm. Further, they juxtapose the finality that is hunting's death with the ceaseless life-giving flow of embodied sexuality. In the end, the longhouse magic spell is men's poem of captured life, as women's poem is their song of moving death.

One of Heidegger's more well known phrases was that "language is the house of being":

> The nature of Language does not exhaust itself in signifying, nor is it merely something that has the character of sign or cipher. It is because language is the house of being, that we reach what is by constantly going through this house. When we go to the well, when we go through the woods, we are always already going through the word "well," through the word "woods." . . . (1971a: 132)

For me this brings to mind Malinowski's characterization of Trobriand magic: "It does not function as an expression of thought or communication of ideas but as a part of concerted activity" (1965: 8). But insofar as both Heidegger and Malinowski integrally link the movement and activity of our bodies with our speech, it could also be said that "the house is the being of language." By this I do not mean *only* that the house provides the central setting or context for the Foi's most compelling experiences of speech, oratory, and poem. I mean also that the house is founded upon what the linguistic capacity enables: the magic spell and its ability to unite ghosts and humans in a mirror image of death-in-life. To enable a longhouse community to celebrate the death of its men in poems, the ghosts of the house must also be fixed into the architecture through magic. The magic spell obliterates death; the poem reaffirms its existential status as a condition of life.

As with the Black Forest cottage, it is in the Foi house that ghosts and men dwell together. And it is in the house that men join the earth and sky together, for them, the path to the domain of the animals upon which they subsist (the Foi still believe that game animals ascend the trees and from there to their home in the sky when the clouds of the rainy season lift around October of each year). The joining of these four realms is an integral part of any dwelling the Foi build. In the clay and earth of their fireplaces, in both the longhouse and their bush houses, men and women do not neglect to insert the feathers of birds of paradise and white cockatoos, so that pearl shells and pigs may be "drawn" to the house and allow its inhabitants to flourish.

The detotalization of Yibumena's body, the ensuing corporeal imagery of the longhouse, the spells that "fix" the animals of the sky realm into the architec-

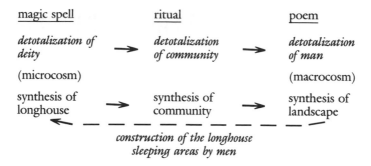

Figure 8–2   Synthesis of Foi Space and Language

ture, the dead body laid out in state in the middle of the central corridor, the rows of men at their fireplaces—all of these spatial images are so inextricably intertwined that it is pointless to separate them. It is simpler to say that the longhouse provides all the dimensions necessary to man's true being: earth and sky, divinity and mortals. Heidegger maintained that these are the dimensions that are always invoked by true poetic language.

NOTES

1. *Hai* means "dog" in Foi, and *Kiri* here refers to the rope with which a pig is tied. They "name" a man and woman by reference to their associated domestic animals.
2. Pesquet's parrot.
3. Either the harpy eagle or peregrine falcon.
4. See Mimica 1981 for a discussion of the embodiment of the Ikwaye cult house.
5. A description of the *bi'a'a guabora* rites can be found in Weiner 1987 and Williams 1977.

9   THE EMPTY HOUSE

Are not the mountains, waves and skies a
part
Of me and of my soul, as I of them?
          —Byron

THE PRECEDING CHAPTER demonstrated that poetry, space and dwelling are inextricably linked for the Foi, and that within the Foi longhouse unfolds the discursive re-creation of life and death as spatial and temporal processes. I suggest that this is a feature of poetry generally, and that it is no more or less than the revealing of the embodied, spatial nature of discourse itself in its authentic lived condition. Before I conclude this book, I would like to examine one other example of how poetry embodies space elsewhere in the tribal world.

The aborigines of the central desert of Australia have long been known for the centrality of territoriality in their society, and Roy Wagner has in fact already commented on the central role of embodied inscriptivity in central Australian discursive techniques (Wagner 1986). For the Walbiri people, the landscape was created by the original movements of ancestral creator beings.

> The ancestors and the times in which they travelled are called *djugurba*, a term that also means "dream." Walbiri men say that the ancestors, sleeping in their camps at different sites, dreamed their songs, graphic designs, and ceremonial paraphernalia. These phenomena record their travels, and the gist of the Walbiri views on this matter seems to be that they also dreamed the world they create in their travels; as one man suggested, they dreamed their track *(yiriyi)*. (Munn 1973b: 195)

The Walbiri possess a corpus of song poetry that describes the actions of these ancestors at the various sites they created during their sojourns. The songs themselves, then, are linked and have lines or tracks, and the singing of them discursively unfolds the temporal and spatial nature of that track. "The fact that the term *yiri(yi)* can cover both verbal forms and visual marks . . .

points to the Walbiri view that designs and songs constitute a single complex"
(Munn 1973a: 145).

These designs or iconographs are stylized graphic patterns that bear a resemblance to the marks left on the earth by the inscriptive activities of men, spirits, and animals. As Munn describes them, "The designs are forms external to individual subjectivity that are thought of as having originally been part of subjective experience, that is, of the interior vision (dream) of ancestors" (1973b: 33). But as Roy Wagner points out, the designs (and songs) also image in an important way the Walbiri people's own spatiotemporally creative movement:

> The country of these people is, of course, known and experienced through the know trails and landmarks that such continuities represent. Indeed, since the traditional Walbiri must perforce, as hunters and gatherers, not only gain their living by following tracks (in hunting), but also spend their lives constantly *making* tracks themselves, that life in all of its acts became a process of *inscription*. . . . The life of a person is the sum of his tracks, the total inscription of his movements, something that can be traced out along the ground. (Wagner 1986: 21)

The ancestral track, whether represented graphically through the iconism of Walbiri designs or discursively through the sequence of linked songs, expands simultaneously into ritual and "everyday life" as a re-creation of the landscape in its primordial form. Like the Foi, through dream, ritual, and poetic discourse the Walbiri "tap" an ancestral creativity. Human life becomes a daily working out of this primordial design for movement and space, and every act is intelligible as a negotiation between the creativity of the ancestors and the present-day Walbiri. For new "dreamings" are constantly perceived by Walbiri men and women, and their creativity is essential to the constitution of that of the ancestors.

> Warlpiri make a distinction between songs that are newly received and those that are not, and the process by which the former becomes the latter seems to involve "rediscovering" and "recreating" songs series received earlier. . . . Recreating song series in the process of rediscovering them . . . is only one means among several of recreating the *jukurrpa*. (Wild 1987: 109)

The same process is at work in the creation of the Foi spatial lifeworld. Women "reveal" the life tracks of the deceased in their songs, and this constitutes the Foi landscape as a double image of ancestrally constituted places over which are inscribed the currently creative movements of the present-day Foi. Women re-create the spatial world of the departed through song and by doing so keep alive the memory of men as temporal beings. Men, on the other hand, confirm the atemporal (and nonspatial) world of ghostly movement through their perception of spells in dreams.

But each needs the other to complete its significance within a communally confirmed world of space and time. The legitimacy of ghostly power is perceived to be necessary because man's productive capacities are insufficient. Men confront sickness, madness, hunger, the deaths of animals and children, all the stark reminders of life's brutal temporality. They can only invoke the motion-holding power of ghosts to create an artificial world "as if" life did not come to an end.

But because ghostly power lacks the temporality to which mortal man is subject, it is without moral "vector." Morality is, after all, the result of a social understanding of temporality, of the comprehension of the effect of one's actions upon others and upon the world. When men obtain the atemporal power of ghosts, it can be used for both good and evil. Men may obtain healing power through ghostly intercession, but this healing power can also be employed as lethal sorcery. A place where powerful spells were once performed is a source of power and revelation for men, it is true, but usually it is simply avoided by people, for it can make weaker adult men ill and can kill women, children, and domestic animals. The places where ghosts have lingered become places of death, just as the places where men lived are those of life in women's song. Magic re-creates the intentions and movements of ghosts; it implements the ghosts' subjective constitution of the landscape. Poetry does the same thing for mortal, temporal man's understanding of the instrumentality of the earth. These two discursive modes in their mirroring of each other encompass the totality of Foi spatial and temporal processes that underwrite their moral world of action and purpose.

The movement of Walbiri and Foi people across the earth in the course of their appropriative sojourning "models" the macrocosmic creation of their topographical world, in which life and death have been historically inscribed. The individual's life's path both iterates an ancestral-historical world and creates a personalized and particular hodologic trace.

In the same way, speech is both iterative and creative. It is constrained by convention, itself made possible by the very scission between sound and object. In chapters 3 and 4, I suggested that the iconism of Foi spatial and temporal lexemes constitutes the background against which referential conventionality, the "arbitrariness" of lexical motivation, emerges. But because language is constituted through the *mutual* interaction between speaker and world—*mutual* and not *causal*—the arbitrariness of Foi representation can also serve as the background against which the motivated fusion of language and world becomes meaningful. Let me give an example of what I mean by this. When I listened to Foi people conversing among themselves, I noted a high degree of variation in the way they used words. Of course I kept a word list, and when I heard a new word I would dutifully insert it in its proper place. But I noticed a common tendency, exemplified by the following:

ka'arudi- *ka'arukegeredi-* *ka'arurudi-* *karudi-* *karukarudi-* *karodi-* }	to bang the sides of a canoe when paddling
kurukurudi– *ku'uduru(di)-* }	to bubble, boil
hahūdi- *heheme dani-* *heherabudi-* }	to be short of breath
huaburuma- *hudafiādi-* *hudafodi-* *hudinimudi-* }	to bump into something accidentally

If Foi motion words are subject to a high degree of iconic motivation, then it is not unreasonable to suppose there would be lexical variation that did not affect meaning. To a Foi, it seems, as long as the word *sounds* correct, it will convey the proper meaning, especially as it is also well contextualized by the heavily anaphoric properties of the ubiquitous Foi deictics.

To put it more succinctly, if no dictionary exists, then it is only by the appropriateness of one's utterance that the fitness of a word is judged. For the Foi, this appropriateness—in other words, the conventionality of referential designation—is a matter as much of *sensual* and *aesthetic* as of *lexical* fitness. Because the Foi language has this aesthetic dimension built into its most basic lexical constitution, the contrast between poetic image as embodied and temporal, and magical metaphor as cryptic and atemporal thus becomes first and foremost an aesthetic contrast.

I have maintained that Foi poetry embodies a moving image, that this image has spatial and acoustic properties which stem from the manner in which it is moved as well as recited by the human body in motion. The flowing, rushing, hissing water has to be heard as such, seen in its white frothiness; the empty house has to be seen in its shabby disrepair, its weed-covered obliteration, heard in its very stillness. Dell Hymes reports a marvelous communication from Gary Snyder, who has translated Chinese Han Shan poetry:

> The problem, in a sense, is not one of "writing" but one of "visualizing." I have found this to be very true of Chinese poetry translation. I get the verbal meaning into mind as clear as I can, but then make an enormous effort of visualization, to "see" what the poem says, nonlinguistically, like a movie in my mind; and to feel it. If I can do this . . . then I write the scene down in English. It is not a translation of the words, it is the same poem in a different language. . . . (Hymes 1981: 60)

Of course, Snyder can be said to be taking his cue straight from Ernest Fenollosa, who commented on the necessity of appreciating the pictorial quality of Chinese characters and poetry: "In reading Chinese we do not seem to be juggling mental counters, but to be watching *things* work out their own fate" (1967: 363). And Ricoeur, in his powerful analysis of Heidegger's hermeneutics, points out that communication for Heidegger was a matter not of communicating with another person but of revealing the structures of being that enable it. For Heidegger "the question of language is only introduced after the questions of situation, understanding, and interpretation" (Ricoeur 1978: 155).

This is the essence of Heidegger's insistence that poetry de-severs the distances that separate us from things in their true being. These distances arise as a result of the everydayness of our life experiences, the routines that fade into impassive one-dimensionality. Insofar as poetry can be said to have a "function," it is the "spatial" one of bringing into our present nearness things that have receded into the distance of our historical attention. Foi poetry simply brings the dead back to life, as Foi magic brings ghosts back to the longhouse from their exile in distant *Haisureri*. Such a statement is not the trite formula of some voodoo aesthetic but the synthetic moment of the creation of a living community in its historical being.

Many times we came upon old and abandoned houses in the bush in various states of decay and disrepair. As a Foi house is left unoccupied, its floor beams sag, its sago mid-rib wall slats become unfastened and crookedly hang down. Shafts of light enter the resulting gaps in the wall as well as through the holes in the insect-eaten sago-leaf roof and illuminate the dusty floor through which tall grass is starting to poke its tops. The steps are broken; maybe they are missing altogether. The bright daylight shines on the interior of the house, through the gaps and holes that have formed in its fabric, in a way that it never does in a lived-in house. Yet it serves to illuminate an absence, to light up the empty space of a house that has lost its fundamental instrumentality and is now merely a shell of degradable forest material, decomposing, losing its opacity, and returning to its original vegetative state.

> A single piece of equipment is worn out and used up; but at the same time the use itself also falls into disuse, wears away, and becomes usual. Thus, equipmentality wastes away, sinks into mere stuff. In such wasting, reliability vanishes. This dwindling, however, to which use-things owe their boringly obtrusive usualness, is only one more testimony to the original nature of equipmental being. (Heidegger 1971a: 35)

Heidegger reached these conclusions after reflecting upon van Gogh's painting of a peasant's shoes (*Les Souliers*, Stedelij Museum, Amsterdam). The stillness and emptiness of the shoes did not detract in the slightest from their ability to "let us know what shoes are in truth" (ibid.). The shoes speak to us of their *reliability* for the peasant woman who wore them. "By virtue of the reliability of the equipment she is sure of her world" (ibid.: 34), and we see this vital usefulness in all its dimensions in van Gogh's painting.

With these words, Heidegger arrived at the simple obliteration of the Western schism between rational/instrumental and poetic thought. His concern with the origin of the work of art, of which he saw poetry as the primordial, truest form, led him to stipulate that the poet brings to light the poetic nature of the most mundanely instrumental equipment and its uses. In appropriating such things, in making them ready-to-hand, humans infuse them with all the concern, historicity, and care of their being. To say that such equipment "comes alive" with concern may strike some of us as mystical, animistic, or fetishistic, but is not such a reaction to be expected from those who see human being as a subordinate adjunct to a world governed by material law? Who would see a being-for-itself that exists apart from human consciousness? David Halliburton, in his masterful analysis of Heidegger's theories of poetry, reaches the same conclusion:

> Science views the thing as an entity existing over against consciousness and therefore liable to measurement and manipulation. It is not that such measurements and manipulations have nothing human about them. . . . But there are different ways of existing as *Dasein* [Being-there] and, more particularly, different ways of existing with respect to things; and the way poetic thinking favors is a rather more basic way of living with things in a common world, a way so ordinary that it is extraordinary that it ever came to seem *extra*ordinary. According to this way of living, things belong with mortals even as things and mortals belong with language. If language is fundamentally poetic, then all it capacitates will be poetic too. . . . (1981: 172)

The emptiness of an abandoned Foi house is made to speak by Foi poets. The house has not lost its ability to speak of the inscriptivity of human being; it merely requires the life-giving imagination of the poet to do so, just as all of our speech requires the poet in every one of us to maintain its vitality as our fundamental mode of discursive inscriptivity.

Heidegger drew attention to the fact that for speakers of modern European language, the existential link between poetry (art), life, and thinking has been lost. Art is something we passively experience as spectators; professional artists are accorded the privilege and responsibility of "doing" art for us. It is not that art has lost the capacity to move us, but that we have learned to *re*act to it rather than *en*act it ourselves. We compartmentalize the artistic and aesthetic of our life rather than viewing it as as essential feature of our fundamental discourse. By so doing we can then privilege the meaning-generating capacity of art and the artist himself.

The problem with the anthropological study of non-Western aesthetics is not that our ideas about representation, abstraction, and so forth may not apply to their technique. It is that we are incapable of divesting ourselves of the notion of *the artist as a privileged role in society* (cf. Witherspoon 1977: 151–53). We accept the judgments of artists and art critics alike; they are the inauthentic "they" from whose pronouncements we *un*critically fashion our critical faculty. We feel that the artist must first have distanced himself from convention before his particularly displacing work of art can exert its shattering effect. The result is a work of art that first and last *establishes* a distance rather than obliterates it. Foi poetry, however, comes from the terrible nearness of death. No interpretation one can place on Foi poetry can even begin to add anything much more to that original disclosure.

But the distancing of art is only one result of a thoroughgoing distancing of the world of externality from our perception of it. When the self-evident distinction of mind and body is taken as a model for the self-evident contrast between subjective and objective qualities, we learn to deal with the world through the reality of abstraction and representation. The privileging of a Cartesian world of natural fact independent of perception models the form we feel scientific investigation should take. We are satisfied that when we have explained the existence of ghosts as a result of some psychological projection mechanism, or as an index of social tension, we have encompassed its entire meaning. But as Michael Jackson points out, the repositioning of lived experience within an external "objective" world of natural fact and law "serves more as a magical token, bolstering our sense of self in disorienting situations, than as a scientific method for describing those situations as they really are" (1989: 3). We would interpret statements such as "Deities are what man measures himself against" as belonging to the province of the theologian, not the scientist. And yet Heidegger's statement preserves more of the ontology of the religious life than does, for example, Durkheim's formulation.

Don Gardner (1987) recounted a story he heard while living among the Mianmin of the West Sepik Province of Papua New Guinea. A man named Keokub and his father's younger brother, Melabeb, had gone to live with the former's affines. But after a while, Keokub's affines told him they feared that Keokub's father's younger brother was a sorcerer. Keokub felt greatly ashamed and killed Melabeb. When Gardner expressed horror at this story and asked the Mianmin whether they thought it was indeed a terrible thing to kill one's close clansman, the Mianmin replied almost incredulously, "Of course it is a terrible thing, but don't you *know* what shame and humiliation can drive a man to?" When the Foi spoke to me about Sahabo's suicide and about the man Sese's suicide some years later, they spoke of these individuals' despair, their felt inability to alter an intolerable situation, the unbearable pressure that spouses and kinsmen had put on them. I recalled how I used to think that what anthropology was all about was the setting up of a great gulf between oneself and one's host community that could then be overcome through systematic discovery, insight, and the growth of empathy. But what I now know is that that insight and empathy is there right from the start. For Heidegger, being is accessible to humans by virtue of their being able to speak and hear. Any time that humans engage in the unconcealing that is the truth of language, the poetry of authentic discourse, they reveal the inherent affectivity, the danger, despair, and risk of loss in being and discourse. As Kaelin puts it, "The revelation [of meaning] is claimed to be direct, there to be seen or heard by anyone who has eyes and ears *through which* to see and hear" (1967: 67).

Through poetry, the objects of our everyday life are shown to embody this life condition. "It is in the process of the use of the equipment that we must actually encounter the character of equipment," Heidegger writes. "Everything [else] that might interpose between the thing and us in apprehending and talking about it must first be set aside" (1971a: 33, 25). Of course this brings us back to the imagists, who wanted to depict things in terms of the immediacy of our engaged perception of them. To accomplish this, we need not the displacing, devious metaphor of simile, innuendo, and rhetoric, the tool of discursive alienation and bad faith; we need the "affective presence" of the authentic metaphor which repairs the gulf of representation itself.

* * *

"Metaphor," writes Michael Jackson, "reveals unities; it is not a figurative way of denying dualities" (1983: 132), and it is this embodied, instrumental nature of metaphor that the imagists, haiku poets, and Foi women implement. Metaphor is inherently spatial and temporal in its constitution because as the "first language of experience," spatial and temporal differentiation is the ground against which we present, appresent, and represent to ourselves everything in the world.

Max Black felicitously identified metaphor as the juxtaposing of two distinct "*systems of associated commonplaces*" (1962: 40). When we consider the majority of Foi songs, we see that it is indeed "associated common places" that are being used to depict another series—the series of productive events which is the life course of individuals. Associated with each person is a set of places at which he or she performed the common acts of everyday life; these portray the Foi person in their unique historical and spatial constitution. Places are the embodiment of human life activity—they acquire significance insofar as they are quickened by the concernful acts of people. And as others such as Welsh, Fenollosa, and Heidegger have maintained, these integral bodily engagements constitute the first language of metaphor and poetry. Merleau-Ponty also stipulated that the act of speech, itself a kinesthetic activity, is contiguous with the body's other spatial engagements with the world:

> Our body, to the extent that it moves itself about, that is, to the extent that it is inseparable from a view of the world and is that view itself brought into existence,

is the condition of possibility, not only of the geometrical synthesis, but of all expressive operations and all acquired views which constitute the cultural world. (1962: 388)

It is this fundamental inseparability of "sensibility" and "meaning" that prompted Cassirer's masterful analysis of the linguistic expressions of space and spatial relations:

> The step from the world of sensation to that of "pure intuition," which the critique of knowledge shows to be a necessary factor of the I and the pure concept of the object, has its exact counterpart in language. It is in the "intuitive forms" that the type and direction of the spiritual synthesis effected in language are primarily revealed, and it is only through the medium of these forms, through the intuitions of space, time and number that language can perform its essentially logical operation: the forming of impressions into representations. (1953: 198)

Ricoeur maintains that space is itself the critical image for describing how metaphor works: "Things or ideas which were remote appear now as close" (1979: 145). These statements confirm our intuitive appreciation of the embodied, spatial nature of metaphor, something well exploited in Oriental and tribal poetic traditions (of which a noteworthy example is Arnhem Land love song [Berndt 1976]), and long maintained by Western critics such as Pound and Phillip Wheelwright (1968).

Finally, Ricoeur has also commented on the distinction between metaphor and image. Drawing on Heidegger's and Husserl's concepts of *Dasein* and the lifeworld, Ricoeur questions Jakobson's distinction between poetic and nonpoetic metaphor, as I did earlier. Jakobson suggested that nonpoetic metaphor retains a fundamentally *referential* function that poetic metaphor lacks (Jakobson 1962b: 356). But Ricoeur states that

> poetic language is no less *about* reality than any other use of language but refers to it by the means of a complex strategy which implies, as an essential component, a suspension and seemingly an abolition of the ordinary reference attached to descriptive language. This suspension, however, is only the negative condition of a second-order reference. . . . This reference is called second-order reference only with respect to the primacy of the reference of ordinary language. For, in another respect, it constitutes the primordial reference to the extent that it suggests, reveals, unconceals . . . the deep structures of reality to which we are related as mortals who are born into this world and who *dwell* in it for a while. (1979: 151)

I can think of no better way to summarize my intent in this book than that splendid passage, which I will take to be an introduction to the anthropological study of poetry, the language of dwelling in the world.

Mortals are they who can experience death as death.
Animals cannot do so. But animals cannot speak either.
The essential relation between death and language
flashes up before us, but remains still unthought.
        —Heidegger, "The Nature of Language"
        (1971b: 107)

Like the imagists, Heidegger envisioned a return to a more authentic language. "Poetry proper is never merely a higher mode (*melos*) of everyday language. It is rather the reverse: everyday language is a forgotten and therefore used-up poem, from which there hardly resounds a call any longer" (1971a: 208), he wrote. True language embodied that ability to place things in space and time, in their relations of proximity to man and the things with which man measured his sojourn on earth—his deities, his earth, his dwelling.

Humans live and speak in movement: their activities and speech "carve out" a space, as I have been saying, both literally, in terms of the actual iconicity of sound and distance, and figuratively, in the distancing of what is remote and in the drawing near of what is encompassed by our concern.

Foi men define their being by placing limits or checks on the movements that create these dimensions. Their discourse is the discourse of finality and death, but only inauthentically, in the sense that they deny death as man's experience and instead define it as what empowers ghostly efficacy. They then invoke the *distancing* power of ghosts in their quest to place a mediating distantiation between themselves and the objects of their concernful attention—for example, the pearl shells with which they control women and assert a role in procreative flow; the spells with which they augment their productive inscriptivity; the bird-feather decorations which establish their sexual attractiveness as males. Men *sever* the movements of the world and earth and produce the horizons within which human striving acquires its moral impetus and rationale.

Women, on the other hand, always *de-sever* the efforts of men. They bring forth into the clearing of human attention the movement across the earth that is human life, the never-ending cycles of fertility and birth within their own bodies, their spontaneous and unmediated productivity.

Women, too, are allocated the care of the dead body in funeral procedures. As the fetus developed from its constituent fluids of blood and semen within their wombs, so do they surround the body as it begins to decompose and dissolve into its constituent fluids. Underneath the raised exposure coffin in traditional times sat the dead man's widow, her skin covered by the fluids of decomposition dripping down from the open platform.

The essential mirror image of life and death unfolds with this practice: the fluids of life flowing within her and those of death enveloping her in a never-ending cycle of decay and cessation and birth and movement. Out of this image of life's essential conquest over the temporariness of death comes the women's song: a message of life after death, a reassertion of life's spatiality in the space-destroying stillness of death.

BIBLIOGRAPHY

Acker, W.
  1952. *T'ao the Hermit: Sixty Poems by Ta'o Ch'ien*. London: Thames and Hudson.
Armstrong, R.
  1971. *The Affecting Presence: An Essay in Humanistic Anthropology*. Urbana: University of Illinois Press.
Bachelard, G.
  1969. *The Poetics of Space*. Boston: Beacon Press.
———. 1971. *The Poetics of Reverie*. Boston: Beacon Press.
Barth, F.
  1975. *Ritual and Knowledge among the Baktaman*. New Haven: Yale University Press.
Basso, K.
  1984. " 'Stalking with Stories': Names, Places, and Moral Narratives among the Western Apache." In *Text, Play and Story*, edited by Edward Brunner. Washington, D.C.: American Ethnological Society Publications.
———. 1988. " 'Speaking with Names': Language and Landscape among the Western Apache." *Cultural Anthropology* 3(2): 99–130.
Benveniste, E.
  1971. *Problems in General Linguistics*. Coral Gables, Fl.: University of Miami Press.
Berndt, R.
  1976. *Love Songs of Arnhem Land*. Chicago: University of Chicago Press.
Biersack, A.
  n.d. "Histories in the Making: Paiela and Historical Anthropology." Unpublished manuscript.
Black, M.
  1962. *Models and Metaphors: Studies in Language and Philosophy*. Ithaca: Cornell University Press.
Boas, F.
  1911. *Handbook of American Indian Languages, Part I*. Washington, D.C.: Bureau of American Ethnology Bulletin 40, Part I.
Bolinger, D.
  1965. *Forms of English*. Tokyo: Hokuou Publishing Co.
Bourdieu, P.
  1977. *Outline of a Theory of Practice*. Cambridge: Cambridge University Press.
Bruzina, R.
  1978. "Heidegger on the Metaphor and Philosophy." In *Heidegger and Modern Philosophy*, edited by Michael Murray. New Haven: Yale University Press. Pp. 184–200.
Cassirer, E.
  1953. *The Philosophy of Symbolic Forms (Volume 1: Language)*. New Haven: Yale University Press.

Feld, S.
>   1982. *Sound and Sentiment: Birds, Weeping, Poetics, and Song in Kaluli Expression*. Philadelphia: University of Pennsylvania Press.
———. 1984. "Sound Structure as Social Structure." *Ethnomusicology* 28(3): 383–409.
———. 1988. "Aesthetics as Iconicity of Style." *Yearbook for Traditional Music* 20.
———. n.d. "Wept Thoughts: The Voicing of Kaluli Memories." Unpublished manuscript.
Fenollosa, E.
>   1967. "The Chinese Written Character as a Medium for Poetry." Reprinted in *Instigations*, edited by E. Pound. London: Books for Libraries Press. Pp. 357–88.
Fernandez, J.
>   1982. *Bwiti: An Ethnography of the Religious Imagination in Africa*. Princeton: Princeton University Press.
Fortune, R.
>   1932. *Sorcerers of Dobu*. New York: E. P. Dutton and Co.
Franklin, K.
>   1978. *A Kewa Dictionary (With Supplementary Grammatical and Anthropological Materials)*. Pacific Linguistics Monographs Series C, no. 53. Australian National University, Department of Linguistics, Research School of Pacific Studies.
Gardner, D. S.
>   1987. "Spirits and Conceptions of Agency among the Mianmin of Papua New Guinea." *Oceania* 57(3): 161–77.
Gèfin, L.
>   1982. *Ideogram: History of a Poetic Method*. Austin: University of Texas Press.
Gell, A.
>   1979. "The Umeda Language Poem." *Canberra Anthropology* 2(1): 44–62.
Glickman, J.
>   1978. "Creativity in the Arts." In *Philosophy Looks at the Arts*, edited by J. Margolis. Philadelphia: Temple University Press.
Glynn, S.
>   1982. "Preface: Phenomenology and Embodiment." *Journal of the British Society for Phenomenology* 13(3): 212–15.
Goodman, N.
>   1978. "Reality Remade." In *Philosophy Looks at the Arts,* edited by J. Margolis. Philadelphia: Temple University Press.
Greenburg, J.
>   1985. "Some Iconic Relationships among Place, Time, and Discourse Deixis." In *Iconicity in Syntax*, edited by John Haiman. Typological Studies in Language vol. 6. Amsterdam: John Benjamins Publishing Co. Pp. 271–87.
Haiman, J.
>   1980. "The Iconicity of Grammar: Isomorphism and Motivation." *Language* 56(3): 515–40.
Haiman, J., ed.
>   1985. *Iconicity in Syntax*. Typological Studies in Language vol. 6. Amsterdam: John Benjamins Publishing Co.
Halliburton, D.
>   1981. *Poetic Thinking: An Approach to Heidegger*. Chicago: University of Chicago Press.

Harries, K.
    1978. "Fundamental Ontology and the Search for Man's Place." In *Heidegger and Modern Philosophy,* edited by Michael Murray. New Haven: Yale University Press. Pp. 65-79.
———. 1979. "Metaphor and Transcendence." In *On Metaphor,* edited by S. Sacks. Chicago: University of Chicago Press. Pp. 71–88.

Harrison, S.
    1982. *Laments for Foiled Marriages: Love Songs from a Sepik River Village.* Port Moresby: Institute of Papua New Guinea Studies.

Heeschen. V.
    1982. "Some Aspects of Spatial Deixis in Papuan Languages." In *Here and There,* edited by J. Weissenborn and W. Klein. Amsterdam: John Benjamins Publishing Co. Pp. 81–109.

Heidegger, M.
    1949. "Hölderlin and the Essence of Poetry." In *Existence and Being,* translated by D. Scott. Chicago: Regnery.
———. 1959. *An Introduction to Metaphysics.* New Haven: Yale University Press.
———. 1962. *Being and Time.* London: Basil Blackwell.
———. 1971a. *Poetry, Language, Thought.* New York: Harper and Row.
———. 1971b. *On the Way to Language.* New York: Harper and Row [1959].
———. 1982. *The Basics Problems of Phenomenology.* Edited by Alfred Hofstadter. Bloomington: Indiana University Press.

Henderson, H. G.
    1958. *An Introduction to Haiku.* New York: Doubleday Anchor Books.

Hoijer, H.
    1964. "Cultural Implications of Some Navajo Linguistic Categories." In *Language in Culture and Society,* edited by D. Hymes. New York: Harper and Row. Pp. 143–53.

Husserl, E.
    1960. *Cartesian Meditations: An Introduction to Philosophy.* The Hague: Martinus Nijhoff.

Hymes, D.
    1981. *"In Vain I Tried to Tell You": Essays in Native American Ethnopoetics.* Philadelphia: University of Pennsylvania Press.

Ihde, D.
    1976. *Listening and Voice: A Phenomenology of Sound.* Athens: Ohio University Press.

Jackson, M.
    1983. "Thinking through the Body: An Essay on Understanding Metaphor." *Social Analysis* 14: 127–49.
———. 1989. *Paths toward a Clearing: Radical Empiricism and Ethnographic Inquiry.* Bloomington: Indiana University Press.

Jakobson, R.
    1962a. "Why 'Mama' and 'Papa'?" In *Selected Writings Volume I.* The Hague: Mouton and Co.
———. 1962b. *Selected Writings Volume II.* The Hague: Mouton and Co.

Jakobson, R., and Waugh, L.
    1979. *The Sound Shape of Language.* Berlin: Mouton de Gruyter.

Jarevella, R., and Klein, W., eds.
    1982. *Speech, Place and Action: Studies in Deixis and Related Topics.* Chichester: John Wiley and Sons.

Kaelin, E. F.
     1967. "Notes toward an Understanding of Heidegger's Aesthetics." In *Phenomenology and Existentialism*, edited by E. Lee and M. Mandelbaum. Baltimore: Johns Hopkins University Press. Pp. 59–92.
Keil, C.
     1979. *Tiv Song*. Chicago: University of Chicago Press.
Kelly, R.
     1976. "Witchcraft and Sexual Relations." In *Man and Woman in the New Guinea Highlands*, edited by P. Brown and G. Buchbinder. Washington, D.C.: American Anthropological Association Special Publication no. 8.
————. 1977. *Etoro Social Structure*. Ann Arbor: University of Michigan Press.
Kenner, H.
     1951. *The Poetry of Ezra Pound*. London: Faber and Faber.
Kockelmans, J.
     1972. *On Heidegger and Language*. Evanston: Northwestern University Press.
Kultgen, J.
     1975. "Phenomenology and Structuralism." *Annual Review of Anthropology* 4: 371–87.
LaFlesch, F.
     1917–1918. "The Osage Tribe: Rite of Vigil." *39th Annual Report of the Bureau of American Ethnology*: 31–630.
Langacker, R.
     1972. *Fundamentals of Linguistic Analysis*. New York: Harcourt, Brace and Jovanovich.
Langlas, C.
     1974. "Foi Land Use, Residence and Prestige Economics: A Processual Analysis." Unpublished Ph.D. thesis, University of Hawaii.
Langlas, C., and Weiner, J.
     1988. "Big-Men, Population Growth and Longhouse Fission among the Foi, 1965–1979." In *Mountain Papuans*, edited by J. Weiner. Ann Arbor: University of Michigan Press.
Leach, E.
     1971. "More about 'Mama' and 'Papa.' " In *Rethinking Kinship and Marriage*, edited by R. Needham. London: Tavistock. Pp. 75–98.
LeRoy, J.
     1978. "Burning Our Trees: Metaphors in Kewa Songs." *Yearbook of Symbolic Anthropology* I: 51–72.
Lévi-Strauss, C.
     1963. *Structural Anthropology*, New York: Basic Books.
————. 1966. *The Savage Mind*. Chicago: University of Chicago Press.
Malinowski, B.
     1965. *Coral Gardens and Their Magic, Vol. II: The Language of Magic and Gardening*. Bloomington: Indiana University Press [1935].
Merleau-Ponty, M.
     1962. *Phenomenology of Perception*. London: Routledge and Kegan Paul.
————. 1973. *Consciousness and the Acquisition of Language*. Translated by Hugh J. Silverman. Evanston: Northwestern University Press.
Mimica, J.
     1981. "Omalyce: An Ethnography of the Ikwaye View of the Cosmos." Ph.D. thesis, Department of Prehistory and Anthropology, Australian National University.

————. 1988. *Intimations of Infinity: The Mythopoeia of the Iqwaye Counting System and Number.* Oxford, New York, Hamburg: Berg.

Munn, N.
1973a. *Walbiri Iconography: Graphic Representation and Cultural Symbolism in a Central Australian Society.* Ithaca: Cornell University Press.

————. 1973b. "The Spatial Presentation of Cosmic Order in Walbiri Iconography." In *Primitive Art and Society,* edited by A. Forge. London: Oxford University Press.

O'Neill, J., ed.
1974. *Phenomenology, Language and Sociology: Selected Essays of Maurice Merleau-Ponty.* London: Heineman.

Paige, D. D., ed.
1950. *The Letters of Ezra Pound, 1907–1941.* New York: Harcourt, Brace and Co.

Pound, E.
1913. "A Few Don'ts by an Imagist." *Poetry* 1: 200.

————. 1916. *Gaudier-Brzeska: A Memoir.* London and New York: John Lane.

————. 1951. *The ABC of Reading.* London: Faber and Faber.

Radcliffe-Brown, R.
1952. *Structure and Function in Primitive Society.* New York: Basic Books.

Relph, E.
1976. *Place and Placelessness.* London: Pion Limited.

Ricoeur, P.
1977. *The Rule of Metaphor.* Toronto: University of Toronto Press.

————. 1978. "The Task of Hermeneutics." In *Heidegger and Modern Philosophy*, edited by Michael Murray. New Haven: Yale University Press. Pp. 141–60.

————. 1979. "The Metaphorical Process as Cognition, Imagination and Feeling." In *On Metaphor*, edited by Sheldon Sacks. Chicago: University of Chicago Press. Pp. 141–57.

Rosaldo, R.
1980. *Ilongot Headhunting, 1883–1974: A Study in Society and History.* Palo Alto: Stanford University Press.

Rule, M.
1977. "A Comparative Study of the Foe, Huli and Pole Languages of Papua New Guinea." Oceania Linguistic Monograph no. 20.

Sacks, S., ed.
1979. *On Metaphor.* Chicago: University of Chicago Press.

Sapir, E.
1912. "Language and Environment." *American Anthropologist* 14: 226–42.

Sartre, J. P.
1956. *Being and Nothingness.* New York: Pocket Books.

Saussure, F. de
1966. *Course in General Linguistics.* New York: McGraw Hill.

Schieffelin, E.
1976. *The Sorrow of the Lonely and the Burning of the Dancers.* New York: St. Martin's Press.

————. 1980. "Reciprocity and the Construction of Reality." *Man*, n.s. 15(3): 502–17.

Schutz, A.
1967. *The Phenomenology of the Social World.* Evanston: Northwestern University Press.

Schutz, A., and Luckmann, T.
1973. *The Structures of the Life-World.* Evanston: Northwestern University Press.

Seamon, D., and Mugerauer, R., eds.
     1985. *Dwelling, Place and Environment: Towards a Phenomenology of Person and World*. The Hague: Martinus Nijhoff.
Sefler, G.
     1974. *Language and the World: A Methodological Synthesis within the Writings of Martin Heidegger and Ludwig Wittgenstein*. Atlantic Highlands, N.J.: Humanities Press.
Shaw, R. D., and Shaw, K.
     1973. "Location: A Linguistic and Cultural Focus." *Kivung* 6(3): 158–72.
Shimkin, D. B.
     1964. "On Wind River Shoshone Literary Forms: An Introduction." In *Language in Culture and Society*, edited by Dell Hymes. New York: Harper and Row. Pp. 344-55.
Silverstein, M.
     1981. "Metaforces of Power in Traditional Oratory." Unpublished manuscript.
Spicer, J.
     1957. *Letter to Lorca*. Reprinted in *The New American Poetry*, edited by Donald M. Allen. Evergreen Books. New York: Grove Press [1960].
Strathern, A.
     1975. "Veiled Speech in Mt. Hagen." In *Political Language and Oratory in Traditional Society*, edited by M. Bloch. London, New York: Academic Press.
Strathern, M.
     1972. *Women in Between*. New York: Academic Press.
Straus, E.
     1966. *Phenomenological Psychology*. New York: Basic Books.
Tormey, A.
     1971. *The Concept of Expression: A Study in Philosophical Psychology and Aesthetics*. Princeton: Princeton University Press.
Vycinas, V.
     1961. *Earth and Gods: An Introduction to the Philosophy of Martin Heidegger*. The Hague: Martinus Nijhoff.
Wadsworth, E.
     1914. "Review of Kandinsky's *Über das Geistege in der Kunst*." *Blast* 1: 120.
Wagner, R.
     1972. *Habu: The Innovation of Meaning in Daribi Religion*. Chicago: University of Chicago Press.
———. 1975. *The Invention of Culture*. Englewood Cliffs, N.J.: Prentice-Hall.
———. 1977. "Analogic Kinship: A Daribi Example." *American Ethnologist* 4(4): 623–42.
———. 1986. *Symbols That Stand for Themselves*. Chicago: University of Chicago Press.
———. 1988. "Visible Sociality: The Daribi Community." In *Mountain Papuans: Historical and Evolutionary Perspectives from New Guinea Fringe Highlands Societies*, edited by J. F. Weiner. Ann Arbor: University of Michigan Press.
Weiner, J.
     1984. "Sunset and Flowers: The Sexual Dimension of Foi Spatial Orientation." *Journal of Anthropological Research* 40(4): 577–88.
———. 1986. "Men, Ghosts and Dreams among the Foi: Literal and Figurative Modes of Interpretation." *Oceania* 57: 114–27.
———. 1987. "Diseases of the Soul: Sickness, Agency and the Men's Cult among the Foi of Papua New Guinea." In *Dealing with Inequality: Analyzing Gender Relations in the South West Pacific and Beyond*, edited by M. Strathern. Cambridge: Cambridge University Press. Pp. 255–77.

————. 1988. *The Heart of the Pearl Shell: The Mythological Dimension of Foi Sociality.* Berkeley: University of California Press.

Weiner, J., ed.
1988. *Mountain Papuans: Historical and Comparative Perspectives from New Guinea Fringe Highland Societies.* Ann Arbor: University of Michigan Press.

Welsh, A.
1978. *Roots of Lyric: Primitive Poetry and Modern Poetics.* Princeton: Princeton University Press.

Wheelwright, P.
1968. *The Burning Fountain: A Study in the Language of Symbolism.* Bloomington: Indiana University Press.

White, D.
1978. *Heidegger and the Language of Poetry.* Lincoln: University of Nebraska Press.

Wild, S.
1987. "Recreating the *Jukurrpa*: Adaptation and Innovation of Songs and Ceremonies in Warlpiri Society." *In Songs of Aboriginal Australia,* edited by M. Clunies-Ross, T. Donaldson, and S. Wild. *Oceania Monographs* no. 32.

Williams, F. E.
1977. "Natives of Lake Kutubu, Papua." In *The Vailala Madness and Other Essays,* edited by E. Schwimmer. Honolulu: University of Hawaii Press.

Witherspoon, G.
1977. *Language and Art in the Navajo Universe.* Ann Arbor: University of Michigan Press.

Yasuda, K.
1957. *The Japanese Haiku.* Rutland, Vt., and Tokyo: Charles E. Tuttle Co.

Zuckerkandl, V.
1956. *Sound and Symbol: Music and the External World.* Bollingen Series XLIV. Princeton: Princeton University Press.

INDEX

JAMES F. WEINER is Lecturer in Social Anthropology at the University of Manchester. Author of *The Heart of the Pearl Shell: The Mythological Dimension of Foi Sociality* and editor of *Mountain Papuans*, Weiner has spent two and a half years with the Foi people of Papua New Guinea.